印度尼西亚
涉商法律文件汇编

李杰 姜一飞 ◎ 编译

A Collection of Indonesian Laws concerning Business

INDONESIA

暨南大学出版社
JINAN UNIVERSITY PRESS

中国·广州

图书在版编目（CIP）数据

印度尼西亚涉商法律文件汇编 = A Collection of Indonesian Laws concerning Business/李杰，姜一飞编译 . —广州：暨南大学出版社，2015.11
ISBN 978 - 7 - 5668 - 1581 - 1

Ⅰ.①印…　Ⅱ.①李…②姜…　Ⅲ.①商法—汇编—印度尼西亚　Ⅳ.①D934.239.9

中国版本图书馆 CIP 数据核字（2015）第 175850 号

出版发行：暨南大学出版社

地　　址：中国广州暨南大学
电　　话：总编室（8620）85221601
　　　　　营销部（8620）85225284　85228291　85228292（邮购）
传　　真：（8620）85221583（办公室）　　85223774（营销部）
邮　　编：510630
网　　址：http://www.jnupress.com　http://press.jnu.edu.cn

排　　版：广州市天河星辰文化发展部照排中心
印　　刷：佛山市浩文彩色印刷有限公司

开　　本：787mm×1092mm　1/16
印　　张：17.75
字　　数：400 千
版　　次：2015 年 11 月第 1 版
印　　次：2015 年 11 月第 1 次

定　　价：45.00 元

前　言

　　随着全球经济一体化的迅速发展和中国加入世界贸易组织，"走出去"开拓国际市场成为中国企业今后生存和发展的必由之路。开拓海外市场，由于其行为发生在国外，除应遵照我国颁布的有关法律法规和政策，接受我国在当地大使馆、领事馆的指导和监督外，还要严格遵循国际法的基本准则以及国际惯例，并在企业注册登记、财务运营、设备折旧、税收筹划及外汇管制等方面遵守业务所在国的法律法规，尊重当地的文化习俗，并严格按照所在国的法律及政策办事。唯其如此，才能确保海外项目的顺利进行，并取得预期的经济效益。

　　印度尼西亚（以下简称印尼）位于亚洲东南部，是世界上最大的群岛国家。印尼拥有2.4亿人口，是世界第四人口大国。印尼是中国在东盟投资最多的国家之一，目前赴印尼寻求投资合作的中国企业不断增多，涉及能源、矿产、交通、通信、机械、金融、农业、渔业等诸多领域，大型投资项目不断涌现，充分显示了中国与印尼经贸合作的勃勃生机。据国家统计数据显示，至2014年4月，中国为印尼非油气产品的最大出口国和进口国，且一直是印尼非油气产品的第一大贸易伙伴，日本和美国分居第二和第三位。

　　为了更好地开拓印尼市场，对其相关法律法规进行深入的调查研究，将能起到举足轻重的作用。《印度尼西亚涉商法律文件汇编》对印尼的相关法律法规进行了系统介绍，旨在为我国企业在海外业务及投资中有效规避并控制法律风险提供参考及借鉴，以利于我国企业海外投资项目的顺利进行。本书包括5部法律，分别是劳动法、油气法、税法通则、所得税法和增值税法。为准确与实用起见，本书采用中英文对照的方式进行编排。

　　由于法律资料来源不同，译校水平有限，本书难免存在不足之处，敬请广大读者批评指正。

编译者

2015 年 6 月

目　录

PRESIDENT OF THE REPUBLIC OF INDONESIA
ACT NUMBER 13 YEAR 2003
CONCERNING MANPOWER

CHAPTER I   GENERAL PROVISIONS

Article 1

Under this Act, the following definitions shall apply:

1. Manpower Affairs refer to every matter that is related to people who are needed or available for a job before, during and after their employment.

2. Manpower is every one who is able to work in order to produce goods and/or services for fulfilling the need of either the relevant person or the society.

3. A Worker/Laborer is any person who works and receives wages or other forms of remuneration.

4. An Employer is individual, entrepreneur, legal entity, or other agency that employ manpower by paying them wages or other forms of remuneration.

5. An Entrepreneur is:

a. an individual, a partnership or a legal entity that operates a self-owned enterprise;

b. an individual, a partnership or a legal entity that independently operates a non-self-owned enterprise;

c. an individual, a partnership or a legal entity located in Indonesia, and representing an enterprise as mentioned under point a and point b that is domiciled outside the territory of Indonesia.

6. An Enterprise is:

a. every form of business, whether a legal entity or not, owned by an individual, a partnership or a legal entity that is either privately owned or state-owned, which employs workers/laborers by paying them wages or other forms of remuneration;

b. social and other businesses with officials in charge and which employ people by paying wages or other forms of remuneration.

7. Manpower Planning is the process of making a manpower plan systematically that is used as a basis and reference for formulating the policy, strategy and implementation of a sustainable

manpower development program.

8. Manpower Information is a group, a set or series and an analysis of data in the form of processed numbers, texts and documents that have specific meanings, values and messages concerning labor.

9. Job Training is the whole activity of providing workers or potential workers with, and paving the way for them to acquire, enhance and develop job competence, productivity, discipline, work attitude and ethics until a desired level of skills and expertise that match the grade and qualification required for a position or a job is reached.

10. Work Competence or Competency is the capability of each individual that covers aspects of knowledge, skill and work attitude which accords with prescribed standards.

11. Apprenticeship is a part of a job training system that integrates training at a training institute with working directly under the tutelage and supervision of an instructor or a more experienced worker/laborer in the process of producing goods and/or services in an enterprise in order to master a certain skill or trade.

12. Job Placement Service is an activity aimed at matching up manpower with employers so that manpower gets jobs that are suitable to their talents, interests and capabilities, and employers get the manpower they need.

13. A Foreign Worker is a visa holder of foreign citizenship with the intention to work in Indonesia's territory.

14. A Work Agreement is an agreement made between a worker/laborer and an entrepreneur or an employer that specifies work requirements, rights and obligations of the parties.

15. An Employment Relation is a relationship between an entrepreneur and a worker/laborer based on a work agreement, which contains the elements of job, wage and work order.

16. The Industrial Relations is a system of relations that is formed among actors in the process of producing goods and/or services, which consists of employers, workers/laborers and the government, which is based on the values of the Pancasila and the 1945 Constitution of the Republic of Indonesia.

17. A Trade Union/Labor Union is an organization that is formed from, by and for workers/laborers either inside or outside an enterprise, which is free, open, independent, democratic, and responsible in order to strive for, defend and protect the rights and interests of the workers/laborers and increase the welfare of the workers/laborers and their families.

18. A Bipartite Cooperation Institute is a communication and consultation forum on matters pertaining to industrial relations in an enterprise whose members consist of entrepreneurs and trade/labor unions that have been registered at a government agency responsible for manpower affairs or workers/laborers' representatives.

19. A Tripartite Cooperation Institute is a communication, consultation and deliberation forum on manpower issues (problems) whose members consist of representatives from entrepreneurs' organizations, workers/laborers' organizations and the government.

20. Company Regulations is a set of written rules and regulations made by an entrepreneur that specifies work requirements and the enterprise's discipline and rules of conduct.

21. A Collective Labor Agreement is an agreement resulted from negotiations between a trade/labor union or several trade/labor unions registered at a government agency responsible for manpower affairs and an entrepreneur or several entrepreneurs or an association of entrepreneurs that specifies work requirements, rights and obligations of the parties.

22. An Industrial Relations Dispute is a difference of opinion that results in a conflict between an entrepreneur or an association of entrepreneurs and a worker/laborer or a trade/labor union because of dispute over rights, interests and termination of employment and dispute between a trade/labor union and another trade/labor union in the same enterprise.

23. A Strike is a collective action of workers/laborers, which is planned and carried out by a trade/labor union to stop or slow down work.

24. A Lockout is the entrepreneur's action of refusing the worker/laborer in whole or in part to perform work.

25. The Termination of an Employment Relationship is termination of employment relationship because of a certain thing that results in the coming of an end of the rights and obligations of the workers/laborer and/or the entrepreneur.

26. A Child is every person who is under 18 (eighteen) years old.

27. Day is a period of time between 6 a. m. to 6 p. m.

28. One (1) day is a period of time of 24 (twenty-four) hours.

29. A Week is a period of 7 (seven) days.

30. A Wage is the right of the worker/laborer that is received and expressed in the form of money as remuneration from the entrepreneur or the employer to worker/laborer, whose amount is determined and paid according to a work agreement, consensus, or laws and regulations, including allowances for the worker/laborer and their family for a job and/or service that has been performed or will be performed.

31. Workers/Laborers' Welfare is a fulfillment of material and spiritual needs and/or necessities (of the worker) either inside or outside the employment relationships that may directly or indirectly enhance work productivity in a working environment that is safe and healthy.

32. Labor Inspection is the activity of controlling and enforcing the implementation of laws and regulations in the field of manpower.

33. Minister is the minister responsible for manpower affairs.

CHAPTER II   STATUTORY BASIS, BASIC PRINCIPLES AND OBJECTIVES

Article 2

Manpower development shall have the Pancasila and the 1945 Constitution as its statutory basis.

Article 3

Manpower development shall be carried out based on the basic principle of integration through functional, cross-sector, central, and provincial/municipal coordination.

Article 4

Manpower development aims at:

a. empowering and making efficient use of manpower optimally and humanely;

b. creating equal opportunity and providing manpower (supply of manpower) that in accordance with the need of national and provincial/municipal developments;

c. providing protection to manpower for the realization of welfare; and

d. improving the welfare of manpower and their family.

CHAPTER III   EQUAL OPPORTUNITIES

Article 5

Every worker/laborer shall have the same opportunity to get a job without discrimination.

Article 6

Every worker/laborer has the right to receive equal treatment without discrimination from their employer.

CHAPTER IV   MANPOWER PLANNING AND MANPOWER INFORMATION

Article 7

(1) For the sake of manpower development, the government shall establish manpower policy and develop manpower planning.

(2) Manpower planning shall include:

a. macro manpower planning; and

b. micro manpower planning.

(3) In formulating policies, strategies, and implementing sustainable manpower development programs, the government must use the manpower planning as mentioned under sub-article (1) as guidelines.

Article 8

(1) Manpower planning shall be developed on the basis of manpower information, which, among others, includes information concerning:

a. population and manpower;

b. employment opportunity;

c. job training including work competence;

d. workers' productivity;

e. industrial relations;

f. working environment condition;

g. wage system and workers' welfare; and

h. social insurance for the employed.

(2) The manpower information as mentioned under sub-article (1) shall be obtained from all related parties, including both government and private agencies.

(3) Provisions concerning procedures for acquiring manpower information as well as procedures for the formulation and implementation of manpower planning as mentioned under sub-article (1) shall be regulated with a Government Regulation.

CHAPTER V   JOB TRAINING

Article 9

Job training is provided and directed to provide, enhance, and develop job competence in order to improve capability, productivity and welfare.

Article 10

(1) Job training shall be carried out by taking into account the need of the job market and the need of the business community, either inside or outside the scope of employment relations.

(2) Job training shall be provided on the basis of training programs that refer to job competence standards.

(3) Job training may be administered step by step.

(4) Provisions concerning procedures for establishing job competence standards as mentioned

under sub-article (2) shall be regulated with a Ministerial Decision.

Article 11

Manpower has the right to acquire and/or improve and/or develop job competence that is suitable to their talents, interests and capabilities through job training.

Article 12

(1) Entrepreneurs are responsible for improving and/or developing their workers' competence through job training.

(2) Entrepreneurs who have met the requirements stipulated with a Ministerial Decision are under an obligation to improve and/or develop the competence of their workers as mentioned under sub-article (1).

(3) Every worker/laborer shall have equal opportunity to take part in job training that is relevant to his/her field of duty.

Article 13

(1) Job training shall be provided by government job-training institutes and/or private job-training institutes.

(2) Job training may be provided in a training place or in the workplace.

(3) In providing job training, government job-training institutes as mentioned under sub-article (1) may work together with the private sector.

Article 14

(1) A private job-training institute can take the form of an Indonesian legal entity or individual proprietorship.

(2) Private job-training institutes as mentioned under sub-article (1) are under an obligation to have a permission or registration from the agency responsible for manpower affairs in the local district/city.

(3) A job-training institute run by a government agency shall register its activities at the government agency responsible for manpower affairs in the local district/city.

(4) Provisions concerning procedures for acquiring a permission from the authorities and registration procedures for job-training institutes as mentioned under sub-article (2) and sub-article (3) shall be regulated with a Ministerial Decision.

Article 15

Job training providers are under an obligation to make sure that the following requirements are met:
a. the availability of trainers;
b. the availability of a curriculum that is suitable to the level of job training to be given;
c. the availability of structures and infrastructure for job training; and
d. the availability of fund for the perpetuation of the activity of providing job training.

Article 16

(1) Licensed private job-training institutes and registered government-sponsored job-training institutes may obtain accreditation from accrediting agencies.

(2) The accrediting agencies as mentioned under sub-article (1) shall be independent, consisting of community and government constituents, and shall be established with a Ministerial Decision.

(3) The organization and procedures of work of the accrediting agencies as mentioned under sub-article (2) shall be regulated with a Ministerial Decision.

Article 17

(1) The government agency responsible for labor/manpower affairs in a district/city may temporarily terminate activities associated with the organization and administration of a job training in the district/city if it turns out that the implementation of the job training:

a. is not in accordance with the job training directions as mentioned under Article 9; and/or

b. does not fulfill the requirements as mentioned under Article 15.

(2) The temporary termination of activities associated with the organization and administration of job training as mentioned under sub-article (1) shall be accompanied with the reasons for the temporary termination and corrective suggestions and shall apply for no longer than 6 (six) months.

(3) The temporary termination of the implementation of the administration of job training only applies to training programs that do not fulfill the requirements as specified under Article 9 and Article 15.

(4) Job training providers who, within a period of 6 (six) months, do not fulfill and complete the suggested corrective suggestions as mentioned under sub-article (2) shall be subjected to a sanction that rules the termination of their training programs.

(5) Job training providers who do not obey and continue to carry out the training programs that have been ordered for termination as mentioned under sub-article (4) shall be subjected to a sanction that revokes their licenses and cancels their registrations as job training providers.

(6) Provisions concerning procedures for temporary termination, termination, revocation of license, and cancellation of registration shall be regulated with a Ministerial Decision.

Article 18

(1) Manpower shall be entitled to receive job competence recognition after participating in job training provided by government job-training institutes, private job-training institutes, or after participating in job training in the workplace.

(2) The job competence recognition as mentioned under sub-article (1) shall be made through job competence certification.

(3) Manpower with experience in the job may, despite their experience, takes part in the job training as mentioned under sub-article (1) in order to obtain job competence certification as mentioned under sub-article (2).

(4) To provide job competence certification, independent profession-based certification agencies shall be established.

(5) Provisions concerning the procedures for the establishment of certification agencies as mentioned under sub-article (4) shall be regulated with a Presidential Decision.

Article 19

The provision of job training to disabled manpower shall take into account the type, degree of disability and their capability.

Article 20

(1) To support the improvement of job training for the sake of manpower development, a national job-training system that serves as a reference for the administration of job training in all fields of work and/or all sectors shall be developed.

(2) Provisions concerning the form, mechanism and institutional arrangements of the national job-training system as mentioned under sub-article (1) shall be regulated with a Government Regulation.

Article 21

Job training may be administered by means of apprenticeship systems.

Article 22

(1) Apprenticeship shall be carried out based on a written apprenticeship agreement between the participant and the entrepreneur.

(2) The apprenticeship agreement as mentioned under sub-article (1) shall at least have stipulations explaining the rights and obligations of both the participant and the entrepreneur as well as the period of apprenticeship.

(3) Any apprenticeship administered without an apprenticeship agreement as mentioned under sub-article (2) shall be declared illegal and as a consequence, the status of the apprenticeship's participants shall change to be the workers/laborers of the enterprise.

Article 23

Manpower that has completed an apprenticeship program is entitled to get their job competence and qualifications recognized by enterprises or by certification agency.

Article 24

Apprenticeship can take place within the enterprise or at the place where job training is organized, or at another enterprise, inside or outside Indonesia's territory.

Article 25

(1) The apprenticeship which is conducted outside Indonesia's territory must obtain a license from the Minister or the appointed official.

(2) In order to obtain the license as mentioned under sub-article (1) , the organizer of the apprenticeship must be in the form of an Indonesian legal entity in accordance with the prevailing laws and regulations.

(3) Provisions concerning the procedures for obtaining license for apprenticeship organized outside Indonesia's territory as mentioned under sub-article (1) and (2) shall be regulated with a Ministerial Decision.

Article 26

(1) Any apprenticeship organized outside Indonesia's territory must take into account:

a. the dignity and status of Indonesians as a nation;

b. mastery of a higher level of competence; and

c. protection and welfare of apprenticeship participants, including their rights to perform religious obligations.

(2) The Minister or appointed official may order the termination of any apprenticeship taking place outside Indonesia's territory if it turns out that its organization is not pursuant to sub-article (1).

Article 27

(1) The Minister may require qualified enterprises to organize apprenticeship programs.

(2) In determining the requirements for organizing apprenticeship programs as mentioned under sub-article (1) , the Minister must take into account the interests of the enterprise, the society and the State.

Article 28

(1) In order to provide recommendation and consideration in the establishment of policies and coordination of job training and apprenticeship activities, a national job-training coordinator institute shall be established.

(2) The formation, membership and procedures of work of the national job-training coordinator institute as mentioned under sub-article (1) shall be regulated with a Presidential Decision.

Article 29

(1) The Central Government and/or Regional Governments shall develop job training and apprenticeship.

(2) The development of job training and apprenticeship shall be directed to improve the relevance, quality, and efficiency of job training administration and productivity.

（3）Efforts to improve productivity as mentioned under sub-article （2） shall be made through the development of productive culture, work ethics, technology and efficiency of economic activities directed towards the realization of national productivity.

Article 30

（1）In order to enhance productivity as mentioned under sub-article （2） of Article 29, a national productivity institute shall be established.

（2）The national productivity institute as mentioned under sub-article （1） shall be in the form of an institutional productivity enhancement service network, which supports cross-sector and cross-regional activities/programs.

（3）The formation, membership and procedures of work of the national productivity institute as mentioned under sub-article （1） shall be regulated with a Presidential Decision.

CHAPTER VI   JOB PLACEMENT

Article 31

Every manpower shall have equal right and opportunity to choose a job, get a job, or move to another job and earn decent income irrespective of whether they are employed at home or abroad.

Article 32

（1）Job placement shall be carried out based on transparency, freedom, objectivity, fairness and equal opportunity without discrimination.

（2）Job placement shall be directed to place manpower in the right job or position which best suits their expertise, skills, talents, interests and capabilities by observing their dignity and human rights as well as legal protection.

（3）Job placement shall be carried out by taking into account the equal distribution of opportunity and the provision of manpower in accordance with the needs of the national and regional development programs.

Article 33

The placement of manpower consists of:

a. domestic manpower placement; and

b. overseas manpower placement.

Article 34

Provisions concerning the placement of manpower in foreign countries as mentioned under Article 33 point b shall be regulated with an act.

Article 35

(1) Employers who need workforce may recruit by themselves the workforce they need or have them recruited through job placement agencies.

(2) Job placement agencies as mentioned under sub-article (1) are under an obligation to provide protection to manpower that they try to find a placement for since their recruitment takes place until their placement is realized.

(3) In employing people who are available for a job, the employers as mentioned under sub-article (1) are under an obligation to provide protection which shall include protection for their welfare, safety and health, both mentally and physically.

Article 36

(1) The placement of manpower by a job placement agency as mentioned under sub-article (1) of Article 35 shall be carried out through the provision of job placement service.

(2) Job placement service as mentioned under sub-article (2) shall be provided/rendered in an integrated manner within a job placement system of which the following elements are parts:

a. job seekers;

b. job vacancies;

c. job market information;

d. inter-job mechanisms; and

e. institutional arrangements for job placement.

(3) Activities connected with the elements of the job placement system as mentioned under sub-article (2) can take place separately and are aimed at the realization of the placement of manpower.

Article 37

(1) Job placement agencies as mentioned under sub-article (1) of Article 35 consist of:

a. government agencies responsible for manpower affairs; and

b. private agencies with legal status.

(2) In order to provide job placement service, the private agency as mentioned under sub-article (1) point b is under an obligation to possess a written permission from the Minister or the appointed official.

Article 38

(1) Job placement agencies as mentioned under point a sub-article (1) of Article 37 are prohibited from collecting placement fees, either directly or indirectly, in part or in whole, from people available for work whom they find a placement for and their users.

(2) Private job placement agencies as mentioned under point b sub-article (1) of Article 37 may only collect placement fees from users of their service and from workers of certain ranks and

occupation whom they have placed.

(3) The ranks and occupation as mentioned under sub-article (2) shall be regulated with a Ministerial Decision.

CHAPTER VII   EXPANSION OF JOB OPPORTUNITIES

Article 39

(1) The government is responsible for making efforts to expand job opportunities both inside and outside the employment relationships.

(2) The government and the society shall jointly make efforts to expand job opportunities both inside and outside the employment relationships.

(3) All the government's policies, at the central or regional level and in each sector, shall be directed to realize the expansion of job opportunities both inside and outside the employment relationships.

(4) Financial institutions, either banks or non-banks, and the business society need to help and facilitate each activity of the society which can create or develop expansion of job opportunities.

Article 40

(1) Expansion of employment opportunities outside employment relationships shall be undertaken through the creation of productive and sustainable activities by efficient use of natural resource potentials, human resources, and effective practical technologies.

(2) Expansion of employment opportunities as mentioned under sub-article (1) shall be undertaken through patterns of formation and development for the self-employed, the application of labor-intensive system, the application and development of effective practical technology, and efficient use of volunteers or other patterns that may encourage the creation of job opportunity expansion.

Article 41

(1) The government shall determine policies on manpower affairs and job opportunity expansion.

(2) The government and the society shall jointly exercise control over the implementation of the policies as mentioned under sub-article (1).

(3) In implementing the duty as mentioned under sub-article (2), a coordinating body with government and society constituents as its members may be established.

(4) Provisions concerning the expansion of job opportunities as mentioned under Article 39 and Article 40, and the formation of a coordinating body as mentioned under sub-article (3) of this Article shall be regulated with a Government Regulation.

CHAPTER VIII   EMPLOYMENT OF FOREIGN WORKERS

Article 42

(1) Every employer that employs foreign workers is under an obligation to obtain written permission from the Minister.

(2) Individual employers are prohibited from employing foreign workers.

(3) The obligation to obtain permission from the Minister as mentioned under sub-article (1) shall not apply to foreign representative offices in Indonesia that employ foreign citizens as their diplomatic and consular employees.

(4) Foreign workers can be employed in Indonesia in employment relations for certain positions and for a certain period of time only.

(5) Provisions concerning certain positions and certain periods of time as mentioned under sub-article (4) shall be regulated with a Ministerial Decision.

(6) Foreign workers as mentioned under sub-article (4) whose working period has expired and cannot be extended may be replaced by other foreign workers.

Article 43

(1) Employers of foreign workers must have a plan concerning the assignment of foreign workers that are legalized by the Minister or the appointed official.

(2) The plans for the assignment of foreign workers as mentioned under sub-article (1) shall at least contain the following information:

a. the reasons why the service of foreign workers is needed or required;

b. the position and/or occupation of the foreign workers within the organizational structure of the enterprise;

c. period of assignment; and

d. the appointment of Indonesian workers as associate for the foreign workers.

(3) The provision as mentioned under sub-article (1) shall not apply to government agencies, international agencies and representative diplomatic offices of foreign countries.

(4) The provisions concerning the procedures for the legalization of plans concerning the assignment of foreign workers shall be regulated with a Ministerial Decision.

Article 44

(1) Employers of foreign workers are under an obligation to obey the prevailing regulations concerning occupations and competence standards.

(2) The provisions concerning occupations and competence standards as mentioned under sub-article (1) shall be regulated with a Ministerial Decision.

Article 45

(1) Employers who employ foreign workers are under obligations:

a. to appoint an Indonesian worker as an associate for the foreign worker whereby the foreign worker shall transfer technologies and his/her expertise to his/her Indonesian associate; and

b. to educate and train the Indonesian worker, as mentioned under point a, until he/she has the qualifications required to occupy the position currently occupied by the foreign worker.

(2) The provision as mentioned under sub-article (1) shall not apply to foreign worker who occupy the position of director and/or commissioner.

Article 46

(1) A foreign worker is not allowed to occupy positions that deal with personnel affairs and/or occupy certain positions.

(2) The certain positions as mentioned under sub-article (1) shall be regulated with a Ministerial Decision.

Article 47

(1) Employers are obliged to pay compensation for every foreign worker that they employ.

(2) The obligation to pay compensation as mentioned under sub-article (1) shall not apply to government agencies, international agencies, social and religious institutions and certain positions in educational institutions.

(3) The provisions concerning certain positions in educational institutions as mentioned under sub-article (2) shall be regulated with a Ministerial Decision.

(4) The provisions concerning the amount of compensation and its allocation shall be regulated with a Government Regulation.

Article 48

Employers who employ foreign workers are under an obligation to repatriate the foreign workers to their countries of origin after the working relations expire.

Article 49

Provisions concerning the procedures for the assignment of foreign workers and the implementation of education and training for their Indonesian associates shall be regulated with a Government Regulation.

CHAPTER IX   EMPLOYMENT RELATIONS

Article 50

Employment relation exists because of the work agreement between the entrepreneur and the worker/laborer.

Article 51

(1) Work agreements can be made either orally or in writing.

(2) Work agreements that specify requirements in writing shall be carried out in accordance with valid legislation.

Article 52

(1) A work agreement shall be made based on:

a. bilateral agreement;

b. the capability or competence of taking legal actions;

c. the availability/existence of the job which the parties have agreed about;

d. the notion that the job which the parties have agreed about is not against public order, morality and what is prescribed in the prevailing laws and regulations.

(2) If a work agreement, which has been made by the parties, turns out to be against what is prescribed under point a and point b of sub-article (1), may be abolished/cancelled.

(3) If a work agreement, which has been made by the parties, turns out to be against what is prescribed under point c and point d of sub-article (1), shall be declared null and void by law.

Article 53

Everything associated with, and/or the costs needed for, the making of a work agreement shall be borne by, and shall be the responsibility of, the entrepreneur.

Article 54

(1) A written work agreement shall at least include:

a. the name, address and line of business;

b. the name, sex, age and address of the worker/laborer;

c. the occupation or the type of job;

d. the place, where the job is to be carried out;

e. the amount of wages and how the wages shall be paid;

f. job requirements stating the rights and obligations of both the entrepreneur and the worker/laborer;

g. date of commencement and validity period of the work agreement;

h. where and when the work agreement is made; and

i. the signatures of the parties involved in the work agreement.

(2) The provisions in a work agreement as mentioned under point e and point f of sub-article (1) are concerned must not contravene the company regulations, the collective labor agreements and prevailing laws and regulations.

(3) A work agreement as mentioned under sub-article (1) shall be made in 2 (two) counterparts which have the same legal force, 1 (one) copy of which shall be kept by the entrepreneur and the other by the worker/laborer.

Article 55

A work agreement cannot be withdrawn and/or changed unless the parties agreed otherwise.

Article 56

(1) A work agreement may be made for a specified or unspecified time.

(2) A work agreement for a specified time shall be made based on:

a. a period; or

b. the completion of a certain job.

Article 57

(1) A work agreement for a specified time shall be made in writing and must be written in the Indonesian language with Latin alphabets.

(2) A work agreement for a specified time, if not made in writing and against what is prescribed under sub-article (1), shall be regarded as a work agreement for an unspecified time.

(3) If a work agreement is written in both the Indonesian language and a foreign language and then differences in interpretation arise, then the Indonesian version of the agreement shall validate.

Article 58

(1) A work agreement for a specified time cannot stipulate probation.

(2) If a work agreement as mentioned under sub-article (1) stipulates the probation, it shall then be declared null and void by law.

Article 59

(1) A work agreement for a specified time can only be made for a certain job, which, because of the type and nature of the job, will finish in a specified time, that is:

a. work to be performed and completed at once, or work which is temporary by nature;

b. work whose completion time is estimated not too long and no longer than 3 (three) years;

c. seasonal work; or

d. work that is related to a new product, a new activity or an additional product that is still in the experimental stage or try-out phase.

(2) A work agreement for a specified time cannot be made for jobs that are permanent by nature.

(3) A work agreement for a specified time can be extended or renewed.

(4) A work agreement for a specified time may be made for a period of no longer than 2 (two) years and can only be extended one time that is not longer than 1 (one) year.

(5) Entrepreneurs who intend to extend the work agreement for a specified time shall notify the relevant workers/laborers of the intention in writing within a period of no later than 7 (seven) days prior to the expiration of the work agreement.

(6) The renewal of a work agreement for a specified time can only be made after a grace period of 30 (thirty) days is over from the work agreement for a specified period comes to an end; the renewal of a work agreement for a specified time can only be made once that is no longer than 2 (two) years.

(7) Any work agreement for a specified time that does not fulfill the requirements mentioned under sub-article (1), (2), (4), (5) and (6) shall, by law, become a work agreement for an unspecified time.

(8) Other matters that have not been regulated under this article shall be further regulated with a Ministerial Decision.

Article 60

(1) A work agreement for an unspecified time may require a probation period for no longer than 3 (three) months.

(2) During the probation period as mentioned under sub-article (1), the entrepreneur is prohibited from paying wages less than the applicable minimum wage.

Article 61

(1) A work agreement shall expire if:

a. the worker dies; or

b. the period of work agreement comes to an end; or

c. a court decision and/or a resolution or order of the industrial relations disputes settlement institution, which has permanent legal force; or

d. there is a certain situation or incident prescribed in the work agreement, the company regulations, or the collective labor agreement which may effectively result in the termination of employment.

(2) A work agreement does not end because the entrepreneur dies or because the ownership of the company has been transferred because the company has been sold, bequeathed to an heir, or awarded as a grant.

(3) In the event of a transfer of ownership of an enterprise, the new entrepreneur shall bear the responsibility of fulfilling the entitlements of the worker/laborer unless otherwise stated in the transfer agreement, which must not reduce the entitlements of the worker/laborer.

(4) If the individual entrepreneur dies, his or her heir may terminate the work agreement after negotiating with the worker/laborer.

(5) If a worker/laborer dies, his or her heir has a rightful claim to acquire the worker's entitlements according to the prevailing laws and regulations, or to the entitlements that have been prescribed in the work agreement, the company regulations, or the collective labor agreement.

Article 62

If either party in a work agreement for a specified time shall terminates the employment relations prior to the expiration of the agreement, or if their work agreement has to be ended for reasons other than what is given under subsections of Article 61, the party that terminates the relation is obliged to pay compensation to the other party in the amount of the workers/laborers' wages until the expiration of the agreement.

Article 63

If a work agreement for an unspecified time is made orally, the entrepreneur is under an obligation to issue a letter of appointment for the relevant worker/laborer. Such letter of appointment shall at least contain information concerning:

a. the name and address of the worker/laborer;

b. the date the worker starts to work;

c. the type of job or work; and

d. the amount of wages.

Article 64

An enterprise may subcontract part of its work to another enterprise under a written agreement of contract of work or a written agreement for the provision of the worker/labor.

Article 65

(1) The subcontract of part of work to another enterprise shall be performed under a written agreement of contract of work.

(2) Work that may be subcontracted as mentioned under sub-article (1) must meet the following requirements:

a. the work can be done separately from the main activity;

b. the work is to be undertaken under either a direct or an indirect order from the party commissioning the work;

c. the work is an entirely auxiliary activity of the enterprise; and

d. the work does not directly inhibit the production process.

(3) The other enterprise as mentioned under sub-article (1) must be in the form of a legal entity.

(4) The protection and working conditions provided to workers/laborers at the other enterprise as mentioned under sub-article (2) shall be at least the same as the protection and working conditions provided at the enterprise that commissions the contract or in accordance with the prevailing laws and regulations.

(5) Any change and/or addition to what is required under sub-article (2) shall be regulated further with a Ministerial Decision.

(6) The employment relationship in undertaking the work as mentioned under sub-article (1) shall be regulated with a written employment agreement between the other enterprise and the worker/laborer it employs.

(7) The employment relationship as mentioned under sub-article (6) may be based on an employment agreement for an unspecified time or on an employment agreement for a specified time if it meets the requirements under Article 59.

(8) If what is stipulated under sub-article (2) and sub-article (3), is not met, the status of working relations between the worker/laborer and the enterprise receiving contract shall change into working relations between the worker/laborer and the enterprise giving the job by law.

(9) In the event of change of employer from the contractor to the contracting enterprise as mentioned under sub-article (8), the employment relationship between the worker/laborer and the contracting enterprise shall be subjected to the employment relationship as mentioned under sub-article (7) .

Article 66

(1) Workers/laborers from labor suppliers must not be utilized by employers to carry out their enterprises' main activities or activities that are directly related to production process except for auxiliary service activities or activities that are indirectly related to production process.

(2) Labor suppliers which receiving labor for auxiliary service activities or activities indirectly related to production process must fulfill the following requirements:

a. there is employment relationship between the worker/laborer and the labor provider;

b. the applicable employment agreement in the employment relationship as mentioned under point a above shall be employment agreement for a specified time which fulfills the requirements under Article 59 and/or work agreement for an unspecified time made in writing and signed by both parties;

c. the labor provider shall be responsible for wages and welfare protection, working conditions and disputes that may arise; and

d. the agreements between enterprises serving as labor providers and enterprises using the labor they provide shall be made in writing, and shall include provisions as mentioned under this act.

(3) Labor providers/suppliers shall take the form of a legal entity business with license from a government agency responsible for manpower affairs.

(4) If what is stipulated under sub-article (1), point a, b and d of sub-article (2) and (3) is not fulfilled, the status of working relations between the worker/laborer and the enterprise receiving the worker/laborer service shall shift to working relations between the worker/laborer and the enterprise providing the job by law.

CHAPTER X PROTECTION, WAGES AND WELFARE

Section One Protection

Subsection One Disabled Persons

Article 67

(1) Entrepreneurs who employ disabled workers are under an obligation to provide protection to the workers in accordance with the type and degree of their disability.

(2) The protection for disabled workers as mentioned under sub-article (1) shall be administered in accordance with prevailing laws and regulations.

Subsection Two Children

Article 68

Entrepreneurs are not allowed to employ children.

Article 69

(1) Exemption from what is stipulated under Article 68 may be made for the employment of children aged between 13 (thirteen) years old and 15 (fifteen) years old for light work as long as the job does not stunt or disrupt their physical, mental and social developments.

(2) Entrepreneurs who employ children for light work as mentioned under sub-article (1) must meet the following requirements:

a. the entrepreneurs must have written permission from the parents or guardians of the children;

b. there must be a work agreement between the entrepreneur and the parents or guardians;

c. maximum working time 3 (three) hours a day;

d. conducting during the day without disturbing school time;

e. occupational safety and health;

f. a clear employment relations; and

g. receiving wages in accordance with the prevailing provisions.

(3) The provisions as mentioned under point a, b, f and g of sub-article (2) shall not apply to children who work in a family business.

Article 70

(1) Children may work at a workplace as part of their school's education curriculum or

training legalized by the authorities.

(2) The children as mentioned under sub-article (1) shall be at least 14 (fourteen) years of age.

(3) The job as mentioned under sub-article (1) can be performed on the conditions:

a. given clear instructions on how to do the job as well as guidance and supervision on how to carry out the work; and

b. given the occupational safety and health.

Article 71

(1) Children may work in order to develop their talents and interests.

(2) Entrepreneurs who employ children as mentioned under sub-article (1) are under an obligation to meet the following requirements:

a. put under direct supervision of their parents or guardians;

b. maximum working time 3 (three) hours a day; and

c. the working conditions and environment do not disrupt their physical, mental and social developments as well as school time.

(3) Provisions concerning children who work to develop their talents and interests as mentioned under sub-article (1) and (2) shall be regulated with a Ministerial Decision.

Article 72

In case children are employed together with adult workers/laborers, the children's workplace must be separated from the workplace for adult workers/laborers.

Article 73

Children shall be assumed to be at work if they are found in a workplace unless there is evidence to prove otherwise.

Article 74

(1) Anyone shall be prohibited from employing and involving children in the worst forms of child labor.

(2) The worst forms of child labor as mentioned under sub-article (1) include:

a. all kinds of job in the form of slavery or practices similar to slavery;

b. all kinds of job that make use of, procure, or offer children for prostitution, the production of pornography, pornographic performances or gambling;

c. all kinds of job that make use of, procure, or involve children for the production and trade of alcoholic beverages, narcotics, psychotropic substances and other addictive substances; and/or

d. all kinds of job that are harmful to the health, safety and moral.

(3) The types of jobs that damage the health, safety or moral of the children as mentioned

under point d of sub-article （2） shall be regulated with a Ministerial Decision.

Article 75

（1） The government is under an obligation to make efforts to overcome problems concerning with children who work outside employment relationship.

（2） The efforts as mentioned under sub-article （1） shall be regulated with a Government Regulation.

Subsection Three   Women

Article 76

（1） It is prohibited to employ female workers/laborers aged less than 18 （eighteen） years of age between 11 p. m. and 7 a. m.

（2） Entrepreneurs are prohibited from employing pregnant workers/laborers who, according to a doctor's certificate, are at risk of harming the safety of themselves and the baby if they work between 11 p. m. and 7 a. m.

（3） Entrepreneurs who employ female workers/laborers to work between 11 p. m. and 7 a. m. are under an obligation：

a. to provide them with nutritious food and drink； and

b. to maintain decency/morality and security in the workplace.

（4） Entrepreneurs are under an obligation to provide returned/roundtrip transport for female workers/laborers who work between 11 p. m. and 5 a. m.

（5） Provisions as mentioned under sub-article （3） and （4） shall be regulated with a Ministerial Decision.

Subsection Four   Working Hours

Article 77

（1） Every entrepreneur is under an obligation to observe the provision concerning working hours.

（2） The working hours as mentioned under sub-article （1） cover：

a. 7 （seven） hours a day and 42 （forty-two） hours a week for 6 （six） workdays in a week； or

b. 8 （eight） hours a day and 40 （forty） hours a week for 5 （five） workdays in a week.

（3） The provisions concerning the working hours as mentioned under sub-article （2） do not apply to certain business sectors or certain types of work.

（4） The provisions concerning working hours for certain business sectors or certain types of work as mentioned under sub-article （3） shall be regulated with a Ministerial Decision.

Article 78

(1) Entrepreneurs who require their workers/laborers to work longer than the working hours determined under sub-article (2) of Article 77 must meet the following requirements:

a. approval of the relevant workers/laborers;

b. maximum overtime work of 3 (three) hours in a day and 14 (fourteen) hours in a week.

(2) Entrepreneurs who require their workers/laborers to work overtime as mentioned under sub-article (1) are under an obligation to pay overtime wage.

(3) The provisions concerning overtime as mentioned under sub-article (1) point b do not apply to certain business sectors or certain jobs.

(4) The provisions concerning overtime and overtime wages as mentioned under sub-article (2) and (3) shall be regulated with a Ministerial Decision.

Article 79

(1) Entrepreneurs are under an obligation to allow their workers/laborers to take a rest and leave.

(2) The period of rest and leave as mentioned under sub-article (1) shall include:

a. the period of rest between working hours at least half an hour after working for 4 (four) hours consecutively and this period of rest shall not be inclusive of working hours; The weekly period of rest is 1 (one) day after 6 (six) workdays in a week or 2 (two) days after 5 (five) workdays in a week;

b. the yearly period of rest is 12 (twelve) workdays after the worker/laborer works for 12 (twelve) months consecutively; and

c. a long period of rest of no less than 2 (two) months, which shall be awarded in the seventh and eighth year of work each for a period of 1 (one) month to workers/laborers who have been working for 6 (six) years consecutively at the same enterprise on the condition that the workers/laborers will no longer be entitled to their annual period of rest in 2 (two) current years. This provision shall henceforth be applicable every 6 (six) years of work.

(3) The application of the provision concerning the period of rest as mentioned under point c of sub-article (2) shall be regulated in a work agreement, the company regulations or the collective labor agreement.

(4) The provisions concerning the long period of rest as mentioned under point c of sub-article (2) only apply to workers/laborers who work in certain enterprises.

(5) The certain enterprises as mentioned under sub-article (4) shall be regulated with a Ministerial Decision.

Article 80

Entrepreneurs are under an obligation to provide workers with adequate opportunity to perform their religious obligations.

Article 81

(1) Female workers/laborers who feel pain during their menstruation period and notify the entrepreneur about this are not obliged to come to work on the first and second day of menstruation.

(2) The implementation of what is stipulated under sub-article (1) shall be regulated in work agreements, the company regulations or collective labor agreements.

Article 82

(1) Female workers/laborers are entitled to a 1.5 (one and a half) months period of rest before the time at which they are estimated by an obstetrician or a midwife to give birth to a baby and another 1.5 (one and a half) month period of rest thereafter.

(2) A female worker/laborer who has a miscarriage is entitled to a period of rest of 1.5 (one and a half) months or a period of rest as stated in the medical statement issued by the obstetrician or midwife.

Article 83

Entrepreneurs are under an obligation to provide proverb opportunities to female workers/laborers whose babies still need breast-feeding to breast-feed their babies if that must be performed during working hours.

Article 84

Every worker/laborer who uses her right to take the period of rest as specified under points b, c and d of sub-article (2) of Article 79, Article 80 and Article 82 shall receive her wages in full.

Article 85

(1) Workers/laborers are not obliged to work on formal public holidays.

(2) Entrepreneurs may require their workers/laborers to work during formal public holidays if the types and nature of their jobs must be conducted continuously or under other circumstances based on the agreement between the worker/laborer and the entrepreneur.

(3) Entrepreneurs who require their workers/laborers to work on formal public holidays as mentioned under sub-article (2) are under an obligation to pay overtime wage.

(4) The provisions concerning the types and nature of the jobs mentioned under sub-article (2) shall be regulated with a Ministerial Decision.

Subsection Five   Occupational Safety and Health

Article 86

(1) Every worker/laborer has the right to receive protection on:
a. occupational safety and health;

b. morality and decency; and

c. treatment that shows respect to human dignity and religious values.

(2) In order to protect the safety of workers/laborers and to realize optimal productivity, an occupational health and safety scheme shall be administered.

(3) The protection as mentioned under sub-article (1) and (2) shall be given in accordance with prevailing laws and regulations.

Article 87

(1) Every enterprise is under an obligation to apply an occupational safety and health management system that shall be integrated into the enterprise's management system.

(2) The provisions concerning the application of the occupational safety and health management system as mentioned under sub-article (1) shall be regulated with a Government Regulation.

Section Two   Wages

Article 88

(1) Every worker/laborer has the right to earn a living that is humanely decent.

(2) In order to enable the worker to earn a living that is humanely decent as mentioned under sub-article (1), the government shall establish a wage policy that protects the worker/laborer.

(3) The wage policy that protects workers/laborers as mentioned under sub-article (2) shall include:

a. minimum wage;

b. overtime wage;

c. wage during the absence;

d. wage because of activities outside their jobs that they have to carry out;

e. wage payable because they use the right to take a rest;

f. the form and method of the payment of wage;

g. fines and deductions from wage;

h. other matters that can be calculated with wage;

i. proportional wage structure and scale;

j. wage for the payment of severance pay; and

k. wage for calculating income tax.

(4) The government shall establish/set minimum wage as mentioned under sub-article (3) point a based on the need for decent living by taking into account productivity and economic growth.

Article 89

(1) The minimum wage as mentioned under sub-article (3) point a of Article 88 may

consist of:

    a. provincial or district/city-based minimum wage;

    b. provincial or district/city-based sectoral minimum wage.

（2）The establishment of minimum wage as mentioned under sub-article（1）shall be directed towards meeting the need for decent living.

（3）The minimum wage as mentioned under sub-article（1）shall be determined by the Governors after considering recommendations from the Provincial Wage Councils and/or the District Heads/Mayors.

（4）The components of and the implementation of the phases of achieving the needs for decent living as mentioned under sub-article（2）shall be regulated with a Ministerial Decision.

Article 90

（1）Entrepreneurs are prohibited from paying wages lower than the minimum wage as mentioned under Article 89.

（2）Entrepreneurs who are unable to pay minimum wages as mentioned under Article 89 may be allowed to make postponement.

（3）Procedures for postponing paying minimum wages as mentioned under sub-article（2）shall be regulated with a Ministerial Decision.

Article 91

（1）The amount of wages set based on an agreement between the entrepreneurs and the worker/laborer or trade/labor union must not be lower than the amount of wages set under the prevailing laws and regulations.

（2）In case the agreement as mentioned under sub-article（1）sets a wage that is lower than or contravenes the one that has to be set under the prevailing laws and regulations shall be declared null and void by law, and the entrepreneur shall be obliged to pay the worker/laborer a wage according to the prevailing laws and regulations.

Article 92

（1）Entrepreneurs shall formulate the structure and scale of wage by taking into account the level, position, years of work, education and competence of the worker/laborer.

（2）Entrepreneurs shall review their workers/laborers' wages periodically by taking into account their enterprises' financial ability and productivity.

（3）The provisions concerning the structure and scales of wages as mentioned under sub-article（1）shall be regulated with a Ministerial Decision.

Article 93

（1）No wages will be paid if workers/laborers do not perform work.

（2）However, the provision as mentioned under sub-article（1）shall not apply and the entrepreneur shall be obliged to pay the worker/laborers' wages if they do not perform work because of the following reasons:

a. the workers/laborers are ill so that they cannot perform their work;

b. the female workers/laborers are ill on the first and second day of their menstruation period so that they cannot perform their work;

c. the workers/laborers have to be absent from work because they get married, marry of their children, have their sons circumcised, have their children baptized, or because the worker/laborer's wife gives birth or suffers from a miscarriage, or because the wife or husband or children or children-in-law(s) or parent(s) or parent-in-law(s) of the workers/laborers or a member of the worker/laborers' household die(s);

d. the workers/laborers cannot perform their work because they are carrying out or fulfilling their obligations to the State;

e. the workers/laborers cannot perform their work because they are performing religious obligations ordered by their religion;

f. the workers/laborers are willing to do the job that they have been promised to but the entrepreneur does not employ them, because of the own fault or because of the impediments that the entrepreneur should have been able to avoid;

g. the workers/laborers are exercising their right to take a rest;

h. the workers/laborers are performing their trade union duties with the permission from the entrepreneur; and

i. the workers/laborers are undergoing an education program required by the enterprise.

(3) The amount of wages payable to workers who are taken ill as mentioned under point a of sub-article (2) shall be determined as follows:

a. for the first four months, they shall be entitled to receive 100% (one hundred percent) of their wages;

b. for the second four months, they shall be entitled to receive 75% (seventy-five percent) of their wages;

c. for the third four months, they shall be entitled to receive 50% (fifty percent) of their wages; and

d. For subsequent months, they shall be entitled to receive 25% (twenty-five percent) of their wages prior to the termination of employment by the entrepreneur.

(4) The amount of wages payable to workers/laborers during the period in which they have to be absent from work for reasons specified under point c of sub-article (2) shall be determined as follows:

a. if the workers/laborers are get married, shall be entitled to receive a payment for 3 (three) days;

b. if the workers/laborers marry of their children, shall be entitled to receive a payment for 2 (two) days;

c. if the workers/laborers' child are circumcised, shall be entitled to receive a payment for 2 (two) days;

d. if the workers/laborers' children are baptized, shall be entitled to receive a payment for 2 (two) days;

e. if a workers/laborers' wife gives birth or suffers a miscarriage, shall be entitled to receive a payment for 2 (two) days;

f. if the workers/laborers' spouse, or because either one parent or one of parent-in-law, or because one of children or children-in-law dies, shall be entitled to receive a payment for 2 (two) days; and

g. If a member of the worker/laborer's household dies, shall be entitled to receive a payment for 1 (one) day.

(5) Arrangements for the implementation of what is stipulated under sub-article (2) shall be specified in the work agreements, company regulations or collective labor agreements.

Article 94

If a wage is composed of basic wage and fixed allowances, the amount of the basic wage must not be less than 75% (seventy-five percent) of the total amount of the wage and fixed allowances.

Article 95

(1) Violations by the worker/laborer, either by willful misconduct or negligence, may result in the imposition of a fine.

(2) Entrepreneurs who pay their workers/laborers' wages late either by willful misconduct or negligence shall be ordered to pay a fine whose amount shall correspond to a certain percentage from the worker/laborer's wages.

(3) The government shall regulate the imposition of fine on the entrepreneur and or the worker/laborer in the payment of wages.

(4) In case the enterprise is declared bankrupt or liquidated based on the prevailing laws and regulations, the payment of the workers/laborers' wages shall take priority over the payment of other debts.

Article 96

Any claim for the payment of the worker/laborer's wages and all other claims for payments that arise from an employment relation shall expire after the lapse of 2 (two) years since such the right is arose.

Article 97

The provisions concerning decent income, wages policy, the need for decent living and workers' wage protection as mentioned under Article 88, the setting of minimum wage as mentioned under Article 89, and the provision concerning the imposition of a fine as mentioned under sub-article (1), (2) and (3) of Article 95 shall be regulated with a Government Regulation.

Article 98

(1) In order to provide recommendations and considerations for the formulation of wage policies to be established by the government, and to develop a national wage system, the National Wage Council, the Provincial Wage Councils, and the District/City Wage Councils shall be established.

(2) The councils as mentioned under sub-article (1) shall have representatives from the government, entrepreneurs' organizations, trade/labor unions, universities and experts as their members.

(3) The members of the National-level Wage Council shall be appointed and dismissed by the President while the members of the Provincial Wage Councils and the District/City Wage Councils shall be appointed and dismissed by the Governors/District Heads/Mayors of the respective provinces, districts and cities.

(4) The provisions concerning the procedures for the formation of, membership composition of, procedures for appointing and dismissing members of and duties and working procedures of wage system councils as mentioned under sub-article (1) and (2) shall be regulated with a Presidential Decision.

Section Three   Welfare

Article 99

(1) Workers/laborers and their families shall each be entitled to social security.

(2) The social security as mentioned under sub-article (1) shall be administered in accordance with prevailing laws and regulations.

Article 100

(1) In order to improve the welfare of the workers/laborers and their families, the entrepreneur shall provide welfare facilities.

(2) The provision of welfare facilities as mentioned under sub-article (1) shall be administered by weighing the need of the worker/laborer for welfare facilities against the enterprise's ability to provide such facilities.

(3) The provisions concerning the type and criteria of welfare facilities according to the need of the worker/laborer and the measurement of the enterprise's ability to provide them as mentioned under sub-article (1) and (2) shall be regulated with a Government Regulation.

Article 101

（1）To improve workers/laborers' welfare, workers/laborers' cooperatives and productive business at the enterprise shall be established.

（2）The government, the entrepreneur and the worker/laborer or the trade/labor union shall make efforts to develop workers/laborers' cooperatives and develop productive business as mentioned under sub-article（1）.

（3）Efforts to establish workers/laborers' cooperatives as mentioned under sub-article（1）shall be made in accordance with the prevailing laws and regulations.

（4）Efforts to develop workers/laborers' cooperatives as mentioned under sub-article（2）shall be regulated with a Government Regulation.

CHAPTER XI   INDUSTRIAL RELATIONS

Section One   General

Article 102

（1）In conducting industrial relations, the government shall perform the function of establishing policies, providing services, taking control and taking actions against any violation of statutory manpower laws and regulations.

（2）In conducting industrial relations, workers/laborers and their organizations unions shall perform the function of performing their jobs/work as obliged, working order to ensure production, channeling their aspirations democratically, enhancing their skills and expertise, helping promote the business of the enterprise, and fighting for the welfare of their members and families.

（3）In conducting industrial relations, entrepreneurs and their associations shall perform the function of creating partnership, developing business, diversifying employment and providing welfare to workers/laborers in a transparent and democratic way and in a way that upholds justice.

Article 103

Industrial relations shall be applied through:

a. trade/labor unions;

b. entrepreneurs' organizations;

c. bipartite cooperation institutions;

d. tripartite cooperation institutions;

e. company regulations;

f. collective labor agreements;

g. statutory manpower laws and regulations; and

h. industrial relations dispute settlement institutions.

Section Two   Trade/Labor Union

Article 104

(1) Every worker/laborer has the right to form and become member of a trade/labor union.

(2) In performing functions as mentioned under Article 102, a trade/labor union shall have the right to collect and manage fund and be accountable for the union's finances, including for the provision of a strike fund.

(3) The amount of the strike fund and procedures for collecting it as mentioned under sub-article (1) shall be regulated under the union's constitution and/or the union's by-law.

Section Three   Entrepreneurs' Organization

Article 105

(1) Every entrepreneur has the right to form and become a member of entrepreneurs' organization.

(2) The provisions concerning entrepreneurs' organizations shall be regulated in accordance with prevailing laws and regulations.

Section Four   Bipartite Cooperation Institution

Article 106

(1) Every enterprise employing 50 (fifty) workers/laborers or more is under an obligation to establish a bipartite cooperation institution.

(2) The bipartite cooperation institution as mentioned under sub-article (1) shall function as a forum for communication and consultation on labor issues in an enterprise.

(3) The membership composition of the bipartite cooperation institution as mentioned under sub-article (1) shall include the entrepreneur's representatives and the worker/laborer's representatives who are democratically appointed by workers/laborers to represent the interests of the worker/laborer in the enterprise.

(4) The provisions concerning the procedures for establishing the membership of the bipartite cooperation institution as mentioned under sub-article (1) and (3) shall be regulated with a Ministerial Decision.

Section Five   Tripartite Cooperation Institution

Article 107

（1） Tripartite cooperation institution shall provide considerations, recommendations and opinions to the government and other parties involved in the formulation of policy and settlement of labor issues/problems.

（2） The tripartite cooperation institution as mentioned under sub-article （1） shall consist of:

a. the National Tripartite Cooperation Institution and the Provincial, District/City Tripartite Cooperation Institutions; and

b. the Sector-based National Tripartite Cooperation Institution and Sector-based Provincial, District/City Tripartite Cooperation Institutions.

（3） The membership of tripartite cooperation institutions shall consist of representatives from the government, entrepreneurs' organizations and trade/labor unions.

（4） Procedures and organizational structures of tripartite cooperation institutions as mentioned under sub-article （1） shall be regulated with a Government Regulation.

Section Six   Company Regulations

Article 108

（1） Every enterprise which employs at least 10 （ten） workers/laborers is under an obligation to establish a set of company regulations that shall come into force after legalized by the Minister or appointed official.

（2） The obligation to have a set of legalized company regulations as mentioned under sub-article （1）, however, does not apply to enterprises already having collective labor agreements.

Article 109

Entrepreneurs shall formulate the rules and regulations of their enterprise and shall be responsible for them.

Article 110

（1） Companies regulations shall be formulated by taking into account the recommendations and considerations from the worker/laborer's representatives of the enterprise.

（2） If a trade/labor union have already been established in the enterprise, the worker/laborer's representatives as mentioned under sub-article （1） shall be the trade/labor union's officials.

(3) If there is no trade/labor union in the enterprise, the worker/laborer's representatives mentioned under sub-article (1) shall be the workers/laborers who hold a position in, or are members of, the bipartite cooperation institution and/or has been democratically elected by the workers/laborers in the enterprise to represent them and act on behalf of their interests.

Article 111

(1) Company regulations shall at least contain:

a. the rights and obligations of the entrepreneur;

b. the rights and obligations of the worker/laborer;

c. working conditions;

d. enterprise discipline and rule of conduct; and

e. the period of the validity of the company regulations.

(2) Company regulations shall not contravene the prevailing laws and regulations.

(3) The company regulations is valid for 2 (two) years and shall be renewed upon its expiration.

(4) During the validity of the company regulations, if the trade union within the enterprise request negotiation of the drafting of the collective labor agreement, the entrepreneur is obligated to do so.

(5) If the negotiation as mentioned under sub-article (4) fails to reach an agreement, then the existing company regulations shall remain valid until its expiration.

Article 112

(1) Legalization of company regulations by the Minister or appointed official as mentioned under sub-article (1) of Article 108 must have performed within a period of no later than 30 (thirty) workdays after the draft of the company regulations is received.

(2) If the company regulations have met the requirements under sub-article (1) and (2) of Article 111 and the period of 30 (thirty) workdays for legalizing them as mentioned under sub-article (1) has elapsed but the Minister or the appointed official has not legalized them yet, then the company regulations shall be assumed to have been legalized.

(3) If the company regulations have not met the requirements under sub-article (1) and (2) of Article 111 yet, the Minister or the appointed official must give a written notification to the entrepreneur the correction to the company regulations.

(4) Within a period of no later than 14 (fourteen) workdays after the date on which the written notification is received by the entrepreneur as mentioned under sub-article (3), the entrepreneur is under an obligation to resubmit the corrected version of the company regulations to the Minister or appointed official.

Article 113

(1) Any changes to the company regulations prior to its expiration can only be made on the

basis of an agreement between the entrepreneur and the worker/laborer's representatives.

(2) The company regulations resulting from the agreement as mentioned under sub-article (1) shall be legalized by the Minister or appointed official.

Article 114

The entrepreneur is under an obligation to notify and explain, as well as deliver, the contents of the company regulations or its changes to the workers/laborers.

Article 115

Provisions concerning procedures for making and legalizing the company regulations shall be regulated with a Ministerial Decision.

Section Seven   Collective Labor Agreement

Article 116

(1) A collective labor agreement shall be made between a trade/labor union or several trade unions already recorded at a government agency responsible for manpower affairs and an entrepreneur or several entrepreneurs respectively.

(2) The collective labor agreement as mentioned under sub-article (1) shall be formulated by means of deliberations.

(3) The collective labor agreement as mentioned under sub-article (1) shall be made in writing using Latin alphabets and in the Indonesian language.

(4) In case the collective labor agreement is not written in the Indonesian language, the collective labor agreement must be translated into Indonesian language by a professional translator and the translation shall be considered to have fulfilled the requirements stipulated under sub-article (3).

Article 117

In case the deliberations as mentioned under sub-article (2) of Article 116 fail to reach any consensus, then shall be settled through the procedures of industrial relations disputes settlement.

Article 118

In one enterprise only 1 (one) collective labor agreement can be made that shall apply to all workers/laborers working in the enterprise.

Article 119

(1) If there is only one trade/labor union in an enterprise, the only trade/labor union in the enterprise shall have the right to represent workers/laborers in negotiating a collective labor agreement with the entrepreneur provided that more than 50% (fifty percent) of the total number

of workers/laborers who work in the enterprise are members of the trade/labor union.

(2) In case there is only one trade/labor union in an enterprise as mentioned under sub-article (1) but the number of its members does not exceed 50% (fifty percent) of the total workforce in the enterprise, the trade/labor union may represent workers/laborers in negotiating a collective labor agreement with the entrepreneur provided that a vote that is held on this issue confirms that the trade/labor union wins the support of more than 50% (fifty percent) of the total number of workers in the enterprise.

(3) If the support of more than 50% (fifty percent) of the enterprise's total workforce as mentioned under sub-article (2) is not obtained, then the trade/labor union concerned may once again put forward its request to negotiate a collective labor agreement with the entrepreneur after a period of 6 (six) months since the vote is held in accordance with the procedures as mentioned under sub-article (2).

Article 120

(1) If there are more than 1 (one) trade/labor union in an enterprise, the trade/labor union that wins the support of more than 50% (fifty percent) of the total number of workers in the enterprise has the right to negotiate a collective labor agreement with the entrepreneur.

(2) If the requirement as mentioned under sub-article (1) is not fulfilled, then the trade/labor unions in the enterprise may form a coalition until the coalition gets the support of workers numbering more than 50% (fifty percent) of the total number of workers/laborers in the enterprise so that it is qualified to represent workers/laborers in negotiating a collective labor agreement with the entrepreneur.

(3) In case what is stipulated under sub-article (1) or (2) is not fulfilled, then the trade/labor unions shall establish a negotiating team whose members shall be determined in proportion to the number of members that each trade/labor union has.

Article 121

Membership in a trade/labor union as mentioned under Article 119 and 120 shall be proved with a membership card.

Article 122

The vote as mentioned under sub-article (2) of Article 119 shall be administered by a committee that is composed of workers/laborers' representatives and trade/labor union officials witnessed by the government official responsible for manpower affairs and by the entrepreneur.

Article 123

(1) The validity of the collective labor agreement is 2 (two) years.

(2) The effectiveness of the collective labor agreement as mentioned under sub-article (1) may be extended for no longer than 1 (one) year based on a written agreement between the

entrepreneur and the trade/labor union(s) .

(3) Negotiations for the next collective labor agreement may be started as early as 3 (three) months prior to the expiration of the existing collective labor agreement.

Article 124

(1) A collective labor agreement shall at least contain:

a. the rights and obligations of the employer;

b. the rights and obligations of the trade/labor union and the worker/laborer;

c. the period during which and the date starting from which the collective labor agreement takes effect; and

d. the signatures of those involved in making the collective labor agreement.

(2) The provisions of a collective labor agreement must not contravene prevailing laws and regulations.

(3) Should the contents of a collective labor agreement contravene prevailing laws and regulations as mentioned under sub-article (2), then the contradictory stipulations shall be declared null and void by law and the provision under prevailing laws and regulations shall prevail.

Article 125

If the parties agree to change collective labor agreement, then the changes shall form an inseparable part of the existing collective labor agreement.

Article 126

(1) The entrepreneur, the trade/labor union and/or the worker/laborer is under an obligation to implement the provisions in the collective labor agreement.

(2) The entrepreneur and the trade/labor union are under an obligation to inform the contents of the collective labor agreement or any changes made to it to all workers/laborers.

(3) The entrepreneur must print and distribute the text of collective labor agreement to each worker/laborer at the enterprise's expense.

Article 127

(1) Any work agreement made by the entrepreneur and the worker/laborer shall not contravene the collective labor agreement.

(2) Should there be any provisions under the work agreement mentioned under sub-article (1) contravene the collective labor agreement, then those particular provisions in the work agreement shall be declared null and void by law and the provision on the collective labor agreement shall prevail.

Article 128

If a work agreement does not contain the rules and regulations that are stipulated in the collective labor agreement, then the stipulations specified in the collective labor agreement shall prevail.

Article 129

(1) The entrepreneur is prohibited from replacing the collective labor agreement with the company regulations as long as there is a trade/labor union in the enterprise.

(2) If there is no more trade/labor union in the enterprise and the collective labor agreement is replaced by the company regulations, then the provisions in the company regulations shall by no means be inferior to the provisions in the collective labor agreement.

Article 130

(1) If a collective labor agreement that has expired will be extended or renewed and there is only 1 (one) trade/labor union in the enterprise, then the extension or renewal of the collective labor agreement shall not require the requirements under Article 119.

(2) If a collective labor agreement that has expired will be extended or renewed and there are more than 1 (one) trade/labor union in the enterprise and the trade/labor union that negotiated in the last agreement no longer meet the requirements under sub-article (1) of Article 120, the extension or renewal of the collective labor agreement shall be made by the trade/labor union whose members are more than 50% (fifty percent) of the total number of workers/laborers in the enterprise together with the trade/labor union that negotiated in the last agreement by establishing a negotiating team whose members are proportional to the members of the trade/labor unions represented in the team.

(3) If the expired collective labor agreement will be extended or renewed and there are more than 1 (one) trade/labor unions in the enterprise and none of them meet the requirements under sub-article (1) of Article 120, then the extension or renewal of the collective labor agreement shall be made in accordance with the provision under sub-article (2) and (3) of Article 120.

Article 131

(1) In case of the dissolution of a trade/labor union or the transfer of the enterprise's ownership, then the existing collective labor agreement shall remain valid until it expires.

(2) If an enterprise with a collective labor agreement merges with another enterprise with another collective labor agreement, then the prevailing collective labor agreement is the one that gives the worker/laborer more advantages.

(3) If an enterprise that has a collective labor agreement merges with another enterprise that has no collective labor agreement, then the collective labor agreement of the enterprise that has it shall apply to the enterprise resulted from the merger until the collective labor agreement expires.

Article 132

(1) A collective labor agreement shall take effect on the day it is signed unless otherwise

stated in the relevant collective labor agreement.

（2）A collective labor agreement that has been signed by the parties must be registered by the entrepreneur at a government agency responsible for manpower affairs.

Article 133

The provisions concerning the requirements and procedures for making, extending, changing and registering the collective labor agreement shall be regulated with a Ministerial Decision.

Article 134

In order to realize the rights and obligations of both the worker/laborer and the entrepreneur, the government is under an obligation to control the implementation of manpower laws and regulations and ensure their observance and enforcement.

Article 135

The implementation of manpower laws and regulations in order to realize industrial relations is the responsibility of the worker/laborer, the entrepreneur and the government.

Section Eight　Institutions/Agencies for the Settlement of Industrial Relations Disputes

Subsection One　Industrial Relations Disputes

Article 136

（1）The entrepreneur and the worker/laborer or the trade/labor union are under an obligation to make efforts to settle any industrial relations dispute they have through deliberations aimed at reaching a consensus.

（2）If the deliberations as mentioned under sub-article（1）fail to reach a consensus, then the entrepreneur and the worker/laborer or the trade/labor union shall have the industrial relations dispute settled through procedures for the settlement of industrial relations disputes that are regulated by law.

Subsection Two　Strike

Article 137

Strike is a fundamental right of workers/laborers and trade/labor unions that shall be staged legally, orderly and peacefully as a result of failed negotiation.

Article 138

(1) The workers/laborers and/or trade/labor unions intending to invite other workers/laborers to strike whilst the strike is going on shall be performed without violating laws.

(2) The workers/laborers who are invited to join the strike as mentioned under sub-article (1) may accept or decline the invitation.

Article 139

The implementation of strike staged by the workers/laborers of enterprises that serve the public interests and/or enterprises whose types of activities, will lead to the endangerment of human lives, shall be arranged in such a way so as not to disrupt public interests and/or endanger the safety of other people.

Article 140

(1) Within a period of no less than 7 (seven) days prior to the actual realization of a strike, workers/laborers and trade/labor unions intending to stage a strike are under an obligation to give a written notification of the intention to the entrepreneur and the local government agency responsible for manpower affairs.

(2) The notification as mentioned under sub-article (1) shall at least contain:

a. the time (date and hour) at which they will start and end the strike;

b. the venue of the strike;

c. their reasons for the strike; and

d. the signatures of the chairperson and secretary of the striking union and/or the signature of each of the chairpersons and secretaries of the unions participating in the strike, who shall be held responsible for the strike.

(3) If the strike is staged by workers/laborers who are not members of any trade/labor union, the notification as mentioned under sub-article (2) shall be signed by workers/laborers' representatives who have been appointed to coordinate and/or responsible for the strike.

(4) If a strike is not pursuant to the requirements as mentioned under sub-article (1), then in order to save production equipment and enterprise assets, the entrepreneur may take temporary action by:

a. prohibiting striking workers/laborers from being present at locations where production processes normally take place; or

b. prohibiting striking workers/laborers from being present at the enterprise's premise if necessary.

Article 141

(1) A representative of the government agency and the management who receives the letter notifying the intention to strike as mentioned under Article 140 is under an obligation to issue a

receipt of acknowledgment.

(2) Prior to and during the strike, the government agency responsible for manpower affairs is under an obligation to solve problem that leads to the emergence of strike by arranging a meeting and negotiate between the disputing parties.

(3) If the discussion as mentioned under sub-article (2) reaching an agreement, the agreement shall be made and signed by the parties, and an official from the government agency responsible for manpower affairs shall serve as witness.

(4) In case the discussion as mentioned under sub-article (2) results in no agreement, the official from the government agency responsible for manpower affairs shall immediately refer the problem(s) that cause(s) the strike to the authorized institution for the settlement of industrial relations disputes.

(5) In case the discussion results in no agreement as mentioned under sub-article (4), then on the basis of negotiation between the entrepreneur and the trade/labor union(s) responsible for the strike or the bearer(s) of responsibility for the strike, the strike may be continued or terminated temporarily or terminated at all.

Article 142

(1) Any strike that is staged without fulfilling the requirement under Article 139 and Article 140 is illegal.

(2) The legal consequences of staging an illegal strike as mentioned under sub-article (1) shall be regulated with a Ministerial Decision.

Article 143

(1) Nobody is allowed to prevent workers/laborers and trade/labor unions from using their right to strike legally, orderly and peacefully.

(2) It is prohibited to arrest and/or detain workers/laborers and union officials who are on strike legally, orderly and peacefully pursuant to the prevailing laws and regulations.

Article 144

In the event of a strike performed pursuant to Article 140, the entrepreneur is prohibited from:

a. replacing striking workers/laborers with other workers/laborers from outside of the enterprise; or

b. imposing sanctions on or taking retaliatory actions in whatever form against striking workers/laborers and union officials during and after the strike is performed.

Article 145

Workers/laborers who stage a strike legally in order to demand the fulfillment of their normative rights, which the entrepreneur has indeed violated, shall have their wages.

Subsection Three   Lockout

Article 146

(1) Lockout is a fundamental right of entrepreneurs to prevent their workforce either in part or in whole from performing work as a result from failed negotiation.

(2) Entrepreneurs are not justified to lock out their workforce as retaliation for normative demands raised by workers/laborers and/or trade/labor unions.

(3) Lockouts must be performed pursuant to the prevailing laws and regulations.

Article 147

Lockouts shall be prohibited from taking place at enterprises that serve the public interest and or enterprises whose types of activities, when interrupted by lockouts, will endanger human lives, including hospitals, enterprises that provide networks of clean water supply to the public, centers of telecommunications control, electricity supply center, oil-and-gas processing industries, and trains.

Article 148

(1) An entrepreneur who intends to perform a lockout is under an obligation to give a written notification of the lockout to workers/laborers and/or trade/labor union and the local government agency responsible for manpower affairs no less than 7 (seven) workdays before the lockout takes place.

(2) The lockout notification as mentioned under sub-article (1) shall at least contain:

a. the time (date and hour) will start and end the lockout; and

b. the reason and cause for the lockout.

(3) The notification as mentioned under sub-article (1) shall be signed by the entrepreneur and/or the management of the relevant enterprise.

Article 149

(1) Workers/Laborers or trade/labor unions and government agencies responsible for manpower affairs that directly receive a written notification of the lockout as mentioned under Article 148 must issue receipts acknowledging which state the day, the date, and the hour received.

(2) Before and during the lockout, the government agency responsible for manpower affairs shall immediately try to solve the problem that causes of the lockout by arranging a meeting and between the disputing parties.

(3) If the discussion as mentioned under sub-article (2) reaching an agreement, an agreement shall be made and signed by the parties and an official from the government agency

responsible for manpower affairs shall serve as witness.

(4) In case the discussion as mentioned under sub-article (2) results in no agreement, the official from the government agency responsible for manpower affairs shall immediately refer the problem(s) that cause(s) the strike to the authorized institution for the settlement of industrial relations disputes.

(5) In case the discussion results in no agreement as mentioned under sub-article (4), then, on the basis of negotiation between the entrepreneur and the trade/labour union, the lockout may be continued or terminated temporarily or terminated at all.

(6) Notification as mentioned under sub-article (1) and (2) of Article 148 is not needed if:

a. the workers/laborers or trade/labor unions violate the strike procedures as mentioned under Article 140;

b. the workers/laborers or trade/labor unions violate the normative provisions stipulated under the work agreements, company regulations, collective labor agreements or prevailing laws and regulations.

CHAPTER XII   TERMINATION OF EMPLOYMENT

Article 150

The provisions concerning termination of employment under this act shall cover termination of employment that happens in a business undertaking which is a legal entity or not, a business undertaking owned by an individual, by a partnership or by a legal entity, either owned by the private sector or by the State, as well as social undertakings and other undertakings which have administrators/officials and employ people by paying them wages or other forms of remuneration.

Article 151

(1) The entrepreneur, the worker/laborer and or the trade/labor union, and the government must make all efforts to prevent termination of employment.

(2) Despite all efforts made termination of employment remains inevitable, the intention to carry out the termination of employment must be negotiated between the entrepreneur and the trade/labor union to which the affected worker/laborer belongs as member, or between the entrepreneur and the worker/laborer to be dismissed if the worker/laborer is not a union member.

(3) If the negotiation as mentioned under sub-article (2) fails to result in any agreement, the entrepreneur may only terminate the employment of the worker/laborer after receiving a decision from the institution for the settlement of industrial relations disputes.

Article 152

(1) A request for a decision of the institution for the settlement of industrial relations

disputes to allow termination of employment shall be addressed in writing to the institution by stating the underlying reasons for the request.

(2) The request for such a decision as mentioned under sub-article (1) may be accepted by the institution for settlement of industrial relations disputes if it has been negotiated as mentioned under sub-article (2) of Article 151.

(3) The decision on the request for termination of employment can only be made by the institution for the settlement of industrial relations disputes if it turns out that the intention to carry out the termination of employment has been negotiated but that the negotiation results in no agreement.

Article 153

(1) The entrepreneur is prohibited from terminating the employment of a worker/laborer because of the following reasons:

a. the worker/laborer is absent from work because of illness as attested by a written statement from the doctor provided that it is for a period of longer than 12 (twelve) months consecutively;

b. the worker/laborer is absent from work because he or she is fulfilling his or her obligations to the State in accordance with the prevailing laws and regulations;

c. the worker/laborer is absent from work because he or she is practicing what is required by his or her religion;

d. the worker/laborer is absent from work because he or she is getting married;

e. the worker/laborer is absent from work because she is pregnant, giving birth, having a miscarriage, or breast-feeding her baby;

f. the worker/laborer is related by blood and/or through marriage to another worker within the enterprise unless so required in the collective labor agreement or the company regulations;

g. the worker/laborer establishes, becomes a member of and/or an official of a trade/labor union; the worker/laborer carries out trade/labor union activities outside working hours, or during working hours with approval from the entrepreneur, or according to that which has been stipulated in the work agreement, or the company regulations, or the collective labor agreement;

h. the worker/laborer reports to the authorities the crime committed by the entrepreneur;

i. because of different understanding/belief, religion, political orientation, ethnicity, color, race, sex, physical condition or marital status;

j. the worker/laborer is permanently disabled, ill as a result of a work accident, or ill because of an occupational disease whose period of recovery cannot be ascertained as attested by the written statement made by the physician.

(2) Any termination of employment that takes place for reasons mentioned under sub-article (1) shall be declared null and void by law. The entrepreneur shall then be obliged to re-employ the affected worker/laborer.

Article 154

The decision of the institute for the settlement of industrial relations disputes as mentioned under sub-article (3) of Article 151 is not needed if:

a. the affected worker/laborer is still on probation provided that such has been stipulated in writing beforehand;

b. the affected worker/laborer makes a written request for resignation at his/her own will with no indication of being pressurized or intimidated by the entrepreneur; or the employment relationship comes to an end according to the work agreement for a specified time for the first time;

c. the affected worker/laborer has reached the retirement age as stipulated under the work agreement, company regulations, collective labor agreements, or laws and regulations; or

d. the affected worker/laborer dies.

Article 155

(1) Any termination of employment without the decision of the institution for the settlement of industrial relations disputes as mentioned under sub-article (3) of Article 151 shall be declared null and void by law.

(2) As long as there is no decision from the institution for the settlement of industrial relations disputes, the entrepreneur and the worker/laborer must keep on performing their obligations.

(3) The entrepreneur may violate the provision under sub-article (2) by suspending the worker/laborer who is still in the process of having his/her employment terminated provided that the entrepreneur continues to pay the worker/laborer's wages and other entitlements that worker/laborer normally receives.

Article 156

(1) Should termination of employment take place, the entrepreneur is obliged to pay the dismissed worker severance pay and/or a sum of money as a reward for service rendered during his or her term of employment and compensation pay for rights or entitlements.

(2) The calculation of severance pay as mentioned under sub-article (1) shall at least be as follows:

a. 1 (one)-month wages for years of employment less than 1 (one) year;

b. 2 (two)-month wages for years of employment up to 1 (one) year or more but less than 2 (two) years;

c. 3 (three)-month wages for years of employment up to 2 (two) years or more but less than 3 (three) years;

d. 4 (four)-month wages for years of employment up to 3 (three) years or more but less than 4 (four) years;

e. 5 (five)-month wages for years of employment up to 4 (four) years or more but less than

5 (five) years;

f. 6 (six)-month wages for years of employment up to 5 (five) years or more but less than 6 (six) years;

g. 7 (seven)-month wages for years of employment up to 6 (six) years or more but less than 7 (seven) years;

h. 8 (eight)-month wages for years of employment up to 7 (seven) years or more but less than 8 (eight) years;

i. 9 (nine)-month wages for years of employment up to 8 (eight) years or more.

(3) The calculation of the sum of money paid as reward for service rendered during the worker/laborer's term of employment shall be determined as follows:

a. 2 (two)-month wages for years of employment up to 3 (three) years or more but less than 6 (six) years;

b. 3 (three)-month wages for years of employment up to 6 (six) years or more but less than 9 (nine) years;

c. 4 (four)-month wages for years of employment up to 9 (nine) years or more but less than 12 (twelve) years;

d. 5 (five)-month wages for years of employment up to 12 (twelve) years or more but less than 15 (fifteen) years;

e. 6 (six)-month wages for years of employment up to 15 (fifteen) years or more but less than 18 (eighteen) years;

f. 7 (seven)-month wages for years of employment up to 18 (eighteen) years but less than 21 (twenty-one) years;

g. 8 (eight)-month wages for years of employment up to 21 (twenty-one) years but less than 24 (twenty-four) years;

h. 10 (ten)-month wages for years of employment up to 24 (twenty-four) years or more.

(4) The compensation pay that the dismissed worker/laborer ought to have as mentioned under sub-article (1) shall include:

a. annual leaves that have not expired and not have taken;

b. costs or expenses for transporting the worker/laborer and his or her family back to the place of hire;

c. compensation for housing allowance, medical and health care allowance is determined at 15% (fifteen percent) of the severance pay and or reward for years of service pay for those who are eligible;

d. other compensations that are stipulated under the work agreement, company regulations or collective labor agreements.

(5) Changes concerning the calculation of the severance pay, the sum of money paid as reward for service during term of employment and the compensation pay that the worker/laborer ought to have as mentioned under sub-article (2), (3) and (4) shall be regulated with a

Government Regulation.

Article 157

(1) Wage components used as the basis for calculating severance pay, money paid as reward for service rendered, and money paid to compensate for entitlements that should have been received, which are deferred, are composed of:

a. basic wages;

b. all forms of fixed allowances that are provided to workers/laborers and their families, including the price of buying ration provided to the worker/laborer free of change whereby if the ration must be paid by workers/laborers with subsidies, the difference between the buying price of the ration and the price that must be paid by the worker/laborer shall be considered as wage.

(2) In case the worker/laborer's wages is paid on the basis of daily calculation, a one-month wage shall be equal to 30 times a one-day wage.

(3) In case the worker/laborer's wage is paid on a piece-rate or commission basis, a day's wage shall equal the average daily wage for the last 12 (twelve) months on the condition that the wages must not be less than the provisions for the provincial or district/city minimum wage.

(4) In case the work depends on the weather and the wage is calculated on a piece-rate basis, the amount of one month's wage shall be calculated from the average wage in the last 12 (twelve) months.

Article 158

(1) An entrepreneur may terminate the employment of a worker/laborer because the worker/laborer has committed the following grave wrongdoings:

a. stealing or smuggled goods and/or money that belong to the enterprise;

b. giving false or falsified information that causes the enterprise to incur losses;

c. being drunk, drinking intoxicating alcoholic drinks, consuming and or distributing narcotics, psychotropic substances and other addictive substances in the working environment;

d. committing immorality/indecency or gambling in the working environment;

e. stacking, battering, threatening, or intimidating his or her co-workers or the entrepreneur in the working environment;

f. persuading his or her co-workers or the entrepreneur to do something that is against the laws and regulations;

g. carelessly or intentionally destroying or exposing the property of the entrepreneur to danger, which caused the enterprise to incur losses;

h. intentionally or carelessly leting his or her co-workers or the entrepreneur exposed to danger in the workplace;

i. unveiled or leaked the enterprise's secrets, which is supposed to keep secret unless otherwise required by the State; or

j. committed other wrongdoings within the working environment, which call for imprisonment for 5 (five) years or more.

(2) The grave wrongdoings as mentioned under sub-article (1) must be supported with the following evidence:

a. the worker/laborer is caught red-handed;

b. the worker/laborer admits committed a wrongdoing; or

c. other evidence in the form of reports of events made by the authorities at the enterprises and confirmed by no less than 2 (two) witnesses.

(3) Workers/Laborers whose employment is terminated because of reasons as mentioned under sub-article (1) may receive compensation pay for entitlements as mentioned under sub-article (4) of Article 156.

(4) Workers/Laborers as mentioned under sub-article (1) whose duties and functions do not directly represent the interest of the entrepreneur shall be given detachment money whose amount and the procedures or methods associated with its payment shall be determined and stipulated in the work agreements, company regulations, or collective labor agreements.

Article 159

If the worker/laborer is unwilling to accept the termination as mentioned under sub-article (1) of Article 158, the worker/laborer may file a suit to the institution for the settlement of industrial relations disputes.

Article 160

(1) In case the worker/laborer is detained by the authorities because he or she is alleged to have committed a crime and this happens not because of the complaint filed by the entrepreneur, the entrepreneur is not obliged to pay the worker/laborer's wage but is obliged to provide assistance to the family who are his or her dependents according to the following provisions:

a. for 1 (one) dependent, the entrepreneur is obliged to pay 25% (twenty-five percent) of the worker/laborer's wages;

b. for 2 (two) dependents, the entrepreneur is obliged to pay 35% (thirty-five percent) of the worker/laborer's wages;

c. for 3 (three) dependents, the entrepreneur is obliged to pay 45% (forty-five percent) of the worker/laborer's wages;

d. for 4 (four) dependents or more, the entrepreneur is obliged to pay 50% (fifty percent) of the worker/laborer's wages.

(2) The assistance as mentioned under sub-article (1) shall be provided for no longer than 6 (six) months of calendar year starting from the first day the worker/laborer is detained by the authorities.

(3) The entrepreneur may terminate the employment of the worker/laborer who after the passing of 6 (six) months are unable to perform his or her work as worker/laborer because of the legal process associated with the legal proceedings as mentioned under sub-article (1).

(4) In case the court decides the case prior to the passing of 6 (six) months as mentioned under sub-article (3) and the worker/laborer is declared not guilty, the entrepreneur is obliged to reemploy the worker/laborer.

(5) In case the court decides the case prior to the passing of 6 (six) months and the worker/laborer is declared guilty, the entrepreneur may terminate the employment of the worker/laborer.

(6) The termination of employment as mentioned under sub-article (3) and (5) is carried out without the decision of the institution for the settlement of industrial relations disputes.

(7) The entrepreneur is obliged to pay to the worker/laborer whose employment is terminated as mentioned under sub-article (3) and (5) reward pay for service rendered during his/her period of employment 1 (one) time of what is stipulated under sub-article (3) of Article 156 and compensation pay that the worker/laborer ought to have as mentioned under sub-article (4) of Article 156.

Article 161

(1) In case the worker/laborer violates the provisions that are specified under work agreement, the company regulations, or the collective labor agreement, the entrepreneur may terminate the employment after the entrepreneur precedes it with the issuance of the first, second and third warning letters consecutively.

(2) Each warning letter issued as mentioned under sub-article (1) shall expire after 6 (six) months unless otherwise stated in the work agreement or the company regulations or the collective labor agreement.

(3) Workers/Laborers whose employment is terminated for reasons as mentioned under sub-article (1) shall be entitled to severance pay amounting to 1 (one) time of the amount of severance pay stipulated under sub-article (2) of Article 156, reward pay for period of employment amounting to 1 (one) time of the amount stipulated under sub-article (3) of Article 156, and compensation pay for entitlements according to the provision under sub-article (4) of Article 156.

Article 162

(1) Worker/Laborer who resign on his/her own will, shall be entitled to compensation pay in accordance with sub-article (4) of Article 156.

(2) Workers/Laborers who resign of their own will, whose duties and functions do not directly represent the interest of the entrepreneur shall, in addition to the compensation pay payable to them according to sub-article (4) of Article 156, be given detachment money whose amount and the procedures/methods associated with its payment shall be regulated in the work agreements, company regulations or collective labor agreements.

(3) A worker/laborer who resigns as mentioned under sub-article (1) must fulfill the following requirements:

a. submiting a resignation letter no later than 30 (thirty) days prior to the date of resignation;

b. not being bound by a contract to serve the enterprise; and

c. continuing to carry out his or her obligations until the date of his or her resignation.

(4) Termination of employment for the reason of own will resignation shall be carried out without the decision of the institution for the settlement of industrial relations disputes.

Article 163

(1) The entrepreneur may terminate the employment of his or her workers/laborers in the event of change in the status of the enterprise, merger, fusion, or change in the ownership of the enterprise and the workers/laborers are not willing to continue their employment, the worker/laborer shall be entitled to severance pay 1 (one) time the amount of severance pay stipulated under sub-article (2) of Article 156, reward pay for period of employment 1 (one) time the amount stipulated under sub-article (3) of Article 156, and compensation pay for entitlements that have not been used according to what is stipulated under sub-article (4) of Article 156.

(2) The entrepreneur may terminate the employment of his or her workers/laborers in the event of change in the status of the enterprise, merger, fusion, or change in the ownership of the enterprise and the entrepreneur is not willing to accept the workers/laborers to work in the new enterprise. The worker/laborer shall be entitled to severance pay twice the amount of severance pay stipulated under sub-article (2) of Article 156, reward pay for period of employment 1 (one) time the amount stipulated under sub-article (3) of Article 156, and compensation pay for entitlements according to what is stipulated under sub-article (4) of Article 156.

Article 164

(1) The entrepreneur may terminate the employment of workers/laborers because the enterprise has to be closed down due to continual losses for 2 (two) years consecutively or force majeure. The workers/laborers shall be entitled to severance pay amounting to 1 (one) time the amount of severance pay stipulated under sub-article (2) of Article 156, reward pay for period of employment amounting to 1 (one) time the amount stipulated under sub-article (3) of Article 156, and compensation pay for entitlements according to sub-article (4) of Article 156.

(2) The continual losses as referred to in sub-article (1) must be proved in the enterprise's financial reports over the last 2 (two) years that have been audited by public accountants.

(3) The entrepreneur may terminate the employment of its workers/laborers because the enterprise has to be closed down and the closing down of the enterprise is caused neither by continual losses for 2 (two) years consecutively nor force majeure but because of rationalization. The workers/laborers shall be entitled to severance pay twice the amount of severance pay stipulated under sub-article (2) of Article 156, reward for period of employment pay amounting to 1 (one) time the amount stipulated under sub-article (3) of Article 156, and compensation pay for entitlements according to sub-article (4) of Article 156.

Article 165

The entrepreneur may terminate the employment of the enterprise's workers/laborers because the enterprise goes bankrupt. The workers/laborers shall be entitled to severance pay amounting to 1 (one) time the amount of severance pay stipulated under sub-article (2) of Article 156, reward pay for period of employment amounting to 1 (one) time the amount stipulated under sub-article (3) of Article 156, and compensation pay for entitlements according to sub-article (4) of Article 156.

Article 166

If an employment relationship comes to an end because the worker/laborer dies, to the worker's heirs shall be given a sum of money whose amount shall be the same as twice of severance pay as stipulated under sub-article (2) of Article 156, reward pay for period of employment worked by the worker/laborer amounting to 1 (one) time the amount stipulated under sub-article (3) of Article 156, and compensation pay for entitlements according to sub-article (4) of Article 156.

Article 167

(1) An entrepreneur may terminate the employment of its workers/laborers because they enter pension age, entrepreneur has included the workers/laborers in a retirement benefit program, the workers/laborers are not entitled to severance pay according to what is stipulated under sub-article (2) of Article 156, reward pay for period of employment in accordance with what is stipulated under sub-article (3) of Article 156, and compensation pay for entitlements according to sub-article (4) of Article 156.

(2) If the amount of retirement benefit that they get as a single lump-sum payment as a result of their participation in a pension program as mentioned under sub-article (1) turns out to be lower than twice the amount of the severance pay stipulated under sub-article (2) of Article 156, reward pay for period of employment in accordance with what is stipulated under sub-article (3) of Article 156, and compensation pay for entitlements according to sub-article (4) of Article 156, the entrepreneur shall pay the difference.

(3) If the entrepreneur has included the worker/laborer in a pension program whose contributions/premiums are paid by the entrepreneur and the worker/laborer, then that which is calculated with the severance pay shall be the pension whose contributions/premiums have been paid by the entrepreneur.

(4) Arrangements other than what is stipulated under sub-article (1), (2) and (3) may be made in the work agreement, company regulations or collective labor agreements.

(5) If the entrepreneur does not include workers/laborers whose employment is terminated because they enter pension age in a pension program, the entrepreneur is obliged to pay them severance pay twice the amount of severance pay as stipulated under sub-article (2) of Article

156, reward pay for period of employment amounting to 1 (one) time the amount stipulated under sub-article (3) of Article 156, and compensation pay for entitlements according to sub-article (4) of Article 156.

(6) The worker/laborer's entitlement to retirement benefit as mentioned under sub-article (1), (2) and (3) shall not eliminate their entitlement to the old age benefit that is compulsory according to prevailing laws and regulations.

Article 168

(1) An entrepreneur may terminate the employment of a worker/laborer if the worker/laborer has been absent from work for 5 (five) workdays or more consecutively without submitting to the entrepreneur a written explanation supplemented with valid evidence and the entrepreneur has properly summoned him or her twice in writing, by qualify the worker/laborer as resigning.

(2) The written explanation supplemented with valid evidence as mentioned under sub-article (1) must be submitted at the latest on the first day on which the worker/laborer comes back to the workplace.

(3) In the event of the termination of employment as mentioned under sub-article (1), the worker/laborer shall be entitled to compensation pay for her/his entitlements according to sub-article (4) of Article 156 and they shall be given detachment money whose amount and the procedures and methods associated with its payment shall be regulated in the work agreement, company regulations, or collective labor agreement.

Article 169

(1) A worker/laborer may file an official request to the institution for the settlement of industrial relations disputes to terminate his/her employment relationship if his/her entrepreneur committing the following actions:

a. battering, rudely humiliating or intimidating the worker/laborer;

b. persuading and/or ordering the worker/laborer to commit acts that violating statutory laws and regulations;

c. not paying wages at a prescribed time for three months consecutively or more;

d. not performing obligations promised to workers/laborers;

e. ordering the worker/laborer to perform work outside what has been agreed upon; or

f. ordering the worker/laborer to carry out work that endangered life, safety, health and morality of the worker/laborer which is not mentioned in the work agreement.

(2) The termination of employment because of reasons as mentioned under sub-article (1), the worker/laborer is entitled to receive severance pay amounting to twice the amount of severance pay stipulated under sub-article (2) of Article 156, reward pay amounting to 1 (one) time the amount of reward pay for period of employment worked stipulated under sub-article (3) of Article 156, and compensation pay for entitlements according to sub-article (4) of Article 156.

(3) In case the entrepreneur is found not guilty of committing the acts mentioned under sub-

article (1) by the institution for the settlement of industrial relations disputes, the entrepreneur may terminate the employment of the worker/laborer without having the decision of the institution for the settlement of industrial relations disputes and the worker/laborer in question is not entitled to severance pay as mentioned under sub-article (2) of Article 156 and reward pay for period of employment worked as mentioned under sub-article (3) of Article 156.

Article 170

Any termination of employment that is carried out without fulfilling sub-article (3) of Article 151 and Article 168 except sub-article (1) of Article 158, sub-article (3) of Article 160, Article 162, and Article 169 shall be declared null and void by law and the entrepreneur is obliged to re-employ the worker/laborer and pay all the wages and entitlements which the worker/laborer should have received.

Article 171

If workers/laborers whose employment is terminated without the decision of the institution for the settlement of industrial relations disputes as mentioned under sub-article (1) of Article 158, sub-article (3) of Article 160 and Article 162 cannot accept the termination of their employment, the workers/laborers may file a lawsuit to the institution for the settlement of industrial relations disputes within a period of no later than 1 (one) year since the date on which their employment was terminated.

Article 172

Workers/Laborers who are continuously ill for a very long time, and who are disabled as a result of a work accident and are unable to perform their work may, after they have been in such a condition for more than the absenteeism limit of 12 (twelve) months consecutively, request that their employment be terminated upon which they shall be entitled to receive severance pay amounting to twice the amount of severance pay stipulated under sub-article (2) of Article 156, reward pay for the period of employment they have worked amounting to twice the amount of such reward pay stipulated under sub-article (3) of Article 156, and compensation pay amounting to 1 (one) time the amount of that which is stipulated under sub-article (4) of Article 156.

CHAPTER XIII   MANPOWER DEVELOPMENT

Article 173

(1) The government shall make efforts to develop and build up elements and activities related to manpower.

(2) The efforts to develop manpower-related elements and activities as mentioned under sub-

article (1) may invite participation of entrepreneurs' organizations, trade/labor unions and other related organizations of professions.

(3) The efforts to develop manpower as mentioned under sub-article (1) and sub-article (2) shall be carried out in a well-integrated and well-coordinated way.

Article 174

For the purpose of manpower development, the government, associations of entrepreneurs, trade/labor unions and other professions organizations may establish international cooperation in the field of labor according to the prevailing laws and regulations.

Article 175

(1) The government may award persons or institutions that have done meritorious service in the field of manpower development.

(2) The award as mentioned under sub-article (1) may be given in the form of a charter, money and/or other forms of reward.

CHAPTER XIV   LABOR INSPECTION

Article 176

Labor inspection shall be carried out by government labor inspectors who have the competence and independency to ensure the implementation of the labor laws and regulations.

Article 177

The labor inspectors as mentioned under Article 176 shall be determined by the Minister or appointed officials.

Article 178

(1) Labor inspection shall be carried out by a separate working unit of a government agency whose scope of duty and responsibility are in the field of labor at the Central Government, Provincial Governments and District/City Governments.

(2) The implementation of labor inspection as mentioned under sub-article (1) shall be regulated further with a Presidential Decision.

Article 179

(1) The working units for labor inspection as mentioned under Article 178 at the Provincial Governments and District/City Governments are obliged to submit reports on the implementation of labor inspection to Minister.

(2) Procedures for submitting the reports as mentioned under sub-article (1) shall be regulated with a Ministerial Decision.

Article 180

Provisions concerning the requirements for the appointment of, the rights and obligations of, the authority of, labor inspectors as mentioned under Article 176 pursuant to the prevailing laws and regulations.

Article 181

In carrying out their duties as mentioned under Article 176, labor inspectors are obliged:

a. to keep secret everything that, by its nature, needs or is worthy to be kept secret;

b. to refrain from abusing their authority.

CHAPTER XV   INVESTIGATION

Article 182

(1) Special authority to act as civil servant investigators may also be given, in addition to the one assigned to the investigating officials of the Police of the State of the Republic of Indonesia, to labor inspectors in accordance with the prevailing laws and regulations.

(2) The civil servant investigators as mentioned under sub-article (1) shall have the authority:

a. to examine whether or not reports and explanations about labor crimes are true;

b. to investigate individuals suspected of having committed a labor crime;

c. to require explanations and evidences from persons or legal entity considered to be relevant to the labor crime being investigated;

d. to examine or confiscate objects or evidences found in a case of labor crime;

e. to examine papers and/or other documents related with labor crimes;

f. to request the help of experts in performing labor-related criminal investigations; and

g. to stop investigation if there is not enough evidence to prove that a labor crime has been committed.

(3) The authority of civil servant investigators as mentioned under sub-article (2) shall be exercised in accordance with the prevailing laws and regulations.

CHAPTER XVI   CRIMINAL PROVISIONS AND ADMINISTRATIVE SANCTIONS

Section One   Criminal Provisions

Article 183

(1) Whosoever violates the provision under Article 74 shall be subjected to a criminal sanction in jail for a minimum of 2 (two) years and a maximum of 5 (five) years and/or a fine of a minimum of Rp 200,000,000 (two hundred million rupiah) and a maximum of Rp 500,000,000 (five hundred million rupiah) .

(2) The criminal action mentioned under sub-article (1) shall be legally categorized as a felony.

Article 184

(1) Whosoever violates what is mentioned under sub-article (5) of Article 167 shall be subjected to a criminal sanction in jail for a minimum of 1 (one) year and a maximum of 5 (five) years and/or a fine of a minimum of Rp 100,000,000 (one hundred million rupiah) and a maximum of Rp 500,000,000 (five hundred million rupiah) .

(2) The criminal action mentioned under sub-article (1) shall be legally categorized as a felony.

Article 185

(1) Whosoever violates what is stipulated under sub-article (1) and (2) of Article 42, Article 68, sub-article (2) of article 69, Article 80, Article 82, sub-article (1) of Article 90, Article 139, Article 143, and sub-article (4) and (7) of Article 160 shall be subjected to a criminal sanction in jail for a minimum of 1 (one) year and a maximum of 4 (four) years and/or a fine of a minimum of Rp 100,000,000 (one hundred million rupiah) and a maximum of Rp 400,000,000 (four hundred million rupiah) .

(2) The criminal action mentioned under sub-article (1) shall be legally categorized as a felony.

Article 186

(1) Whosoever violates what is stipulated under sub-article (2) and (3) of Article 35, sub-article (2) of Article 93, Article 137, and sub-article (1) of Article 138 shall be subjected to a criminal sanction in jail for a minimum of 1 (one) month and a maximum of 4 (four) years and/or

a fine of a minimum of Rp10,000,000 (ten million rupiah) and a maximum of Rp400,000,000 (four hundred million rupiah).

(2) The criminal action mentioned under sub-article (1) shall be legally categorized as a misdemeanor.

Article 187

(1) Whosoever violates what is stipulated under sub-article (2) of Article 37, sub-article (1) of Article 44, sub-article (1) of Article 45, sub-article (1) of Article 67, sub-article (2) of Article 71, Article 76, sub-article (2) of Article 78, sub-article (1) and (2) of Article 79, sub-article (3) of Article 85, and Article 144 shall be subjected to a criminal sanction in prison for a minimum of 1 (one) month and a maximum of 12 (twelve) months and/or a fine of a minimum of Rp 10,000,000 (ten million rupiah) and a maximum of Rp 100,000,000 (one hundred million rupiah).

(2) The criminal action mentioned under sub-article (1) shall be legally categorized as a misdemeanor.

Article 188

(1) Whosoever violates what is stipulated under sub-article (2) of Article 14, sub-article (2) of Article 38, sub-article (1) of Article 63, sub-article (1) of Article 78, sub-article (1) of Article 108, sub-article (3) of Article 111, Article 114, and Article 148 shall be subjected to a criminal sanction in the form of a fine of a minimum of Rp 5,000,000 (five million rupiah) and a maximum of Rp 50,000,000 (fifty million rupiah).

(2) The criminal action mentioned under sub-article (1) shall be legally categorized as a misdemeanor.

Article 189

Sanctions imposed on entrepreneurs in the form of a jail, prison sentence and/or a fine do not release the entrepreneurs from their obligations to pay entitlements and/or compensations to the workers/laborers.

Section Two   Administrative Sanctions

Article 190

(1) Minister or appointed official shall impose administrative sanctions because of violations under Article 5, Article 6, Article 15, Article 25, sub-article (2) of Article 38, sub-article (1) of Article 45, sub-article (1) of Article 47, Article 48, Article 87, Article 106, sub-article (3) of Article 126, and sub-article (1) and (2) of Article 160 of this act and its implementing regulations. The administrative sanctions as mentioned under sub-article (1) may take the form of:

a. a rebuke;

b. a written warning;

c. restrict/limit the business activities of the affected enterprise;

d. freeze the business activities of the affected enterprise;

e. cancellation of approval;

f. cancellation of registration;

g. temporary termination of partial or the whole production tools/instruments;

h. abolishment/revocation of license or permission to operate.

(2) The provisions concerning administrative sanctions as mentioned under sub-article (1) and (2) shall be regulated further by the Minister.

CHAPTER XVII   TRANSITIONAL PROVISIONS

Article 191

All implementing regulations that regulate manpower affairs shall remain effective as long as they do not against and/or have not been replaced by the new regulations made based on this act.

CHAPTER XVIII   CLOSING PROVISIONS

Article 192

At the time this act starts to take effect, then:

1. Ordinance concerning the Mobilization of Indonesian People to Perform Work outside Indonesia (Statute Book of 1887 Number 8).

2. Ordinance dated December 17, 1925, which is a regulation concerning Restriction of Child Labor and Night Work for Women (Statute Book of 1925 Number 647).

3. Ordinance Year 1926, which is a regulation which regulates the Employment of Child and Youth on Board of A Ship (Statute Book of 1926 Number 87).

4. Ordinance dated May 4, 1936 concerning Ordinance to Regulate Activities to Recruit Candidates/Prospective Workers (Statute Book of 1936 Number 208).

5. Ordinance concerning the Repatriation of Laborers Who Come From or Are Mobilized from Outside of Indonesia (Statute Book of 1939 Number 545).

6. Ordinance Number 9 Year 1949 concerning Restriction of Child Labor (Statute Book of 1949 Number 8).

7. Act Number 1 Year 1951 concerning the Declaration of the Enactment of Employment Act Year 1948 Number 12 from the Republic of Indonesia for All Indonesia (Statute Book of 1951

Number 2).

8. Act Number 21 Year 1954 concerning Labor Agreement between Labor Union and Employer (Statute Book of 1954 Number 69, Supplement to statute Book Number 598a).

9. Act Number 3 Year 1958 concerning the Placement of Foreign Workers (Statute Book of 1958 Number 8).

10. Act Number 8 Year 1961 concerning Compulsory Work for University Graduates Holding Master's Degree (Statute Book of 1961 Number 207, Supplement to statute Book Number 2270).

11. Act Number 7 Year 1963 Serving as the Presidential Resolution on the Prevention of Strike and/or Lockout at Vital Enterprises, Government Agencies in Charge of Public Service and Agencies (Statute Book of 1963 Number 67).

12. Act Number 14 Year 1969 concerning Fundamental Provisions concerning Manpower (Statute Book of 1969 Number 55, Supplement to statute Book Number 2912).

13. Act Number 25 Year 1997 concerning Manpower (Statute Book of 1997 Number 73, Supplement to Statute Book Number 3702).

14. Act Number 11 Year 1998 concerning the Change in the Applicability of Act Number 25 Year 1997 concerning Manpower (Statute Book of 1998 Number 184, Supplement to Statute Book Number 3791).

15. Act Number 28 Year 2000 concerning the Establishment of Government Regulation in lieu of Law Number 3 Year 2000 concerning Changes to Act Number 11 Year 1998 concerning the Change in the Applicability of Act Number 25 Year 1997 concerning Manpower into Act (Statute Book of 2000 Number 204, Supplement to Statute Book Number 4042) shall herewith be declared null and void.

Article 193

This act shall be effective upon the date of its promulgation. For the cognizant of the public, orders the promulgation of this act by having it place on the Statute Book of the Republic of Indonesia.

印度尼西亚共和国总统 2003 年
第 13 号关于劳动力的法令

第一章　总则

第一条

在本法中，以下定义适用：

1. 劳动力事宜是指与某项工作所需人员在其受雇用之前、期间及结束后相关的一切事务。

2. 劳动力是指每一个能够通过工作来生产商品和/或提供服务以满足其自身或社会需要的个体。

3. 劳动者是指通过劳动获取工资或其他形式的报酬的个人。

4. 雇主是指通过支付工资或者以其他支付形式雇用劳动力的个人、企业家、法人实体或其他实体。

5. 企业家是指：

a. 经营自有企业的个人、合伙人或法人；

b. 自主经营非自有企业的个人、合伙人或法人；

c. 属于 a 项和 b 项下的位于印度尼西亚但代表境外企业的个人、合伙人或法人。

6. 企业是指：

a. 私营的或国有的，具有法人资格的或不具有法人资格的，以支付工资或以其他支付方式雇用工人/劳动者的，属于个人、合伙人或者法人的所有商业形式。

b. 由官员负责的以支付工资或其他支付方式雇用人的民生事业或其他社会事业。

7. 人力资源规划是用来系统地制定政策、战略和实施可持续人力发展方案的依据和参考。

8. 劳动力信息是一组、一套或者一系列有关劳动力的具有特定含义、价值和信息的处理后的数字、文本和文件。

9. 职业培训是指对员工或者准员工提供的，或为其提供便利以使其能够获得、加强和发展工作能力、劳动纪律及敬业品德，直到其获得理想的可满足工作需要的工作技能和专业知识为止的一整套活动。

10. 工作技能是个人的工作能力，它包括符合规定标准的知识、技能和工作态度。

11. 学徒制是职业培训制度的一部分，它把在培训机构里的培训和在企业里直接在前辈指导下的生产和/或服务工作相结合，使学徒能够掌握某项技能或商务能力。

12. 就业服务是一种旨在将劳动力与雇主相匹配的活动，以使劳动者能得到与其天分、兴趣和才能相适应的工作，使雇主获得他们所需要的劳动力。

13. 外籍员工是指持有签证并愿意在印度尼西亚工作的外国公民。

14. 劳动协议是劳动者和企业/雇主之间签订的用以明确具体工作要求、双方各自权利和义务的协议。

15. 雇佣关系是指企业家和工人/劳动者之间的关系，它建立在工作协议基础之上，包含工作、工资和工作要求要素。

16. 劳资关系是指在生产和/或服务过程中形成的各方间的关系体系，其中包括雇主、工人/劳动者和政府，它是建立在立国五项基本原则和1945年宪法基础之上的。

17. 工会是由企业内外的工人/劳动者组成的，实现工人/劳动者自身目的的，自由、开放、独立、民主且负责任的组织，其目的是争取和维护工人的权益，并增加工人及其家庭的福利。

18. 双方合作机构是指企业内部关于劳资关系事项的起沟通和协商作用的论坛，其成员包括雇主和在政府相关机构注册的工会或工人/劳动者代表。

19. 三方合作机构是指由雇主代表、工人/劳动者代表和政府组成的，就人力资源问题进行沟通、协商和评议的论坛。

20. 企业规章制度是指雇主以书面形式规定的关于工作要求、劳动纪律和行为规范的一系列规定。

21. 集体劳动协议是指规定了工作要求和各方权利与义务的协议，它是已在相关政府部门注册的企业家和工会之间的协议。

22. 劳资纠纷是指在雇主或雇主联合会和工人/劳动者或工会之间因在劳动者权益和员工资遣等方面因意见分歧而导致的冲突，同时也包括同一企业内不同工会之间的纠纷。

23. 罢工是指由工会策划和组织的劳动者集体停工或怠工的行为。

24. 企业停工是指雇主全部或部分停止劳动者进行生产作业的行为。

25. 员工资遣是指由于某种原因而导致的劳资双方权利和义务的终结。

26. 儿童是指年龄不满十八周岁的个人。

27. 白天是指早上六点到下午六点。

28. 一天指二十四小时。

29. 一周指七天。

30. 工资是指雇主对劳动者以货币形式表明和发放的报酬，其数量按照劳动协议、双方共识或法律法规进行确定，其中包括对劳动者及其家庭已经从事或即将从事的劳动和/或服务而发放的补贴。

31. 福利是对工人/劳动者在其受雇期间或雇佣关系结束之后对其精神和或/物质需求的一种满足，它可以使工人/劳动者在一个安全和健康的工作环境下直接或间接地提高工作效率。

32. 劳动监察是指在劳动力领域监督和强化法律法规执行情况的活动。

33. 部长是指负责劳动力事务的部长。

第二章　法律基础、宗旨和目标

第二条

劳动力发展要以立国五项基本原则和 1945 年宪法为法律基础。

第三条

劳动力发展的执行应基于职能性，跨部门，中央、省级/地方合作等原则进行整合。

第四条

劳动力发展的目标：

a. 最佳地、富有人情味地有效授权和使用劳动力；

b. 创造公平的机会，提供适合国家、省份、地区发展需要的人力资源；

c. 为员工提供保护，以保证员工福利的实现；

d. 提高员工及其家庭的福利。

第三章　平等机会

第五条

任何员工都有相同的获得工作的机会而不受任何歧视。

第六条

每个员工都从雇主处获得平等的待遇而不受任何歧视的权利。

第四章　劳动力规划和劳动力信息

第七条

（1）为了人力资源的发展，政府应建立劳动力政策并制订劳动力规划。

（2）劳动力规划应包括：

a. 宏观劳动力规划；

b. 微观劳动力规划。

（3）在制定政策和战略及实施可持续劳工发展方案上，政府必须以第（1）款中提及的劳动力规划作为指导方针。

第八条

（1）劳动力规划应建立在劳动力信息的基础上，其中包含以下内容：

a. 人口和劳动力；

b. 工作机会；

c. 工作培训，包括工作适任能力；

d. 员工的生产力；

e. 劳资关系；

f. 工作环境条件；

g. 工资体系和员工福利；

h. 员工的社会保障。

（2）第（1）款中提及的劳动力信息应该从所有相关方获得，包括政府和私人中介。

（3）有关第（1）款中提及的获得劳动力信息的程序以及劳动力规划制订和执行的程序之规定不应违背政府法规。

第五章　职业培训

第九条

职业培训应着眼于培养、加强和发展工作能力，以提高个人能力、生产力及福利。

第十条

（1）实施职业培训，无论是在就业期间还是非就业期间，均应考虑就业市场和商业界的需求。

（2）提供的培训要建立在切合工作能力标准程序的基础之上。

（3）职业培训应按一定步骤展开。

（4）关于本条第（2）款中提及的建立工作能力标准程序的规定应由部长令监管。

第十一条

员工有权通过培训获得和/或改进和/或发展适合于自身天赋、兴趣和才能的工作适任能力。

第十二条

（1）企业家有责任通过培训改进和/或发展其员工的工作能力。

（2）已满足部长令要求的企业家有义务提高和/或发展第（1）款中提及的员工的工作能力。

（3）每位员工均拥有平等的机会参加与其负责领域相关的职业培训。

第十三条

（1）职业培训应由政府培训机构和/或私人职业培训机构提供。

（2）职业培训可以在培训地点或工作地点进行。

（3）在提供职业培训过程中，第（1）款所述的政府培训机构可以与私人组织合作。

第十四条

（1）私人职业培训机构可以是印尼法人实体或个人所有制企业。

（2）第（1）款中提及的私人职业培训机构必须拥有许可证或在当地劳动力事务管理部门登记备案。

（3）由政府部门运营的培训机构须在当地劳动力事务管理部门将其活动登记备案。

（4）上述第（2）款和第（3）款中提及的培训机构获得许可证和进行登记程序的规定应由部长令监管。

第十五条

培训提供者有义务确保满足以下要求：

a. 培训师须到位；

b. 提供课程且课程适合培训的水平；

c. 所提供培训呈体系化且有相应的基础设施；

d. 提供足够资金，确保培训活动的长效性。

第十六条

（1）有执照的私人职业培训机构和经注册的由政府发起的培训机构可在认证机构处进行认证。

（2）第（1）款中提及的认证机构应是独立的，其成员由社区和政府人员组成，经部长令同意后成立。

（3）第（2）款中提及的认证机构，其组织机构与工作步骤应由部长令监管。

第十七条

（1）在下列情况下，负责地方性劳动力事务的政府机构可以暂时中止与该地区职业培训相关的组织和管理活动：

a. 不符合第九条中提及的职业培训指导意见；和/或

b. 不能满足第十五条规定的要求。

（2）上述第（1）款中提及的暂时中止行为应有充分理由，并同时提供整改意见，中止时间不得超过六个月。

（3）对培训管理的临时中止行为只限于未满足第九条和第十五条规定的培训项目。

（4）如果培训机构在六个月内未能履行并完成第（2）款所述的整改要求，则将受到终止培训项目的制裁。

（5）如果培训机构不遵守第（4）款所述的处罚规定，继续进行培训活动，将被吊销培训执照并撤销培训机构资格。

（6）中止、终止、吊销执照及撤销培训资格的规定应由部长令监管。

第十八条

（1）员工在参加了由政府培训机构、私人培训机构或职场提供的培训之后，有权得到工作技能认可。

（2）上述工作技能认可应采用工作适任证书的形式。

（3）即使是具有工作经验的员工，也要参加第（1）款所述的培训，以期获得第（2）款所述的工作适任证书。

（4）须建立独立的专业性认证机构以提供工作适任证书。

（5）第（4）款中提及的认证机构的建立程序应由总统令监管。

第十九条

为残疾人士提供的培训要考虑其伤残的类型、严重程度以及个人能力。

第二十条

（1）应建立国家级职业培训体系，作为各行各业和/或各工作领域内职业培训的参照，借以对人力资源的发展和提高提供支持。

（2）第（1）款中提及的关于国家级职业培训系统的形式、机制和机构安排应由政府法规监管。

第二十一条

培训可以采用学徒制形式。

第二十二条

（1）学徒制度的实施基础是学徒和企业书面签订的学徒制合同。

（2）第（1）款中提及的学徒制合同应至少约定学徒和企业双方的权利和义务，以及学徒制期限。

（3）任何没有签订第（2）款所述的学徒制合同的学徒关系将被视为非法的，并且学徒的身份要变成企业的正式工人。

第二十三条

完成学徒计划的员工有权得到企业或认证中介的工作技能资格认证。

第二十四条

学徒计划可以在企业内部、职业培训地或其他企业进行，在印尼境内、境外均可。

第二十五条

（1）在印尼境外进行的学徒制培训必须获得由部长或指定官员签发的许可证。

（2）为了能得到第（1）款中提及的许可证，学徒培训的组织者必须是符合现行相关法律法规的印尼法人实体。

（3）第（1）款及第（2）款中提及的对获得许可证程序的规定应由部长令监管。

第二十六条

（1）任何在印尼境外进行的学徒制培训必须考虑到如下几点：

a. 印度尼西亚作为一个独立国家的尊严和地位；

b. 掌握更高水平的技能；

c. 学徒的保护和福利，包括履行宗教义务的权利。

（2）如果学徒制培训不能满足第（1）款中提及的要求，部长或指定官员可终止任何在印尼境外进行的学徒制培训。

第二十七条

（1）部长可要求有资格的企业组织学徒制培训。

（2）在落实第（1）款中提及的组织学徒制计划的需求时，部长须考虑企业、社会和国家的利益。

第二十八条

（1）为了能够在制定培训政策时提供建议和意见，应建立国家级职业培训协调者机构。

（2）上述机构的建立、成员构成和工作步骤应由总统令监管。

第二十九条

（1）中央政府和/或地方政府要大力开展职业培训和学徒制计划。

（2）开展职业培训和学徒制计划应着眼于提高职业培训管理上的实用性、质量和效率以及生产力。

（3）第（2）款所述的为提高生产力所做的努力应通过发展卓有成效的企业文化、职业道德、技术水平以及经济活动的效率，进而实现国民生产力的提高。

第三十条

（1）为提高第二十九条第（2）款中提及的生产力，应建立国家级生产力机构。

（2）上述国家级生产力机构应采用公共生产力强化服务网络形式，借以支持跨部门、跨地区的经济活动或计划。

（3）第（1）款所述机构的建立、成员结构和工作步骤应由总统令监管。

第六章　工作安置

第三十一条

不管是在国内或国外工作，每位员工都应有平等的权利和机会选择、获得或更换工作，并且获得体面的收入。

第三十二条

（1）工作安置应透明、自由、客观、公平、平等，并且没有歧视。

（2）工作安置应尽量做到人尽其才，使各岗位能够最大限度地适应员工的行业、技能、天赋、兴趣及能力，并保证其人格获得尊重，权利获得法律保护。

（3）按照国家和地区发展计划的需求情况，在进行工作安置时，应考虑工作机会的平等分配以及劳动力的有效供给。

第三十三条

劳动力的工作安置包括：

a. 劳动力在国内的工作安置；

b. 劳动力在国外的工作安置。

第三十四条

第三十三条 b 项所述的劳动力在国外的工作安置应由法规监管。

第三十五条

（1）需要劳动力的雇主可自行招聘雇工，也可通过职业中介聘用雇工。

（2）从开始招聘到落实工作这一过程中，第（1）款所述的职业中介有义务为其所招聘的雇工提供保护。

（3）在招聘过程中，第（1）款所述的雇主有义务保障受雇人员的福利、安全以及身心健康。

第三十六条

（1）第三十五条第（1）款中提及的由职业中介进行的劳动力安排要通过提供工作安置服务完成。

（2）第三十五条第（2）款中提及的工作安置服务应在工作安置体系中以一体化方式得到提供，该体系包含以下各要素：

a. 求职者；

b. 职位空缺；

c. 职业市场信息；

d. 工作间机制；

e. 制度安排。

（3）与第（2）款中所述的工作安置体系要素相关的活动可以独立进行，并以落实劳动力安排为目标。

第三十七条

（1）第三十五条第（1）款中提及的职业中介包括：

a. 政府中负责劳动力事务的部门；

b. 合法的私人职业中介。

（2）为提供雇用服务，上述的私人职业中介须获得部长或其他指定官员的许可。

第三十八条

（1）无论间接还是直接，部分还是全部，第三十七条第（1）款 a 项中提及的职业中介均不得从申请人或用人单位处收取工作安置费。

（2）第三十七条第（1）款 b 项中提及的私人职业中介只可从用人单位和已经安置好的具有一定级别或特定职业的员工处收取工作安置费。

（3）第（2）款所述的级别和职业应由部长令监管。

第七章　增加就业机会

第三十九条

（1）政府有责任致力于在雇佣关系之内或之外增加工作机会。

（2）政府和社会要共同致力于在雇佣关系之内或之外增加工作机会。

（3）所有政府政策，无论是国家层面的还是地方层面的，抑或是出自任何部门，皆应着眼于增加雇佣关系之内或之外的工作机会。

（4）对于那些可以创造或增加就业机会的社会活动，银行业或非银行业的金融机构以及整个商业界都要提供帮助和便利。

第四十条

（1）应通过有效利用自然资源潜力、人力资源及有效的实用技术来创造生产性的可持续的活动，借以增加劳动关系之外的就业机会。

（2）上述就业机会的增加应通过以下模式实现：个人自营模式、劳动密集型系统的应用、实用型技术的开发和应用、志愿者的有效使用、其他可增加就业机会的模式。

第四十一条

（1）政府应制定有关劳动力和增加就业机会的政策。

（2）政府和社会应共同对第（1）款所述政策的执行进行监管。

（3）在执行第（2）款所述职责时，可建立一个协调机构，其成员为政府代表和社会人士。

（4）第三十九条和第四十条中关于增加就业机会的规定以及本条第（3）款关于组建协调机构的相关事宜应由政府法规监管。

第八章　外籍员工的雇用

第四十二条

（1）任何雇用外籍员工的雇主均须获得部长许可状。

（2）私人雇主禁止雇用外籍员工。

（3）驻印尼的外国外交机构代表处雇用外籍的外交和领事人员无须获得第（1）款所述的部长许可状。

（4）外籍雇员只能在特定岗位和特定期限在印尼工作。

（5）第（4）款所述的特定岗位和特定期限应由部长令监管。

（6）第（4）款所述的外籍雇员，如其工作期限已满且不能延长，可由其他外籍人员替代。

第四十三条

（1）雇用外籍员工的雇主必须具有关于安排外籍员工的计划，且该计划须由部长或授权官员在法律上认可。

（2）上述计划应至少包含以下内容：

a. 需要外籍员工服务的原因；

b. 外籍员工在企业组织架构中的职位和/或职业；

c. 使用外籍员工的期限；

d. 指定印尼员工作为外籍员工的搭档。

（3）第（1）款的规定不适用于政府部门、国际组织以及外国的外交机构代表处。

（4）使用外籍员工的计划，其合法程序应由部长令监管。

第四十四条

（1）雇用外籍员工的雇主须遵守有关职业与技能标准的法律规定。

（2）第（1）款所述的职业与技能标准应由部长令监管。

第四十五条

（1）雇用外籍员工的雇主须履行如下义务：

a. 指定印尼员工作为外国员工的搭档，使得外籍员工能将其技术和技能传授给印尼同事。

b. 教育和培训印尼员工，直到其可以担任目前由外籍员工担任的职位。

（2）第（1）款的规定不适用于担任主管和/或专员职位的外籍员工。

第四十六条

（1）外籍员工不得居于与人事相关的职位和/或某些特定职位。

（2）上述特定职位应由部长令监管。

第四十七条

（1）雇主必须向其雇用的外国员工支付报酬。

（2）上述支付报酬的规定不适用于政府部门、国际组织、社会和宗教团体或教育机构的某些岗位。

（3）第（2）款所述的关于教育机构中某些特定岗位应由部长令监管。

（4）对报酬金额及分配的规定应由政府法规监管。

第四十八条

当外籍员工雇用期满后，雇主应将其遣返原籍国。

第四十九条

关于使用外籍员工的程序及对印尼搭档的教育和培训工作的规定应由政府法令监管。

第九章　雇佣关系

第五十条

雇佣关系因雇主与工人/劳动者之间存在劳动协议而存在。

第五十一条

（1）劳动协议可以是书面的，也可以是口头的。

（2）以书面形式明确具体要求的工作协议，应遵照现行法律执行。

第五十二条

（1）劳动协议应以下述条款为基础：

a. 双方一致同意；

b. 采取法律诉讼的行为能力；

c. 存在双方一致认可的工作；

d. 双方认可的工作不能有违公序良俗或现行法律法规中的规定。

（2）如果双方签订的劳动协议违反第（1）款中的 a 项和 b 项，可被废止或取消。

（3）如果双方签订的劳动协议违反第（1）款中的 c 项和 d 项，则该协议可被依法宣布无效。

第五十三条

雇主应承担与签订劳动协议相关的所有事项和/或所需费用。

第五十四条

（1）书面劳动协议应至少包括以下内容：

a. 企业名称、地址及所属行业；

b. 工人/劳动者的姓名、性别、年龄和住址；

c. 职业或工作类别；

d. 工作地点；

e. 工资总额和支付方式；

f. 指明劳资双方的权利和义务的工作要求；

g. 劳动协议的生效日期和有效期；

h. 劳动协议的签订日期和地点；

i. 双方当事人签字。

（2）第（1）款 e 项和 f 项中提及的劳动协议不得违反公司规定、集体劳动协议及现行法律法规。

（3）第（1）款所述的劳动协议一式两份，具有同等法律效力，企业和工人/劳动者各持一份。

第五十五条

除非双方另有约定，否则劳动协议不得终止和/或更改。

第五十六条

（1）劳动协议可以是有期限的，也可以是无限期的。

（2）期限劳动协议应以下述条件为基础：

a. 期限；或

b. 完成某项工作。

第五十七条

（1）限期劳动协议应采用书面形式，使用拉丁字母形式的印尼语。

（2）限期劳动协议，如未采用书面形式而违反第（1）款规定的，应视为无限期劳动协议。

（3）如劳动协议同时以印尼语和某一外语书写，当在解释上出现分歧时，以印尼语版本为准。

第五十八条

（1）具有明确履行时间规定的劳动协议不能约定试用期。

（2）如果本条第（1）款中提及的劳动协议规定了试用期，则依法视为无效。

第五十九条

（1）限期协议只可适用于某些工作，由于其类型和性质，这些工作将在指定时间内完成，详情如下：

a. 可一次性完成或属临时性质的工作；

b. 预计最长不超过三年可完成的工作；

c. 季节性工作；

d. 与新产品、新活动或仍处于试验阶段的附加产品相关的工作。

（2）长期性质的工作不可签订限期协议。

（3）限期协议可以延期或续签。

（4）可以签订不长于两年的限期协议，只可延期一次，且延期以一年为限。

（5）雇主如欲延长劳动协议，应至少在协议期满七天前书面通知员工。

（6）当限期协议到期时，需经过三十天的缓冲期，方可续签协议。协议只能续签一次，以两年为限。

（7）不能满足第（1）款、第（2）款、第（4）款、第（5）款和第（6）款规定的劳动协议将依法变为无限期协议。

（8）本条中未尽事宜由部长令监管。

第六十条

（1）在无限期劳动协议下，可规定最长三个月的试用期。

（2）试用期间，雇主支付的工资不得低于最低工资标准。

第六十一条

（1）在下列情况下劳动合同终止：

a. 员工死亡；或

b. 劳动协议到期；或

c. 法庭判决和/或具有法律效力的劳资纠纷协调机构的指令；或

d. 劳动协议、公司章程或集体劳动协议中规定的某些情况导致的雇佣关系的终止。

（2）如雇主死亡，公司所有权转移，公司出售、传给子嗣或赠送他人的，劳动协议仍然有效。

（3）公司所有权发生转移时，除非转让协议另有规定，否则新雇主有责任保护员工的权益，且该协议不得削减员工的福利待遇。

（4）如雇主个人去世，其继承人在与员工协商后可终止劳动协议。

（5）如员工去世，其子嗣有权主张法律规定的员工权益，也有权主张在劳动协议、公司章程或集体劳动协议中规定的员工权益。

第六十二条

在限期劳动协议中，如任何一方在协议期满前终止雇佣关系，或劳动协议由于第六十一条各款所述以外的原因而不得不终止，则终止协议的一方须向另一方支付补偿金，其金额相当于协议期满前的员工剩余工资总额。

第六十三条

如无限期劳动协议是口头形式的，则雇主须向相关员工签发一份任命书。该任命书应至少包括以下内容：

a. 员工的姓名和住址；

b. 员工开始工作的日期；

c. 工作类型；

d. 工资总额。

第六十四条

公司可以通过书面工作合同或符合相关员工法规的书面协议将部分工作转包给另一公司。

第六十五条

（1）转包部分工作给另一公司应签订书面承包协议。

（2）上述可分包的工作必须满足下列要求：

a. 该工作可以与主体活动分开完成；

b. 该工作是在发包方直接或间接的指令下完成；

c. 该工作完全是公司的一项辅助活动；

d. 该工作不直接影响生产过程。

（3）第（1）款所述的承包商必须是法律实体。

（4）第（2）款所述的承包商所提供的劳动保护和工作条件，至少应与发包商所提供的相同或符合现行法律法规的规定。

（5）第（3）款在内容上如有变动和/或增加，应由部长令监管。

（6）为完成第（1）款中提及的工作而产生的雇佣关系应采用书面雇佣协议的形式加以规定，雇佣协议的双方为承包商及其雇用的员工。

（7）第（6）款中所述的雇佣关系可采用无限期劳动协议，如满足第五十九条的要求，也可采用限期协议。

（8）如未能满足第（2）款和第（3）款的规定，则发包商应依法变为承包商所雇用的员工的雇主。

（9）如第（8）款所述，如果雇主从承包商变为发包商，则员工和发包商之间的劳动关系应服从于第（7）款所述的劳动关系。

第六十六条

（1）雇主不可使用劳务公司提供的员工从事企业的主要活动或与生产过程直接相关的活动，辅助性服务或与生产过程间接相关的活动除外。

（2）为企业提供辅助性服务人员或与生产过程间接相关人员的劳务公司应满足下列条件：

a. 员工和劳务公司之间有雇佣关系；

b. 上述劳动关系中的适用劳动协议应为具有固定期限的劳动协议（该协议需满足第五十九条的要求）和/或经双方签字的无固定期限书面工作合同；

c. 劳务公司负责劳动者的工资、福利保障、工作条件及解决可能出现的纠纷；

d. 劳务公司与雇主之间的协议应采用书面形式，并包括本法所提到的相应条款。

（3）劳务公司须为法律实体，并且拥有政府人力资源部门颁发的营业执照。

（4）如未能满足上述第（1）款，第（2）款项下的 a 项、b 项和 d 项以及第（3）款的规定，则使用劳务公司所提供服务的企业有责任依法成为劳务公司所提供的员工的雇主。

第十章　保障、工资和福利

第一节　保障

第一小节　残疾员工

第六十七条

（1）雇用残疾员工的雇主须根据其残疾的类型和严重程度为残疾员工提供保护。

（2）上述保护应遵照现行法律法规执行。

第二小节　童工

第六十八条

企业不准雇用童工。

第六十九条

（1）企业如雇用十三到十五岁的儿童从事轻体力工作，则可免于第六十八条的规定，但前提是该项工作不能影响儿童在生理和心理上的正常发育及其在社会上的健康成长。

（2）雇用第（1）款中提及的儿童从事轻体力劳动的雇主应符合以下规定：

a. 雇主须获得儿童父母或监护人的书面同意；

b. 雇主须和儿童父母或监护人签订劳动协议；

c. 一天最长工作时间为三个小时；

d. 白天工作不得影响学校上课时间；

e. 职业安全与健康；

f. 清晰的雇佣关系；

g. 按照现行规定领取工资。

（3）第（2）款中 a 项、b 项、f 项和 g 项不适用于在家族企业中工作的儿童。

第七十条

（1）儿童在工厂的工作可作为法定的学校课程或培训的一部分。

（2）第（1）款中提及的儿童至少要满十四岁。

（3）第（1）款中提及的工作应具备以下条件：

a. 就如何开展工作给予明确的指令，同时就如何完成工作提供指导和监督；

b. 保障职业安全与健康。

第七十一条

（1）儿童可以工作，借以开发自身的天赋和兴趣。

（2）第（1）款中提及的雇用童工的雇主应满足以下要求：

a. 处于其父母或监护人的直接监督下；

b. 每天最多工作三小时；

c. 工作条件和工作环境不能影响儿童的身心健康、在社会上的健康成长及上学时间。

（3）第（1）款和第（2）款提及的有关儿童参加工作，借以开发其天赋和兴趣的规定应由部长令监管。

第七十二条

如儿童和成人一起受雇，则童工的工作场所必须和成人的工作场所分开。

第七十三条

如发现儿童在工作场所，则其应被视为在工作，除非有证据证明并非如此。

第七十四条

（1）任何人不得以恶劣的童工方式雇用儿童。

（2）上述恶劣的童工方式包括：

a. 奴役或类似奴役的工作；

b. 利用、介绍或提供儿童从事卖淫、制作色情产品、进行色情表演或赌博；

c. 利用、介绍或使儿童生产和买卖酒精饮料、麻醉品、精神类药物和其他致瘾性物质；和/或

d. 任何对儿童的健康、安全和精神有害的工作。

（3）第（2）款中所述的有害健康、安全或精神的工作类型的规定应由部长令监管。

第七十五条

（1）对于没有劳动关系的童工在工作中出现的问题，政府有义务努力解决。

（2）上述努力应由政府规章加以规范。

第三小节　女性

第七十六条

（1）禁止雇用十八岁以下的女性员工在晚上十一点至早上七点之间工作。

（2）为避免伤害或影响怀孕员工和其腹中胎儿的健康及安全，禁止雇用孕妇（以医生证明为准）在晚上十一点至早上七点之间工作。

（3）如果企业雇用女性在晚上十一点至早上七点之间工作，雇主应：

a. 提供营养充足的食物和饮品；

b. 保持工作场所的庄重和安全。

（4）企业有义务为在晚上十一点至早上五点之间工作的女性员工提供往返交通工具。

（5）第（3）款和第（4）款所述规定应由部长令监管。

第四小节　工作时间

第七十七条

（1）每位雇主均须遵守关于工作时间的规定。

（2）第（1）款所述工作时间包括：

a. 每天七小时，每周工作六天，总工作时间四十二小时；或

b. 每天八小时，每周工作五天，总工作时间四十小时。

（3）上述关于工作时间的规定不适用于某些业务领域或某些类型的工作。

（4）上述有关特定业务领域或某些工作类型的工作时间之规定应由部长令监管。

第七十八条

（1）如雇主要求员工工作的时间长于第七十七条第（2）款的规定，则必须满足以下

条件：

　　a. 得到相关员工的同意；

　　b. 加班时间每天不得超过三小时，每周不得超过十四小时。

　　（2）雇主要求员工进行上述加班时应付加班费。

　　（3）第（1）款 b 项关于加班的规定不适用于某些业务领域或某些工作。

　　（4）上述关于加班及加班费的规定应由部长令监管。

第七十九条

　　（1）企业必须允许员工休息和休假。

　　（2）上述休息和休假时间包括：

　　a. 连续工作四小时后，至少休息半小时，这半小时不得包括于工作时间中。每周工作六天，则休息一天，每周工作五天，则休息两天；

　　b. 连续工作十二个月后，每年可休息十二天；

　　c. 如员工在同一个企业连续工作六年，作为奖励，其可在第七年和第八年分别享有一个月的休假，前提是该员工在这两年里不能再享受正常的年假，依此类推。

　　（3）关于第（2）款 c 项所述的休假规定的运用情况应在劳动合同、公司规章或集体劳动协议中加以规定。

　　（4）c 项中关于长假的规定只适用于在某些企业工作的工人。

　　（5）第（4）款所述企业应由部长令监督。

第八十条

企业须为员工提供足够的机会以履行宗教义务。

第八十一条

　　（1）如女性员工在例假期间感到疼痛，在通知雇主后，可在例假的第一天和第二天不来上班。

　　（2）上述情况的执行应在劳动协议、公司章程或集体劳动协议中阐明。

第八十二条

　　（1）女性员工在产前和产后各有一个半月的休假，产前时间以产科医生或助产士的推算为准。

　　（2）女性员工在流产后可以休养一个半月，或以产科医生或助产士出具的医疗证明中要求的休养时间为准。

第八十三条

如果女性员工在工作期间需要为婴儿哺乳，企业须为其提供条件。

第八十四条

按照第七十九条第（2）款 b 项、c 项、d 项以及按照第八十条和第八十二条进行的休假，员工应获得全额工资。

第八十五条

（1）公共假日期间，员工可不工作。

（2）如因工作性质、类别或劳动协议中另有特别要求而员工必须连续工作，则企业可以要求员工在公共假期工作。

（3）员工如在上述公共假期工作，则雇主必须支付加班费。

（4）第（2）款所述工作性质或类别的规定应由部长令监管。

第五小节　职业安全和健康

第八十六条

（1）员工有权获得如下保护：

a. 职业安全和健康；

b. 道德和尊严；

c. 人格和宗教价值观受到尊重。

（2）为保障员工安全并实现生产力最大化，应制定职业健康和安全管理方案。

（3）第（1）款和第（2）款所述保护应遵照现行法律法规。

第八十七条

（1）每个企业须建立职业健康与安全管理体系，并列入企业的管理体系当中。

（2）第（1）款所述关于职业安全与健康管理系统的规定应由政府规章加以监管。

第二节　薪金

第八十八条

（1）员工有权获得作为人的体面的生活。

（2）为使员工能够获得上述生活，政府应制定薪酬政策以保障劳动者。

（3）上述的薪酬政策应包括：

a. 最低工资；

b. 加班费；

c. 缺勤期间应付工资；

d. 员工因不得不参加工作以外的活动而缺勤，但应得到的工资；

e. 休息期间应付工资；

f. 工资支付形式和方法；

g. 罚款和工资减扣；

h. 其他可用工资计算的事项；

i. 均衡的工资结构和等级；

j. 资遣费；

k. 所得税。

（4）综合考量生产力和经济发展因素，政府应制定第（3）款 a 项所述的可保证员工体面生活的最低工资标准。

第八十九条

（1）第八十八条第（3）款 a 项所述的最低工资由以下部分组成：

a. 基于省或地市的最低工资；

b. 以省或地市为基础的部门最低工资。

（2）第（1）款所述的最低工资，其制定须以满足体面生活为指导思想。

（3）在充分考虑到省级工资委员会和/或地市行政长官意见的情况下，由省长确定第（1）款所述最低工资标准。

（4）获得第（2）款所述的体面生活之步骤的内涵和执行情况应由部长令监管。

第九十条

（1）雇主支付员工的工资不得低于第八十九条所述的最低工资标准。

（2）如雇主（暂时）无力支付第八十九条所述的最低工资，则允许其推迟支付时间。

（3）推迟支付最低工资的程序须受部长令的监管。

第九十一条

（1）如工资总额是建立在雇主和员工或雇主和工会签订的协议基础之上的，则其数额不得低于现行法律法规所规定的工资额度。

（2）如上述协议确定的工资低于法律规定的最低工资或与现行法律相悖，则该协议依法宣布无效，雇主须支付员工符合现行法律规定的工资。

第九十二条

（1）雇主应根据员工的级别、职位、工龄、教育状况及工作能力制定薪金的结构和等级。

（2）雇主应根据企业的财务状况和生产力程度，定期审查员工工资。

（3）第（1）款所述工资结构和等级须由部长令监管。

第九十三条

（1）如果员工未工作，企业可以不支付工资。

（2）在下列情况下，上述规定不适用，雇主仍应支付员工工资：

a. 员工因病不能工作；

b. 女性员工在例假第一天和第二天因不适而不能工作；

c. 员工因结婚、子女结婚、儿子行割礼、子女洗礼、妻子生产或流产，或配偶、子女及其配偶、（岳）父母或其他家人去世而不能工作；

d. 员工因履行国家义务而不能工作；

e. 员工因履行宗教规定义务而不能工作；

f. 员工愿意遵照承诺工作，但由于雇主并未指示他们工作，或由于雇主自身的过失，或由于雇主原本可以避免的阻碍而使员工不能工作；

g. 员工正在行使休息的权利；

h. 员工在履行工会的义务并得到企业的允许；

i. 员工正在接受企业要求的教育或培训。

（3）如第（2）款所述员工长期生病不能工作，员工的薪金应该按照以下方式计算：

a. 缺勤的前四个月，应得百分之百的工资；

b. 缺勤的第二个四个月，应得百分之七十五的工资；

c. 缺勤的第三个四个月，应得百分之五十的工资；

d. 接下来的四个月，在资遣之前，应得百分之二十五的工资。

（4）由于第（2）款 c 项所列明的原因而缺勤，则员工在此期间应得工资按以下标准计算：

a. 因为结婚应得三天的工资；

b. 因为子女结婚应得两天的工资；

c. 因为儿子行割礼应得两天的工资；

d. 因为子女接受洗礼应得两天的工资；

e. 因为妻子生产或流产而缺勤的员工应得两天的工资；

f. 如果员工的配偶、父母或岳父母之中一人，或子女中有人过世，雇员应得两天的工资；

g. 如果员工家属有人过世，雇员应得一天的工资。

（5）第（2）款中所提及事项的具体执行办法应在劳动协议或集体劳动协议中加以说明，或按公司规定执行。

第九十四条

如果工资由基本工资和固定福利组成，则基本工资不得低于二者总额的百分之七十五。

第九十五条

（1）如员工违规，无论有意或无心，均要受到强制罚款。

（2）如果雇主有意或因疏忽延迟支付员工工资，则雇主要被勒令支付相当于员工薪金一定比例的罚款。

（3）在工资支付方面，政府应对针对企业或员工的强制罚款进行监管。

（4）如企业根据现行法律法规宣告破产或进行清算，在所有债务中，应优先支付员工工资。

第九十六条

所有关于员工工资的索赔事项以及所有其他源于劳资关系的款项之索赔，其有效期为提出索赔申请后两年内。

第九十七条

以下各项均应受政府法规的监管：第八十八条所述关于体面收入、工资政策、体面生

活之所需以及员工工资之保障的规定；第八十九条所述最低工资的设定；第九十五条第
（1）款、第（2）款及第（3）款所述关于强制罚款的规定。

第九十八条

（1）应建立国家薪资委员会、省级薪资委员会和地市级薪资委员会，借以在政府制定
薪资政策时提供建议和意见，并促进国家薪资体系的发展。

（2）上述各级委员会的会员应包括政府代表、企业联合会代表、工会代表、高校代表
及专家代表。

（3）国家级薪资委员会的成员应由总统任免，而省级和地市级薪资委员会成员由省长
地方长官或市长任免。

（4）关于第（1）款和第（2）款所述薪资委员会的设立程序、人员构成、人员任免
程序以及薪资委员会的工作程序和职责之规定由总统令监管。

第三节　福利

第九十九条

（1）企业应为员工及其家属办理社会保险；

（2）上述社会保险应依照现行法律规定进行管理。

第一百条

（1）为提高员工及其家属的福利水平，雇主应提供福利设施。

（2）福利设施的提供应综合考虑员工对福利设施的需求和企业的供给能力。

（3）第（1）款和第（2）款所述关于员工所需的福利设施类型和标准以及对企业提
供福利设施能力的衡量须由政府法规进行监管。

第一百零一条

（1）为提高员工福利，应在企业内部建立员工合作社。

（2）政府、企业、员工和工会应努力发展上述员工合作社。

（3）建立上述员工合作社应依照现行法律法规进行。

（4）发展第（2）款所述员工合作社应受政府法规监管。

第十一章　劳资关系

第一节　总则

第一百零二条

（1）在处理劳资关系方面，政府应履行如下职能：制定政策、提供服务、监控并针对
各种违反人力资源法律法规的行为采取行动。

（2）在处理劳资关系方面，劳动者及工会等组织应履行其应尽的工作义务，保持良好
的工作状态以保障生产、民主地表达诉求、提高工作技能、促进企业业务并为员工及其家

属的福利而奋斗。

（3）在处理劳资关系方面，企业家及企业家组织应建立合作，开展业务，使就业渠道多样化，并以透明、民主和公正的方式为员工提供福利。

第一百零三条

劳资关系应通过以下方式协调：

a. 工会；

b. 企业家组织；

c. 双方协作机构；

d. 三方协作机构；

e. 公司章程；

f. 集体劳动协议；

g. 法定劳动力法律法规；

h. 劳资纠纷调解机构。

第二节　工会

第一百零四条

（1）每个员工都有权组织和加入工会。

（2）在履行第一百零二条提及的职能时，工会有权收取并管理经费，并对包括罢工经费在内的工会财政负责。

（3）第（2）款中提到的罢工经费及收取程序应在工会章程和/或规章制度中加以规定。

第三节　企业家组织

第一百零五条

（1）企业家有权成立和加入企业家组织。

（2）有关企业联合组织的条款应符合现行法律法规。

第四节　双方协作机构

第一百零六条

（1）任何员工人数超过五十人的企业均须建立双方协作机构。

（2）第（1）款所述双方协作机构在企业内应起到沟通和协商劳动力事宜的平台作用。

（3）第（1）款所述协作机构的成员应包括企业家代表和员工代表，员工代表由员工民主选举，代表员工利益。

（4）第（1）款和第（3）款有关确定双方协作机构成员的条款由部长令进行规范。

第五节　三方协作机构

第一百零七条

（1）三方协作机构应向政府和其他政策制定方和问题解决方提供关于劳动力问题的建议和意见。

（2）上述三方协作由以下部分组成：

a. 国家级、省级和地市级三方协作机构；

b. 由不同部门组成的国家级、省级和地市级三方协作机构。

（3）三方协作机构的成员由政府代表、企业家组织代表和工会代表构成。

（4）第（1）款所述三方协作机构的程序和组织结构由政府法令进行规定。

第六节　公司章程

第一百零八条

（1）员工超过十人的企业须建立一套公司章程，由部长或指定官员批准后生效。

（2）第（1）款所述制定公司章程的义务不适用于已有集体劳动协议的企业。

第一百零九条

企业应制定公司规章制度，并对其负责。

第一百一十条

（1）制定公司章程时，应考虑企业员工代表的建议和意见。

（2）企业中已经有工会的，则第（1）款所述员工代表应为工会负责人。

（3）企业中尚无工会的，则第（1）款所述员工代表应为双方合作机构的成员和/或在该机构中任职，或由企业员工通过民主选举方式选出，代表企业员工保障员工的利益。

第一百一十一条

（1）公司章程应至少包括以下内容：

a. 雇主的权利和义务；

b. 员工的权利和义务；

c. 工作条件；

d. 企业纪律和行为准则；

e. 章程的有效期。

（2）公司章程不得违反现行法律法规。

（3）公司章程有效期为两年，到期后须进行更新。

（4）公司章程有效期内，如果工会要求就集体劳动协议的起草进行谈判，则企业有义务照做。

（5）如果上述谈判失败，则现行的公司章程仍然有效，直至期满。

第一百一十二条

（1）在公司章程草案提交给部长或指定官员后，其须在三十个工作日内将其合法化。

（2）如公司章程已满足第一百一十一条的第（1）款和第（2）款之要求，而在第（1）款规定的三十个工作日内部长或指定官员没有做出审批，则公司章程即视为已经合法化。

（3）如公司章程尚未满足第一百一十一条第（1）款和第（2）款之要求，则部长或指定官员须向企业发出书面修改通知。

（4）在收到上述修改通知后十四个工作日内，企业须向部长或指定官员重新提交公司章程修改版。

第一百一十三条

（1）公司章程期满前的任何变更须取得雇主和员工代表的一致同意。

（2）经上述双方一致同意修改后的公司章程应提交部长或指定官员进行合法化审批。

第一百一十四条

企业应向员工通告、解释和传达公司章程的内容及其变更。

第一百一十五条

有关制定和审批公司章程之过程的规定由部长令监管。

第七节　集体劳动协议

第一百一十六条

（1）签订集体劳动协议的双方分别为已在政府人力资源部门注册的某一（或多个）工会和某一（或多个）雇主。

（2）第（1）款中所述的集体劳动协议应通过评议形式而制定。

（3）第（1）款中所述的集体劳动协议应采用拉丁字母和印尼语进行编写。

（4）如果集体劳动协议不是由印尼语编写，必须由专业翻译人员译成印尼语，译本应视为已满足第（3）款列明之要求。

第一百一十七条

如第一百一十六条第（2）款中提及的评议未能达成一致，则应通过劳资关系处理程序加以解决。

第一百一十八条

一个企业只能有一份集体劳动协议，且适用于企业所有员工。

第一百一十九条

（1）如果一个企业中只有一个工会，则此唯一的工会在企业里有权代表员工就集体劳动协议和雇主进行谈判，前提是百分之五十以上的员工为该工会成员。

（2）如第（1）款所述，企业中只有一个工会，但工会成员总数为未超过企业员工总数的百分之五十，工会仍然可以代表员工就集体劳动协议和雇主谈判，前提是须就此事进行投票，确认工会可以获得企业中百分之五十以上员工的支持。

（3）如果工会未能赢得如第（2）款所述百分之五十以上员工的支持，在举行投票六个月后，工会可再次就集体劳动协议提出与企业进行谈判的要求。

第一百二十条

（1）如果在一个企业中有几个工会，则获得百分之五十以上员工支持的工会有权与雇主谈判。

（2）如果未能满足第（1）款的要求，则企业各个工会可结成联盟直至获得百分之五十以上企业员工的支持，故而，该联盟即有资格代表员工与雇主进行集体劳动协议谈判。

（3）如第（1）款和第（2）款所述仍然未果，则各工会应建立一个谈判小组，其成员按各工会人数比例确定。

第一百二十一条

第一百一十九条和第一百二十条所述的工会成员应持有工会会员卡作为凭证。

第一百二十二条

第一百一十九条第（2）款所述之投票应由员工代表和工会官员组成的委员会进行监督管理，并在负责人力资源事务的政府官员以及雇主的见证下进行。

第一百二十三条

（1）集体劳动协议的有效期为两年。

（2）在雇主和工会书面同意的基础上，集体劳动协议的有效期可延长，但不能超过一年。

（3）关于下一次集体劳动协议的谈判最早可在现行集体劳动协议终止前三个月开始。

第一百二十四条

（1）集体劳动协议应至少包括：

a. 雇主的权利和义务；

b. 工会或员工的权利和义务；

c. 集体劳动协议的生效日期和有效期；

d. 制定集体劳动协议各方的签字。

（2）集体劳动协议的条款不能违反现行法律法规。

（3）如集体劳动协议的内容违反现行法律法规，则相悖条款依法视为无效，而以现行法律规定为准。

第一百二十五条

如果双方同意变更集体劳动协议，则所做变更应成为现行集体劳动协议之不可分割的一部分。

第一百二十六条

（1）雇主、工会和/或员工须共同履行集体劳动协议的规定。

（2）雇主和工会有义务就集体劳动协议的内容或其变更告知所有员工。

（3）企业须印制集体劳动协议文本并分发给每位员工，费用由企业承担。

第一百二十七条

（1）企业和员工之间订立的劳动协议不得违反集体劳动协议。

（2）如上述劳动协议中存在与集体劳动协议相悖的条款，则该条款应依法视为无效，而以集体劳动协议中的规定为准。

第一百二十八条

集体劳动协议中规定的但未包括在劳动协议中的条款，适用于劳动协议。

第一百二十九条

（1）企业内有工会的，禁止雇主用公司章程替代集体劳动协议。

（2）企业内没有工会，用公司章程代替集体劳动协议的，则企业在制定公司章程条款时不得低于集体劳动协议中规定的标准。

第一百三十条

（1）如果集体劳动协议到期后需要延期或续签，而企业中只有一个工会，则该集体劳动协议的延期或续签不受第一百一十九条限制。

（2）如果集体劳动协议到期后需要延期或续签，而企业中有数个工会，但在上次协议中谈判的工会无法再满足第一百二十条第（1）款的要求，则该集体劳动协议的延期或续签将由拥有超过百分之五十企业员工的工会和上次协议中签字的工会通过建立谈判小组的形式来进行，谈判小组成员由上述各工会按其会员人数比例组成。

（3）如果集体劳动协议到期后需要延期或续签，而企业中有数个工会，但无一可满足第一百二十条第（1）款的规定，则该集体劳动协议的延期或续签应按照第一百二十条第（2）款和第（3）款的规定进行。

第一百三十一条

（1）如果工会解散或企业所有权发生转移时，则现存的集体劳动协议在期满前仍然有效。

（2）如果企业与另一个企业合并，而双方各有一个集体劳动协议，则以对员工更有利的一个为有效协议。

（3）如果一个有集体劳动协议的企业与另一个没有集体劳动协议的企业合并，则现存的集体劳动协议仍然适用于合并后的企业，直至期满。

第一百三十二条

（1）集体劳动协议自签署之日起生效，除非在集体劳动协议中另有说明。

（2）经双方签订的集体劳动协议须由企业在政府人力资源部门登记备案。

第一百三十三条

有关集体劳动协议的制定、延期、变更和注册的要求和程序的规定应由部长令监管。

第一百三十四条

为实现劳资双方各自的权利和义务，政府有义务监督劳动力法律法规的实施，并确保严格遵守和强制执行。

第一百三十五条

为实现劳资关系而实行劳动力法的责任主体是员工、企业和政府。

第八节　劳资纠纷调解机构和部门

第一小节　劳资纠纷

第一百三十六条

（1）雇主和员工或工会均应通过协商努力解决劳资纠纷，以期达成共识。

（2）如上述协商未果，雇主和员工或工会应通过法律规定程序解决劳资纠纷。

第二小节　罢工

第一百三十七条

因谈判失败而导致的合法、有序、和平的罢工是员工和工会的基本权利。

第一百三十八条

（1）在罢工进行期间，员工和/或工会如邀请其他员工参加罢工，其行为不得违反法律规定。

（2）上述受邀参加罢工的员工可以接受或拒绝该邀请。

第一百三十九条

罢工的员工如果来自从事公共事业的企业和/或活动类型会危及他人生命安全的企业，则其罢工行为应以不危害公共利益和/或不威胁他人生命财产安全为前提。

第一百四十条

（1）在罢工开始至少七天前，员工和工会须向雇主和当地政府人力资源部门发出书面通知。

（2）第（1）款所述通知至少应包括：

a. 罢工起始时间（具体到小时）；

b. 罢工地点；

c. 罢工原因；

d. 罢工工会主席和秘书的签字和/或所有参加罢工的工会主席和秘书的签字，上述人等要对罢工负责。

（3）如果罢工员工非工会成员，则罢工通知应由工人代表签字，其职责是协调和/或对罢工负责。

（4）如果罢工没有遵照第（1）款执行，为保护生产设备和企业财产，雇主可采取以下临时措施：

a. 禁止罢工者进入生产区域；

b. 必要时，禁止罢工者进入企业场所。

第一百四十一条

（1）政府部门代表和管理层在收到第一百四十条所述的罢工通知书后应出具回执。

（2）罢工前和罢工期间，政府人力资源部门有义务通过举行会议来协商双方的纠纷，以解决导致罢工出现的问题。

（3）如果第（2）款所述协商达成一致意见，则该协议书应由争议双方签署，并由政府人力资源部门官员作为见证人。

（4）如第（2）款所述协商未果，则政府人力资源部门的官员应立即将导致罢工的问题提交给经授权的劳资纠纷调解机构加以解决。

（5）如第（4）款所述协商仍未果，则在雇主与负责罢工的工会或罢工负责方谈判的基础上，可以选择继续罢工、中止或终止罢工。

第一百四十二条

（1）未按第一百三十九条和第一百四十条之要求而举行的罢工均不合法。

（2）举行非法罢工的法律后果由部长裁决。

第一百四十三条

（1）只要员工或工会举行的罢工合法、有序、和平，则任何人不得加以阻止。

（2）按照现行法律，禁止逮捕和/或拘押合法、有序、和平进行罢工的员工或工会官员。

第一百四十四条

如按第一百四十条所述举行罢工，则企业不得：

a. 用企业以外的员工代替罢工的员工；

b. 在罢工期间或罢工后以任何方式制裁或报复罢工员工和工会官员。

第一百四十五条

如果工人是为了维护正当权利而罢工，且雇主确实侵犯了这些权利，则工人仍应得到工资。

第三小节 停工

第一百四十六条

（1）停工是企业的基本权利。停工是企业因为谈判失败部分或全部停止工作。

（2）企业不能因为员工和/或工会提出正当要求而停工。

（3）实行停工应当依照现行法律法规。

第一百四十七条

如果停工会威胁人的生命，服务于公共利益的企业禁止停工，具体包括医院、向公众提供清洁用水的机构、电信控制中心、电网中心、石油和天然气加工行业、铁路部门。

第一百四十八条

（1）如企业停工，则雇主须至少提前七个工作日书面通知员工和/或工会及政府人力资源部门。

（2）上述停工通知应至少包括：

a. 停工的开始和结束时间（具体到小时）；

b. 停工的原因。

（3）第（1）款中提及的停工通知应由雇主和/或企业管理层签字。

第一百四十九条

（1）直接收到第一百四十八条所述的书面停工通知的员工、工会和政府人力资源部门应出具回执，申明接到该通知的日期和具体时间。

（2）在停工之前或者停工时，政府人力资源部门应当立即通过安排争议双方会谈并讨论解决争议以解决问题。

（3）如果第（2）款中提及的讨论能够达成一致，协议书应当由争议的双方制定并签署，政府人力资源部门作为见证人。

（4）如果第（2）款中提及的讨论不能达成一致，政府人力资源部门应立即将该问题委托授权的劳资纠纷调解机构处理。

（5）第（4）款中提及的讨论未能达成一致意见，劳资双方依据谈判结果选择继续停工还是中止或终止停工。

（6）以下情形不需要第一百四十八条第（1）款和第（2）款中提及的停工通知：

a. 员工（工会）违反第一百四十条规定的罢工程序；

b. 员工（工会）违反劳动协议、公司章程、集体劳动协议或现行的法律法规的规定。

第十二章　雇用终止

第一百五十条

本法关于员工资遣的规定，其适用范围应包括：法律实体企业或非法律实体企业，私人企业、合伙制企业或法人企业（私有或国有），拥有管理人员并雇用工作人员的事业单位或其他社会组织。

第一百五十一条

（1）雇主、员工或工会以及政府须尽一切可能防止资遣事件发生。

（2）如经过各种努力，资遣仍不可避免，则该资遣意图须由雇主和资遣员工所属工会进行协商。如员工非工会成员，则由雇主和该资遣员工进行协商。

（3）如第（2）款所述协商失败，则雇主必须在接到劳资纠纷调解机构的决议书后方可遣散员工。

第一百五十二条

（1）就员工资遣向劳资纠纷调解机构发出的申请应采用书面形式并列明理由。

（2）只有当资遣问题已经按第一百五十一条第（2）款之规定谈判完毕，则劳资纠纷调解机构可以接受该项资遣申请。

（3）如果实施资遣的意图已经付诸协商但协商无果，则只能由劳资纠纷调解机构就资遣申请做出决定。

第一百五十三条

（1）企业不能因为以下原因开除员工：

a. 员工因病超过十二个月不能工作，并且有医生的书面证明；

b. 员工因履行法律法规规定的国家义务而不能工作；

c. 员工因履行宗教义务而不能工作；

d. 员工因结婚而不能工作；

e. 员工因怀孕、生产、流产或哺乳婴儿而不能工作；

f. 员工与其他同一企业的员工有血缘关系和/或婚姻关系，除非在集体劳动协议或公司章程中有所表述；

g. 员工加入工会和/或成为工会负责人；员工在工作时间外或得到企业允许在工作时间内或根据劳动协议、公司章程、集体劳动协议参与工会活动；

h. 员工向相关部门报告企业的犯罪行为；

i. 因信念、宗教、政治倾向、种族、肤色、性别、生理状况或婚姻状况的不同；

j. 员工因工伤而永久残疾或受伤，或员工在工作中生病并被医生证明恢复时间不确定。

（2）企业如果因上述原因开除员工，将被认为是无效的，企业要重新招聘被解雇的员工。

第一百五十四条

在以下情况中，无须经过第一百五十一条的第（3）款中的步骤：

a. 被解雇的员工还在试用期，并且预先有书面的协定；

b. 被解雇的员工在没有企业强迫和威胁的情况下自愿提交书面的辞职书，或者劳动协议到期；

c. 根据劳动协议、公司章程、集体劳动协议和法律法规规定，员工达到退休年龄；

d. 员工死亡。

第一百五十五条

（1）若未按第一百五十一条第（3）款的规定，所做出的员工资遣没有劳资纠纷调解机构出具的决议书，则该资遣行为依法视为无效。

（2）只要没有劳资纠纷调解机构的决议书，则企业和员工必须继续履行各自义务。

（3）只要企业继续支付雇员工资及其他由雇员的合法福利，则企业不得擅自中止雇员的工作，否则视为违反第（2）款的规定。

第一百五十六条

（1）如果企业解雇员工，企业有义务支付遣散费和/或一部分费用作为奖金和补偿。

（2）遣散费的计算方法如下：

a. 工作不到一年的员工，一个月工资；

b. 工作不到两年的员工，两个月工资；

c. 工作不到三年的员工，三个月工资；

d. 工作不到四年的员工，四个月工资；

e. 工作不到五年的员工，五个月工资；

f. 工作不到六年的员工，六个月工资；

g. 工作不到七年的员工，七个月工资；

h. 工作不到八年的员工，八个月工资；

i. 工作八年以上的员工，九个月工资。

（3）奖金的计算方法如下：

a. 工作三到六年的员工，两个月工资；

b. 工作七到十年的员工，三个月工资；

c. 工作十到十二年的员工，四个月工资；

d. 工作十三到十五年的员工，五个月工资；

e. 工作十六到十八年的员工，六个月工资；

f. 工作十九到二十一年的员工，七个月工资；

g. 工作二十二到二十四年的员工，八个月工资；

h. 工作二十五年或以上的员工，十个月工资。

（4）补偿的计算方法是：

a. 没有过期且没有用掉的年假；

b. 送员工及其家人回到原来地方的交通花费；

c. 住房补助和医疗补助：离职费或服务奖励的百分之十五。

（5）政府应当明确规定有关遣散费，作为工作期间回报的服务费总额和第（2）款、第（3）款、第（4）款中所规定的劳动者应得的补偿发生变化的部分。

第一百五十七条

（1）工资用来作为计算遣散费、奖金及各种权益的补偿费的基础，它包括：

a. 基本工资；

b. 为员工及其家属提供的所有形式的固定津贴，包括免费为其提供的配给购买价；如该配给须员工以津贴方式支付，则该配给购入价与员工须支付价之间的差额应视为工资。

（2）如果员工的工资按天数计算，那么一个月的工资等于一天工资的三十倍。

（3）如果员工的工资按件计酬或按佣金计酬，那么员工的日工资应等于前十二个月内员工的平均日工资，并且不能低于该地区规定的最低工资标准。

（4）如果员工的工作跟气候有关，且按件计酬，那么月工资额应按前十二个月的平均工资进行计算。

第一百五十八条

（1）如果员工有以下行为，企业可以解雇员工：

a. 偷窃或夹带公司产品和/或资金；

b. 提供虚假或伪造信息，并导致公司损失；

c. 在工作场所醉酒，食用或散布毒品、精神药品或其他能上瘾的物品；

d. 有不道德或下流、猥亵的行为或在工作场所赌博；

e. 殴打、胁迫、恐吓其他员工；

f. 唆使其他员工违法；

g. 有意或无意地破坏公司财产或使公司财产受到威胁，并导致公司损失；

h. 在工作场所中，有意或无意地使其他员工受到威胁；

i. 泄漏公司机密；

j. 其他判决五年或以上有期徒刑或无期徒刑的犯罪行为。

（2）第（1）款中涉及的行为必须有以下证据：

a. 员工被当场抓住；

b. 员工承认其行为；或

c. 公安部门的报告并且有最少两个目击证人。

（3）员工因第（1）款中提及的原因被解雇，可以得到第一百五十六条第（4）款中涉及的补偿。

（4）第（1）款中提及的员工，如果其工作职责不直接代表企业利益，则企业仍应支付其遣散费，具体金额及支付方法应在劳动协议或集体劳动协议中加以规定，也可按公司有关规定执行。

第一百五十九条

如果员工不愿接受一百五十八条第（1）款中提及的终止劳动关系，该员工可向劳资纠纷调解机构起诉。

第一百六十条

（1）如果员工被司法部门拘留并且拘留的原因与企业无关，企业不必支付员工工资，但企业有义务对其赡养或抚养人提供补助：

a. 一个赡养或抚养人，工资的百分之二十五；

b. 两个赡养或抚养人，工资的百分之三十五；

c. 三个赡养或抚养人，工资的百分之四十五；

d. 四个或更多赡养或抚养人，工资的百分之五十。

（2）第（1）款中提及的补助不能超过六个月。

（3）如果员工因拘留等司法程序有六个月以上不能工作，则企业可以解雇员工。

（4）第（3）款中提及的六个月内，如果员工被司法部门证明无罪，企业要重新招聘员工。

（5）如果在六个月内，员工被宣判有罪，企业可以解雇员工。

（6）第（3）款和第（5）款中提及的解雇不需要劳资纠纷调解部门的决议书。

（7）员工在第（3）款和第（5）款中提及的情况下被解雇之后有权按第一百五十六条第（4）款的规定得到一倍的奖金和一倍的补偿。

第一百六十一条

（1）如果员工违反了劳动协议、公司章程或集体劳动协议，并且企业给予了第一、二、三次警告信以后，企业可以解雇员工。

（2）第（1）款中提及的每次警告信有效期为六个月，除非在劳动协议、公司章程或集体劳动协议中有特殊规定。

（3）员工因第（1）款中提及的原因被解雇，有权得到一倍的遣散费、一倍的奖金和一倍的补偿。

第一百六十二条

（1）员工如果自愿辞职，有权按第一百五十六条第（4）款的规定得到补偿金。

（2）如果员工自愿辞职，而其工作职责又不直接代表企业利益，则企业除了要支付其补偿金之外，还须按第一百五十六条第（4）款规定支付其遣散费，具体金额及支付方法应在劳动协议或集体劳动协议中加以规定，也可按公司有关规定执行。

（3）如果员工辞职，员工应满足以下要求：

a. 在辞职前至少三十天内递交辞职信；

b. 与企业没有合同牵连；

c. 继续工作直到离职。

（4）自愿辞职不需要劳资纠纷调解部门的决议书。

第一百六十三条

（1）如企业的形态发生变更，如兼并、合并或企业所有权的改变，而员工不愿继续雇佣关系时，则该员工应获得第一百五十六条第（2）款规定的一倍的遣散费、第一百五十六条第（3）款规定的一倍的奖金和第一百五十六条第（4）款规定的一倍的补偿金。

（2）如企业的形态发生变更，如兼并、合并或企业所有权的改变，而雇主不愿继续雇佣关系时，则企业应支付该员工第一百五十六条第（2）款规定的两倍的遣散费、第一百五十六条第（3）款规定的一倍的奖金和第一百五十六条第（4）款规定的一倍的补偿金。

第一百六十四条

（1）如企业连续两年亏损，企业可以裁员，但须支付员工一倍的遣散费、服务奖励和补偿金。

（2）企业应提供财政报告证明第（1）款中提及的连续两年亏损。

（3）如果企业因为改革而裁员，则企业应支付员工第一百五十六条第（2）款规定的两倍的遣散费和第一百五十六条第（3）款规定的一倍的奖金和补偿金。

第一百六十五条

如企业倒闭，企业可以终止合同关系，但应支付员工第一百五十六条第（2）款规定的一倍的遣散费、第一百五十六条第（3）款规定的奖金和第一百五十六条第（4）款规定的一倍的补偿金。

第一百六十六条

如果员工死亡，企业应支付其继承人第一百五十六条第（2）款规定的两倍的遣散费、第一百五十六条第（3）款规定的一倍的奖金和第一百五十六条第（4）款规定的一倍的补偿金。

第一百六十七条

（1）当员工已到退休年龄，而企业已将其纳入退休福利计划，则企业不必支付该员工第一百五十六条第（2）款规定的遣散费、第一百五十六条第（3）款规定的奖金和第一百五十六条第（4）款规定的补偿金。

（2）如果员工一次性获得的第（1）款所述的退休福利金少于第一百五十六条第（2）款规定的遣散费的两倍、第一百五十六条第（3）款规定的奖金和第一百五十六条第（4）款规定的补偿金的总和，则企业应支付差额部分。

（3）如果员工的养老保险的保险金是由企业和职工共同支付的，那么遣散费就是其中企业支付的那部分养老金。

（4）除根据第（1）款、第（2）款、第（3）款的规定，还可以根据劳动协议、公司章程或集体劳动协议安排。可能会在安排劳动协议或公司章程规定或集体劳动协议。

（5）如果员工没有加入养老保险，在员工退休时，企业应支付其第一百五十六条第（2）款规定的两倍的遣散费、第一百五十六条第（3）款规定的奖金和第一百五十六条第（4）款规定的补偿金。

（6）根据第（1）款、第（2）款和第（3）款劳动者退休福利权利不因年老而终止，该规定是基于现行法律的强制性规定。

第一百六十八条

（1）如果员工连续旷工五天以上，没有递交附有效证明的书面解释，并且企业已书面召唤其两次，员工将被视为自动辞职。

（2）附有第（1）款中所述的有效证明的书面解释最迟要在员工重回岗位的第一天递交。

（3）如按第（1）款解除雇佣关系，企业要支付员工第一百五十六条第（4）款规定的补偿金，同时员工还应得到遣散费，其金额及其发放程序和方法在劳动协议、公司章程或集体劳动协议中规定。

第一百六十九条

（1）在下列情形中，员工可向劳资纠纷调解机构提交正式申请，要求解除与雇主的雇佣关系：

a. 员工受到虐待、粗暴地侮辱或威吓；

b. 诱劝和/或命令员工从事违反法律法规的行为；

c. 连续三个月或者更长时间未能按时支付工资；

d. 未向员工履行规定的义务；

e. 命令员工完成劳动协议之外的工作；

f. 要求劳动者进行劳动协议中未规定的危及员工生命、安全、健康以及心理的工作。

（2）由于第（1）款的原因终止雇佣关系的员工，有权根据第一百五十六条第（2）款的规定得到两倍遣散费、根据第一百五十六条第（3）款规定得到工作期间收入一倍的奖金并根据第一百五十六条第（4）款规定得到补偿金。

（3）如经劳资纠纷调解机构调查后未发现企业有第（1）款所述的违法行为，则企业可不经劳资纠纷调解机构的决定，直接终止与该员工的雇佣关系，并且该员工无权获得第一百五十六条第（2）款规定的遣散费和一百五十六条第（3）款规定的奖金。

第一百七十条

如资遣的实施未满足第一百五十一条第（3）款、第一百六十八条［第一百五十八条第（1）款的情形除外］、第一百六十条第（3）款以及第一百六十二条和第一百六十九条之规定，则视为无效，而雇主需重新雇用该员工并支付其应得的全部工资和其他福利。

第一百七十一条

如员工的资遣未能按照第一百五十八条第（1）款、第一百六十条第（3）款和第一百六十二条的规定由劳资纠纷调解机构进行决定，则员工可在雇佣关系终止后一年内向劳资纠纷调解机构提起诉讼。

第一百七十二条

如因员工长期生病或因工伤造成残疾不能从事工作，且连续缺勤超过十二个月时，企业可提出解雇该员工，但应支付该员工第一百五十六条第（2）款规定的遣散费的两倍，第一百五十六条第（3）款规定的员工工作期间奖金的两倍以及第一百五十六条第（4）款规定的补偿金。

第十三章　人力资源开发

第一百七十三条

（1）政府应努力建设与人力资源相关的机制，并开展相关的活动。

（2）在进行第（1）款所述的建设基础和开展活动时，可邀请企业组织、工会和相关的专业组织参加。

（3）第（1）款和第（2）款中所述的开发人力资源机制的努力应采取综合协调的方式进行。

第一百七十四条

为人力资源开发计，政府、企业组织、工会和其他专业组织可遵照现行法律法规在人力资源领域开展国际合作。

第一百七十五条

（1）政府可对在人力资源开发领域做出杰出贡献的个人或者机构进行奖励。

（2）第（1）款所述的奖励可采用奖章、金钱和/或其他形式。

第十四章　劳动监察

第一百七十六条

劳动监察由能够胜任的独立政府劳动监察员负责实施，以确保劳动法的执行。

第一百七十七条

第一百七十六条所述的劳动监察员由部长或其他指定官员决定。

第一百七十八条

（1）劳动监察应由专门的政府工作机构实施，其职责范围包括中央政府、省政府和市政府三个层级。

（2）第（1）款中提及的劳动监察的执行由总统令监管。

第一百七十九条

（1）第一百七十八条提及的省政府和市政府层级的劳动监察单位应向部长提交劳动监察报告。

（2）提交第（1）款中提及的报告的程序由部长令监管。

第一百八十条

有关第一百七十六条中提及的劳动监察员的任命、其权利义务及权限的规定应遵照现行法律法规。

第一百八十一条

在实施第一百七十六条提及的职责时，劳动监察员应：

a. 对具有保密性质的或值得进行保密的一切进行保密；

b. 避免滥用职权。

第十五章　调研

第一百八十二条

（1）遵照现行法律，担任公务调查员的特别权利，除了给予印度尼西亚国家警务调查官员外，也可以给予劳动监察人员。

（2）第（1）款中提及的公务调查员拥有以下权利：

a. 检查有关劳动犯罪的报告和解释是否真实；

b. 调查涉嫌劳动犯罪人员；

c. 要求被认为与调查中的劳动犯罪行为相关的个人或法律实体提供解释和证据；

d. 对在劳动犯罪中的物品或证据予以检查或没收；

e. 检查与劳动犯罪相关的文章或其他文件；

f. 在进行与劳动犯罪相关的调查时，请求专家帮助；

g. 如果没有足够证据证明存在劳动犯罪，须停止调查。

（3）第（2）款中提及的公务调查员的权利应遵照现行法律法规行使。

第十六章　刑事条例和行政制裁

第一节　刑事条例

第一百八十三条

（1）任何人违反第七十四条的规定，将受到最低两年、最高五年的刑事处罚和/或最低两亿卢比、最高五亿卢比的惩罚。

（2）第（1）款所述的犯罪行为，在法律上归为重罪。

第一百八十四条

（1）任何人如违反第一百六十七条第（5）款的规定，将受到最低一年、最高五年的刑事处罚和/或最低一亿卢比、最高五亿卢比的罚款。

（2）第（1）款所述的犯罪行为，在法律上归为重罪。

第一百八十五条

（1）任何人如违反第四十二条第（1）款和第（2）款、第六十八条、第六十九条第（2）款、第八十条、第八十二条、第九十条第（1）款、第一百三十九条、第一百四十三条、第一百六十条第（4）款和第（7）款的规定，将受到最低一年、最高四年的刑事处罚和/或最低一亿卢比、最高四亿卢比的罚款。

（2）第（1）款所述的犯罪行为，在法律上归为重罪。

第一百八十六条

（1）任何人如违反三十五条第（2）款和第（3）款、第九十三条第（2）款、第一百三十七条、第一百三十八条第（1）款的规定，将受到最低一个月、最高四年的刑事处罚和/或最低一千万卢比、最高四千万卢比罚款。

（2）第（1）款所述的犯罪行为，在法律上归为轻罪。

第一百八十七条

（1）任何人如违反第三十七条第（2）款、第四十四条第（1）款、第四十五条第（1）款、第六十七条第（1）款、第七十一条第（2）款、第七十六条、第七十八条第（2）款、第七十九条第（1）款和第（2）款、第八十五条第（3）款、第一百四十四条的规定，将处以最低一个月、最高十二个月刑事处罚和/或最低一千万卢比、最高一亿卢比的罚款。

（2）第（1）款所述的犯罪行为，在法律上归为轻罪。

第一百八十八条

（1）任何人如违反第十四条第（2）款、第三十八条第（2）款、第六十三条第（1）款、第七十八条第（1）款、第一百零八条第（1）款、第一百一十一条第（3）款、第一百一十四条、第一百四十八条的规定，将受到最低五百万卢比、最高五千万卢比的罚款。

（2）第（1）款所述的犯罪行为，在法律上归为轻罪。

第一百八十九条

对雇主施加的监禁、有期徒刑和/或罚款等制裁措施，并不解除雇主向员工支付各种权益金和/或赔偿金的义务。

第二节　行政制裁

第一百九十条

（1）违反本法下列规定的，由部长依法给予行政制裁：第五条、第六条、第十五条、第二十五条、第三十八条第（2）款、第四十五条第（1）款、第四十七条第（1）款、第四十八条、第八十七条、第一百零六条、第一百二十六条第（3）款、第一百六十条第（1）款和第（2）款。上述行政制裁包括下列形式：

a. 谴责；

b. 书面警告；

c. 限制涉嫌企业的经营活动；

d. 停止涉嫌企业的经营活动；

e. 取消协议；

f. 取消登记；

g. 暂时停止部分或全部生产；

h. 吊销营业执照。

（2）第（1）款和第（2）款中提及的行政制裁条例由部长作进一步规定。

第十七章　过渡性条款

第一百九十一条

所有调整劳动力事务的执行条例，如不与本法相冲突和/或未被新法所取代，则仍然有效。

第十八章　最终条款

第一百九十二条

自本法开始生效之日起，以下法律法规同时宣告无效：

1. 关于动员印度尼西亚公民在国外工作的条例（1887 年第 8 号政府公报）。

2. 1925 年 12 月 17 日关于限制使用童工和妇女上夜班的条例（1925 年第 647 号政府公报）。

3. 1926 年关于在船上雇用童工和未成年人的条例（1926 年第 87 号政府公报）。

4. 1936 年 5 月 4 日关于举办招聘活动的条例（1936 年第 208 号政府公报）。

5. 关于遣送在印度尼西亚工作的国外劳动力的条例（1939 年第 545 号政府公报）。

6. 1949 年第 9 号关于限制使用童工的条例（1949 年第 8 号政府公报）。

7. 1951 年第 1 号关于向全体印度尼西亚人民宣告 1948 年第 12 号制定雇佣法的法案（1951 年第 2 号政府公报）。

8. 1954 年第 21 号关于工会和雇主间劳动协议法案（1954 年第 69 号政府公报，第 598a 号政府公报增刊）。

9. 1958 年第 3 号安置外籍劳动力法（1958 年第 8 号政府公报）。

10. 1961 年第 8 号关于硕士研究生义务工作的法案（1961 年第 207 号政府公报，第

2270 号政府公报增刊）。

11. 1963 年第 7 号关于在重点企业和政府公共服务部门预防罢工或停摆的总统令（1963 年 67 号政府公报）。

12. 1969 年第 14 号关于劳动力法基本条例的法案（1969 年第 55 号政府公报，第 2912 号政府公报增刊）。

13. 1997 年第 25 号关于人力资源的法案（1997 年第 73 号政府公报 第 3702 号政府公告增刊）。

14. 1998 年第 11 号关于 1997 年第 25 号劳动力适用范围变化法案的法案（1998 年第 184 号政府公报，第 3791 号政府公告增刊）。

15. 2000 年第 28 号关于建立政府规章以代替 2000 年第 3 号法令的法案（2000 年第 204 号政府公报，第 4042 号政府公报增刊）。

第一百九十三条

本法自颁布之日起生效。为周知计，本法于印度尼西亚政府公报中予以颁布。

REGULATION BY THE MINISTER OF ENERGY AND MINERAL RESOURCES OF THE REPUBLIC OF INDONESIA NUMBER 6 OF 2010 CONCERNING POLICY GUIDELINES TO INCREASE OIL AND GAS OUTPUT

Considering:

a. whereas oil and gas contribute highly to state revenues and to meeting domestic demand for energy and industry raw materials, and at this time oil and gas output is experiencing a decline;

b. whereas there remains potential to optimize oil and gas output, and therefore in order to increase oil and gas output it is essential to establish policy guidelines to increase oil and gas output under a Regulation by the Minister of Energy and Mineral Resources.

In reference to:

1. Law Number 22 of 2001 concerning Oil and Gas (Republic of Indonesia Statute Book Year 2001 Number 136, Republic of Indonesia Statute Book Supplement Number 4152).

2. Government Regulation Number 35 of 2004 concerning Upstream Oil and Gas Enterprises (Republic of Indonesia Statute Book Year 2004 Number 123, Republic of Indonesia Statute Book Supplement Number 4435) as amended two times, more recently under Government Regulation Number 55 of 2009 (Republic of Indonesia Statute Book Year 2009 Number 128, Republic of Indonesia Statute Book Supplement Number 5047).

3. Government Regulation Number 42 of 2002 concerning Implementing Body for Upstream Oil and Gas Enterprises (Republic of Indonesia Statute Book Year 2002 Number 81, Republic of Indonesia Statute Book Supplement Number 4216).

4. Presidential Decree Number 84/P of 2009.

5. Regulation by the Minister of Energy and Mineral Resources Number 0030 of 2005 dated July 20th, 2005 concerning Department of Energy and Mineral Resources Organization and Work Procedures.

Decrees:

To establish: REGULATION BY THE MINISTER OF ENERGY AND MINERAL RESOURCES CONCERNING POLICY UIDELINES TO INCREASE OIL AND GAS OUTPUT.

CHAPTER I   GENERAL PROVISIONS

Article 1

Under this Ministerial Regulation, the following definitions shall apply:

1. Oil and Gas are petroleum and natural gas.

2. Cooperation Contract is a Production Sharing Contract or any other form of cooperation contract for Exploration and Exploitation activities, that is more advantageous to the State and whose output shall be used for the greatest benefit of the people's prosperity.

3. Contractor is a Business Entity or Permanent Establishment designated to conduct Exploration and Exploitation in a Working Area under a Cooperation Contract with the Implementing Body.

4. Exploration is an activity aimed at obtaining information on geological conditions in order to discover and gain an estimate of oil and gas reserves in a specified working area.

5. Exploitation is the sequence of activities aimed at producing oil and gas from a specified working area, consisting of well drilling and completion, construction of transportation, storage and processing facilities in the separation and refining of oil and gas in the field, and supporting activities thereof.

6. Minister is the minister charged with duties and responsibilities that include oil and gas business enterprises.

7. Implementing Body (Badan Pelaksana) is the agency formed to control Upstream Oil and Gas Enterprises.

8. The Directorate General is the directorate general, of which duties and authority include oil and gas enterprises.

9. The Director General is the director general charged with duties and responsibilities in the area of oil and gas.

Article 2

All Exploration and Exploitation enterprises are required to support the achievement of Government program targets determined under the State Budget and other Government policies in support of increasing Oil and Gas output.

CHAPTER Ⅱ IMPLEMENTATION OF POLICIES TO INCREASE OIL AND GAS OUTPUT

PART Ⅰ CONTRACTOR OBLIGATIONS

Article 3

In implementing the provision under Article 2, Contractors shall be required to implement the following:

a. complete exploration activities in the discovery structure and expedite submittal of program proposals for the development of new fields and discovered reserves;

b. accelerate execution of development activities in the first field;

c. accelerate execution of development activities in subsequent fields;

d. endeavor to develop or resume production in fields still having potential, whether previously having been in production, or never having been in production;

e. endeavor to resume production in oil wells still having potential, either individually or in collaboration with another entity.

Article 4

(1) In implementing the provisions under Article 3 item a, item b and item c, Contractor shall be required to:

a. report new oil and gas reserves to Minister through the Implementing Body at the latest within a period of 14 (fourteen) calendar days from determination by the Implementing Body;

b. submit proposal for a new field development program at the latest within a period of 90 (ninety) calendar days from determination of a new oil and gas reserve as referred to in item a;

c. commence field development activities at the latest within a period of 180 (one hundred and eighty) calendar days from the time approval was granted for the field development program;

d. commence oil and/or gas production at the latest within a period of 2 (two) years from the time approval was granted to develop a field.

(2) Contractor shall be required to perform field development referred to in paragraph (1) in accordance with the Work Program and Budget and with provisions under regulations and legislation.

(3) If by reason of technical and/or economic considerations the provisions referred to in paragraph (1) cannot be implemented, the Minister by way of Director General may institute another policy toward accelerating production.

Article 5

(1) In implementing the provisions referred to in Article 3 item d, Contractor shall be

required to:

a. conduct an inventory of fields not in production but still having potential, and to report inventory results to the Implementing Body at the latest within a period of 14 (fourteen) calendar days from issuance of this Ministerial Regulation;

b. report to Minister through the Implementing Body, together with submittal of a production resumption program, at the latest within a period of 30 (thirty) calendar days following completion of inventory referred to in item a.

(2) In the event the production resumption program referred to in paragraph (1) is to be conducted in collaboration with another entity, prior approval from the Minister through the Implementing Body shall be required.

Article 6

In the event Contractor does not submit a program for the enterprise of a field not in output but still having potential as referred to in Article 5 paragraph (1), Contractor shall be required to return the field to the Minister for determination of the policy on its enterprise.

Article 7

(1) In implementing the provision referred to in Article 3 item e, Contractor shall be required to:

a. conduct inventory of wells not in production but still having potential, in a field in production, and to report inventory results to the Implementing Body at the latest within a period of 14 (fourteen) calendar days from issuance of this Ministerial Regulation;

b. report to Minister through the Implementing Body, together with submittal of the production resumption program at the latest within a period of 90 (ninety) calendar days from completion of the inventory referred to in item a.

(2) In the event the production resumption program referred to in paragraph (1) is to be conducted in collaboration with another entity, prior approval from the Minister through the Implementing Body shall be required.

Article 8

Implementation of the provisions under Article 3 through Article 7 shall take into consideration the Cooperation Contract and shall refer to regulations and legislation.

PART II   IMPLEMENTING BODY OBLIGATIONS

Article 9

In implementing the provisions under Article 2, the Implementing Body shall be required to:
a. support the process to expedite preparation and publication of the necessary regulation and

legislation;

b. expedite permit and approval processes associated with increasing output;

c. intensify control and supervision of Cooperation Contract implementation;

d. intensify oversight of Contractor compliance with Cooperation Contract in the execution of rights and obligations;

e. intensify internal coordination toward resolving issues relating to oil operations.

Article 10

In implementing the provision under Article 9 item a, the Implementing Body shall be required to:

a. inventory and evaluate implementation of regulations and legislation relevant to the increase of Oil and Gas output and to report results thereof to the Minister with a copy forwarded to the Director General, at the latest within a period of 30 (thirty) calendar days from issuance of this Ministerial Regulation;

b. provide the Director General with substantial and material inputs toward the preparation of regulations and legislations necessary to oil and gas output increase, at the latest within a period of 30 (thirty) calendar days from completion of the inventory referred to in item a;

c. evaluate implementation of Cooperation Contracts and provide inputs to Director General for the preparation of alternate Cooperation Contract formats and/or key terms and conditions within a period of 90 (ninety) calendar days from issuance of this Ministerial Regulation;

d. adjust and revise work procedure provisions and guidelines at the latest within a period of 30 (thirty) calendar days from issuance of this Ministerial Regulation.

Article 11

In implementing the provision under Article 9 item b, the Implementing Body shall be required to:

a. submit recommendations, together with assessments on the first field development plan (POD I), to the Minister at the latest within a period of 40 (forty) calendar days from receipt of Contractor's complete proposal;

b. approve the subsequent field development (POD) at the latest within a period of 40 (forty) calendar days from receipt of Contractor's complete proposal;

c. approve a Work Program and Budget (Rencana Kerja dan Anggaran) and/or Authorization Financial Expenditure (Otorisasi Pembelanjaan Finansial) at the latest within a period of 40 (forty) calendar days from receipt of Contractor's complete proposal;

d. recommend approval of assignment of rights and obligations (farm in and farm out) at the latest within a period of 14 (fourteen) calendar days from receipt of Contractor's complete proposal;

e. approve the sharing of facilities at the latest within a period of 14 (fourteen) calendar days from receipt of Contractor's complete proposal;

103

f. in the event of a case of unitization, recommend approval to the Minister at the latest within a period of 14 (fourteen) calendar days from receipt of Contractor's complete proposal;

g. recommend importing of goods, oil operation equipment at the latest within a period of 14 (fourteen) calendar days from receipt of Contractor's complete proposal.

Article 12

In implementing the provision under Article 9 item c, the Implementing Body shall be required to:

a. supervise and evaluate execution of first and subsequent PODs in conformance with approved POD agreements;

b. supervise and evaluate execution of Work Programs and Budgets (Rencana Kerja dan Anggaran) and/or Authorization Financial Expenditures (Otorisasi Pembelanjaan Finansial) previously approved by the Implementing Body;

c. intensify supervision of maintenance of oil and gas wells and production facilities.

Article 13

In implementing the provision under Article 9 item d, the Implementing Body shall be required to:

a. intensify monitoring and supervision of Contractor activities;

b. issue admonishment/warning to Contractors failing to meet obligations under their Cooperation Contract;

c. recommending the Minister impose sanction to terminate a Cooperation Contract in the event of breach of Cooperation Contract and/or regulations and legislation.

Article 14

In implementing the provision under Article 9 item e, the Implementing Body shall be required to:

a. facilitate and conduct internal coordination to expedite issue resolution;

b. report to the Minister any unresolved issue toward arriving at a policy thereof.

Article 15

In implementing the provisions under Article 9 through Article 14, the Implementing Body shall be required to:

a. determine the size of a newly discovered oil and gas reserve at the latest within a period of 30 (thirty) calendar days from the time the new discovery was made;

b. allocate an output target for each Contractor, which target shall be adjusted to the national oil and gas output target determined by the Government;

c. oversee compliance with timetable for application of discovered oil and gas reserve field development programs referred to under Article 4 paragraph (1) item b, and to report their development on a monthly basis to the Director General.

PART III DIRECTORATE GENERAL AND DIRECTOR GENERAL OBLIGATIONS

Article 16

In implementing the provision under Article 2, Directorate General shall be required to:

a. expedite preparation and publication of the necessary regulations and legislation;

b. expedite permit and approval processes associated with increasing oil and gas output;

c. intensify guidance, control and supervision of Cooperation Contract implementation;

d. intensify oversight of Contractor compliance with Cooperation Contract in the execution of rights and obligations;

e. intensify internal and cross-sectoral coordination toward resolving issues relating to oil operations.

Article 17

In implementing the provision under Article 16 item a, Director General shall be required to:

a. submit to the Minister an inventory and evaluation of regulations and legislations relevant to the increase of oil and gas output, at the latest within a period of 30 (thirty) calendar days from issuance of this Ministerial Regulation;

b. prepare and draft regulations and legislation needed to increase oil and gas output, at the latest within a period of 30 (thirty) calendar days from completion of the inventory referred to in item a;

c. conduct evaluation of Cooperation Contract formats and key terms and conditions and propose to the Minister alternative Cooperation Contract formats and/or key terms and conditions at the latest within a period of 90 (ninety) calendar days from issuance of this Ministerial Regulation.

Article 18

In implementing the provision under Article 16 item b, Director General shall be required to:

a. submit an assessment to the Minister toward granting approval for a POD I, at the latest within a period of 30 (thirty) calendar days from receipt of the POD I;

b. grant permit/recommendation at the latest within a period of 10 (ten) calendar days from receipt of complete application.

Article 19

In implementing the provision under Article 16 item c, Director General shall be required to:

a. evaluate and analyze execution of Contractor activities relevant to increasing oil and gas output;

b. provide early information on specific matters and submit anticipatory recommendations to the Minister on matters relevant to increasing oil and gas output;

c. take necessary measures to follow up on evaluation reports of the matters referred to in item a and item b.

Article 20

In implementing the provision under Article 16 item d, Director General shall be required to:

a. issue admonishment/warning to a Contractor failing to meet obligations under this Ministerial Regulation;

b. impose sanctions on a Contractor repeating an infringement after issuance of a warning as referred to in item a.

Article 21

In implementing the provision under Article 16 item e, the Director General shall be required to:

a. facilitate, and coordinate with energy and mineral resources sector internal agencies, the expeditious resolution of oil operation issues;

b. facilitate, and undertake cross-sectoral coordination to expedite, resolution of oil operation issues;

c. report to the Minister any unresolved issue towards arriving at a policy thereof.

CHAPTER III MISCELLANEOUS

Article 22

In executing Exploration and Exploitation as referred to under Article 2, Contractor shall be required to place priority on the use of domestic goods, services, technology and engineering and designing skills.

Article 23

Priority shall be placed on designating Exploration and Exploitation production output to meet domestic demand.

Article 24

Policy determination, regulation, guidance and supervision shall be conducted in the context of implementing the provisions referred to under Article 22 and Article 23.

Article 25

In aid of implementation of the program to increase oil and gas output, the Minister may form a Supervisory Team for oil and gas output increase.

CHAPTER IV   CLOSING PROVISIONS

Article 26

Upon this Ministerial Regulation becoming effective, all Ministerial Regulations and implementing regulations thereof in contradiction with this Ministerial Regulation shall be rescinded and pronounced null and void.

Article 27

This Ministerial Regulation shall become effective from the date of issuance. In order for all to be so informed, it shall be ordered for this Ministerial Regulation to be promulgated through posting in the Republic of Indonesia Statute Book.

印度尼西亚共和国 2010 年第 6 号
关于增加油气产量政策指南能源与矿产部部长条例

鉴于：

　　a. 油气对国家收入和满足国内能源及原材料需求有巨大贡献，且目前油气产量正处于下降趋势；

　　b. 油气产量仍有上涨的潜力，故为提高油气产量，以能源与矿产部部长条例之形式建立政策指南至为重要。

参照：

　　1. 2001 年第 22 号油气法（2001 年第 136 号印度尼西亚共和国政府公报，印度尼西亚共和国政府公报第 4152 号增刊）。

　　2. 修改了两次的 2004 年第 35 号关于上游油气企业政府条例（2004 年第 123 号印度尼西亚共和国政府公报，印度尼西亚共和国政府公报第 4435 号增刊），最新的 2009 年第 55 号政府条例（2009 年第 128 号印度尼西亚共和国政府公报，印度尼西亚共和国政府公报第 5047 号增刊）。

　　3. 2002 年第 42 号关于上游油气企业执行机制政府条例（2002 年第 42 号印度尼西亚共和国政府公报，印度尼西亚共和国政府公报第 4216 号增刊）。

　　4. 2009 年第 84/P 号总统令。

　　5. 2005 年 7 月 20 日第 0030 号关于能源与矿产部门组织机构与工作程序之能源与矿产部部长条例。

特制定：

关于增加油气产量政策指南能源与矿产部部长条例。

第一章　总则

第一条

本部长条例中定义如下：

1. 油气指石油和天然气。

2. 合作协议指产量分成合同或其他任何形式的有利于国家的勘探开发合作合同，该合同以提高人民福祉为目的。

3. 承包商是指按照与执行机构签订的合作合同而被指定在工区内进行勘探开发业务

的商业实体或常驻机构。

4. 勘探指为获得地质条件信息的活动，目的是在特定的工区内发现并获取油气储量的估值。

5. 开发是指为在特定工区生产油气而进行的一系列活动，包括钻井与完井、运输建设、储存和在野外对油气进行分离与炼制的处理设施，以及对上述活动的所有支持性措施。

6. 部长指对包括油气企业在内的担负责任的部长。

7. 执行机构指控制上游油气企业的部门。

8. 总局指职权覆盖油气企业的总局。

9. 总干事指担负油气领域职责的总干事。

第二条

所有油气企业均须支持政府，以使其按照预算确定的目标以及其他有利于增加油气产量的国家政策得以实现。

第二章　增加油气产量政策的执行

第一部分　承包商义务

第三条

为实现第二条之规定，承包商应执行如下要求：

a. 进行全面的开发活动，尽快提交新油田及发现储量的开发方案；

b. 加快在第一处油田的开发活动；

c. 加快在后续油田的开发活动；

d. 无论已投产或未投产的油田，只要仍有潜力，则应努力开发或恢复生产；

e. 对仍有潜力的油井，无论独立或与其他实体合作，应努力恢复生产。

第四条

（1）为执行第三条 a、b、c 项，承包商应：

a. 在执行机构测定之后 14 日内通过执行机构向部长报告油气储量；

b. 在确定 a 项所述的新油气储藏后 90 日内提交新油田开发方案；

c. 在油田开发方案获准后 180 日内启动油田开发作业；

d. 获准开发油田后 2 年内开始油和/或气生产。

（2）承包商应按照开发方案和预算以及相关法律规定进行第（1）款所述的油田开发。

（3）如出于技术或和/经济考虑，第（1）款所述规定无法执行，则部长可通过总干事另行制定政策以促进生产。

第五条

（1）为执行第三条 d 项之规定，承包商应：

a. 对未生产但尚有潜力的油田进行清查，并在本部长法令签发之日起 14 日内向执行机构汇报清查结果；

b. 在 a 项所述清查结束后 30 日内通过执行机构向部长汇报并同时提交复产方案。

（2）如上述复产方案与另一实体合作执行，须事先通过执行机构获得部长的批准。

第六条

如承包商未提交关于第五条第（1）款所述未投产但尚有潜力的油田开发方案，则应将油田退还部长，由部长确定开发政策。

第七条

（1）为执行第三条 e 项之规定，承包商应：

a. 将对在产油田未生产但仍有潜力的井口数进行盘点，并在部长条例签发后 14 日内向执行机构汇报盘点结果；

b. 在 a 项所述盘点结束后 90 日内通过执行机构向部长汇报并同时提交复产方案。

（2）如上述复产方案与另一实体合作执行，须事先通过执行机构获得部长的批准。

第八条

在执行第三条至第七条的规定时，应顾及合作协议并应符合相关法规。

第二部分　执行机构的义务

第九条

为执行第二条之规定，执行机构应：

a. 支持工作进程，加快相关法律法规的制定和发布；

b. 加快与增加产量相关的许可和批准进程；

c. 加强在合作协议执行上的控制和监督；

d. 在承包商行使权利和履行义务时，加强对其与合作协议的合规性监督；

e. 强化内部协调，解决好石油作业相关问题。

第十条

为执行第九条 a 项的规定，执行机构应：

a. 清查并评价与增加油气产量相关的法律法规的执行情况并在部长条例签发后 30 日内将结果向部长汇报，并同时向总干事提交副本一份；

b. 在完成 a 项所述清查后 30 日内，向总干事提供增加油气产量所必需的法律法规制定方面的实际投入情况；

c. 评估合作协议的执行情况，并在部长条例签发后 90 日内将替代性合作协议的格式和/或主要条款的制作情况提交总干事；

d. 在部长条例签发后 90 日内调整并修正工作流程规范和指导准则。

第十一条

在执行第九条 b 项的规定时，执行机构应：

a. 在接到承包商完整的方案后 40 日内向部长提交议案，同时提交对首个油田开发方案的评估报告；

b. 在接到承包商完整的方案后 40 日内批准随后的油田开发方案；

c. 在接到承包商完整的方案后 40 日内批准工作计划和预算和/或获准的财务支出；

d. 在接到承包商完整的方案后 14 日内建议批准权利与义务的转让（即承包）；

e. 在接到承包商完整的方案后 14 日内批准设施的分派；

f. 如为联合经营，在接到承包商完整的方案后 14 日内向部长建议批准；

g. 在接到承包商完整的方案后 14 日内建议进口相关商品和石油作业设备。

第十二条

在执行第九条 c 项的规定时，执行机构应：

a. 依照已经批准的开发方案协议监督和评估其后的首个油田开发方案的执行情况；

b. 监督和评估执行机构先前批准的工作计划和预算和/或获准的财务支出；

c. 加强对油气井和生产设施在维修方面的监督。

第十三条

在执行第九条 d 项的规定时，执行机构应：

a. 加强对承包商作业的监测和监督；

b. 对未能履行合作协议规定的义务的承包商提出警告；

c. 如承包商违约和/或违反法律规定，则建议部长进行制裁，终止合作协议。

第十四条

在执行第九条 e 项的规定时，执行机构应：

a. 为加快问题的解决提供便利和进行内部协调；

b. 就未能解决之问题向部长汇报，以期出台相关政策。

第十五条

在执行第九条至第十四条的规定时，执行机构应：

a. 在发现新油田后的 30 日内确定新发现的油气储备规模；

b. 为各承包商分派产量目标，该目标应按政府确定的全国油气产量目标进行调节；

c. 对是否符合第四条第（1）款 b 项所述发现的油气储量现场开发方案的应用时间表进行监督，并向总干事就开发情况提交月报。

第三部分　总局和总干事职责

第十六条

在执行第二条的规定时，总局应：

a. 加快制定和颁布必要的法律法规；

b. 加快与增加油气产量相关的许可和批准进程；

c. 强化对合作协议执行情况的指导、控制和监督；

d. 加强对承包商在行使权利和履行义务时与合作协议之间的合规性监督；

e. 在解决与石油作业相关的问题时，加强内部及跨部门协调工作。

第十七条

在执行第十六条 a 项的规定时，总干事应：

a. 在部长条例签发后 30 日内向部长提交对与增加油气产量相关的法律法规进行清查和评估的报告；

b. 在完成 a 项所述的清查报告后 30 日内筹备和起草增加油气产量所需的法律法规；

c. 在部长条例签发后 90 日内对合作协议格式和主要条款进行评估，并向部长推荐替代性的合作协议和/或主要条款。

第十八条

在执行第十六条 b 项的规定时，总干事应：

a. 在收到首个油田开发方案后 30 日内向部长提交评估报告，以期首个油田开发方案获得批准；

b. 在收到完备的申请书后 10 日内授予许可证或提出建议。

第十九条

在执行第十六条 c 项的规定时，总干事应：

a. 对与增加油气产量相关的承包商作业的执行情况进行评价和分析；

b. 就具体事项向部长提供早期信息，并就与增加油气产量的相关问题向部长提交预期建议；

c. 采取必要措施跟踪 a 项和 b 项所述事宜的评估报告。

第二十条

在执行第十六条 d 项的规定时，总干事应：

a. 向未能履行部长条例项下义务的承包商发出警告；

b. 如在发出上述警告后，承包商仍然违约，则实施制裁措施。

第二十一条

在执行第十六条 e 项的规定时，总干事应：

a. 为快速解决石油作业问题提供便利，并与能源和矿产资源部门内部机构密切协作；

b. 为快速解决石油作业问题提供便利，并承担跨部门协调工作；

c. 就悬而未决的问题向部长汇报，以期对此出台政策。

第三章　其他规定

第二十二条

在进行第二条所述的勘探开发活动时，承包商应优先使用国内的商品、服务、技术以及设计技术。

第二十三条

勘探开发及产量上应被作为重点，以满足国内需求。

第二十四条

政策制定、监管、指导和监督应在落实第二十二条和第二十三条所述规定的情形下实施。

第二十五条

为更好地实施增加油气产量方案，部长可设立增加油气产量监督组。

第四章　最终条款

第二十六条

一旦本部长条例生效，则所有与本条例相悖的部长条例及其执行规定均予以废除并宣告无效。

第二十七条

本部长条例自发布之日起生效。为周知计，本条例将通过印度尼西亚共和国政府公告形式予以颁布。

THE THIRD AMENDMENT TO LAW OF THE REPUBLIC OF INDONESIA NUMBER 6 YEAR 1983 REGARDING TAXATION GENERAL PROVISIONS AND PROCEDURES

(Law No. 28/2007 dated July 17, 2007)

Considering:

a. that in the framework of providing better justice and enhancing service for taxpayers and in order to better provide legal certainty as well as to anticipate development in information technology and material provisions in the taxation sector, it is necessary to amend Law Number 6 of 1983 regarding Taxation General Provisions and Procedures as already amended by Law Number 16 of 2000;

b. that based on the consideration as meant in letter a, it is necessary to enact a law regarding the Third Amendment to Law Number 6 of 1983 regarding Taxation General Provisions and Procedures.

In view of:

1. Article 5 paragraph (1), Article 20 and Article 23 of the 1945 Constitution.

2. Law Number 6 of 1983 regarding Taxation General Provisions and Procedures (of the Republic of Indonesia of 1983 No. 49, Supplement to Statute Book No. 3262) as already amended several times and the latest by Law Number 16 of 2000 (Statute Book of Republic of Indonesia of 2000 No. 126, Supplement to Statute Book No. 3984).

With the approval of THE HOUSE OF REPRESENTATIVES OF THE REPUBLIC OF INDONESIA decides:

To stipulate:

LAW REGARDING THE THIRD AMENDMENT TO LAW NUMBER 6 YEAR 1983 REGARDING TAXATION GENERAL PROVISIONS AND PROCEDURES.

Article 1

Several provisions in Law Number 6 of 1983 regarding Taxation General Provisions and Procedures (Statute Book of the Republic of Indonesia of 1983 No. 49, Supplement to Statute Book No. 3262) have been amended several times and the latest by Law Number 16 of 2000 (Statute Book of the Republic of Indonesia of 2000 No. 126, Supplement to Statute Book

No. 3984) shall be amended as follows:

1. Provisions in Article 1 shall be amended so to read as follows:

"Article 1

Hereinafter referred to as:

1. Taxes shall be compulsory contributions to the state, which are indebted forcefully by individuals or bodies on the basis of law, without obtaining compensation directly and used for the need of the state for the people's welfare maximally.

2. Taxpayers shall be individuals or bodies, covering taxpayers, tax withholders and tax collectors that have taxation rights and obligations in accordance with the provisions of taxation legislation.

3. Body shall be a group of individuals and/or capital that constitutes an integral part, whether undertaking business or not, covering state limited liability company, limited partnership, other limited liability company, state or regional administration owned company in any name and form, firm, commercial association, cooperative, pension fund, alliance, affiliation, foundation, mass organization, socio-political organization or the like, institution, permanent establishment, and other forms of body.

4. Entrepreneur shall be an individual or body in any form that in his/her/its business activity or job produces goods, imports goods, exports goods, does trade, takes advantage of intangible from outside Customs Areas, provides services, or benefits from services from outside customs areas.

5. Taxable Entrepreneur shall be an entrepreneur that delivers taxable goods and/or provide taxable services subject to taxes pursuant to the Value Added Tax Law of 1984 and its amendments.

6. Taxpayer Code Number shall be a code number given to a taxpayer as a means in taxation administration and used as personal identity or identifier of the taxpayer in exercising his/her taxation rights and obligations.

7. Tax Period shall be a period becoming the basis for taxpayers to count, remit and report tax due in a specified period as stipulated in this law.

8. Tax Year shall be a period of 1 (one) calendar year, except if the taxpayer uses a book year, which is not the same as calendar year.

9. Part of Tax Year shall be a part of the period of 1 (one) tax year.

10. Tax Due shall be tax, which must be paid at a certain time, during a tax period, during a tax year or during a part of tax year pursuant to the tax legislation.

11. Tax Return shall be a statement used by a taxpayer to report his/her tax calculations and/or payments, tax objects and/or non-tax objects and/or assets and liabilities, pursuant to the tax

legislation.

12. Periodic Tax Return shall be a tax return for a certain tax period.

13. Annual Tax Return shall be a tax return for a certain tax year or a part of tax year.

14. Tax Payment Form shall be an evidence of payment or remittance of tax already realized by using form or other methods to the state cash through places of payment appointed by the Minister of Finance.

15. Tax Assessment shall be letter of stipulation, covering Underpaid Tax Assessment, Additional Underpaid Tax Assessment, Nil Tax Assessment or Overpaid Tax Assessment.

16. Underpaid Tax Assessment shall be a tax assessment determining the amount of tax principal, the amount of tax credits, the amount of underpaid tax-principal, the amount of administrative sanction and the amount of tax yet to be paid.

17. Additional Underpaid Tax Assessment shall be a tax assessment stipulating an addition to the amount of tax already stipulated.

18. Nil Tax Assessment shall be a tax assessment stipulating that the amount of tax principal is the same as the amount of tax credit or tax is not payable and tax credit is nothing.

19. Overpaid Tax Assessment shall be a tax assessment stipulating the excess of tax payment because the amount of tax credit is bigger than tax due or tax not payable.

20. Tax Collection Form shall be a form used to collect tax and/or administrative sanction in the form of interest and/or fine.

21. Distress Warrant shall be an order issued to pay tax due and the collection costs of tax.

22. Tax Credit for Income Tax shall be tax paid directly by a taxpayer plus the principal tax due in a tax collection form because Income Tax in the current year is unpaid or underpaid plus the withheld or collected tax, plus tax on income paid or indebted abroad, subtracted by the amount of preliminary restitution of overpaid tax, which is deducted from tax due.

23. Tax Credit for Value Added Tax shall be Input Tax, which is creditable following deduction by preliminary restitution of overpaid tax or deduction by tax already compensated, which is subtracted from tax due.

24. Independent Job shall be a job done by an individual who has special expertise as part of effort to earn income, which is not bound by industrial relation.

25. Audit shall be a series of activities carried out to collect and process data, information and/or evidence, which is executed objectively and professionally on the basis of an audit standard to assess a taxpayer's compliance with tax obligations and/or to achieve other goals in the framework of implementing provisions of taxation legislation.

26. Initial Evidence shall be a condition, conduct and/or evidence in the form of information, writing or material which can provide directive for strong allegation that taxation crime committed by whoever, which is potential to inflict loss on the state income is underway or had been underway.

27. Audit of Initial Evidence shall be audit executed to obtain initial evidence related to allegation that taxation crime had been underway.

28. Tax Guarantor shall be an individual or body responsible for paying taxes, including a proxy exercising the rights and fulfilling the obligations of the taxpayer in accordance with provisions of taxation legislation.

29. Accounting shall be a process of recording in a regularly way to collect financial data and information, covering assets, liabilities, capital, income and expenses, as well as acquisition and delivery prices of goods or services, which is closed by making a financial statement in the form of balance sheet and profit/loss statement during the tax year.

30. Examination shall be a series of activities carried out to assess whether or not tax return and its attachments have been filled, including assessing whether or not writing and calculation have been done properly.

31. Investigation of Criminal Offences in the taxation field shall be a series of activities carried out by an investigator to seek and gather evidence to disclose a criminal offence in the taxation field as well as to find suspect.

32. Decision on Rectification shall be a decision issued to correct miswriting, miscalculation, and/or mistakes in the application of certain provisions in taxation legislation, which is found in tax assessment, tax collection form, decision on rectification, decision on objection, decision on the reduction or abolition of administrative sanction, decision on the reduction of tax assessment, decision on nullification of tax assessment or decision on initial restitution of overpaid tax or decision on the granting of interest.

33. Decision on Appeal shall be a decision issued by the Tax Court to appeal filed by a taxpayer against decision on objection.

34. Decision on Objection shall be a decision on objection filed by a taxpayer against tax assessment or the tax withholding or collection by a third party.

35. Decision on Appeal shall be a decision issued by the tax court on appeal against the decision on objection filed by a taxpayer.

36. Decision on Lawsuit shall be a decision issued by the tax court on lawsuit against matters to which lawsuit can be filed on the basis of provisions of taxation legislation.

37. Decision on Judicial Review shall be a decision issued by the Supreme Court on application for judicial review filed by a taxpayer or the Director General of Taxation against decision on appeal or decision on objection issued by the tax court.

38. Decision on Preliminary Restitution of Overpaid Tax shall be decision, which contains the amount of initial refund on overpaid tax for certain taxpayers.

39. Decision on Granting of Interest Compensation shall be a decision determining the amount of interest compensation granted to a taxpayer.

40. Date of Sending shall be the date of post stamp on the sending, date of facsimile, or the

date in letter or decision, in the case of the letter or decision being sending directly.

41. Date of Receipt shall be the date of post stamp of the sending, date of facsimile, or the date in letter or decision, in the case of the letter or decision being sending directly. "

2. The provision of Article 2 shall be amended so as to read as follows:

"Article 2

(1) Any taxpayer fulfilling subjective and objective requirements in accordance with provisions of taxation legislation shall register with the office of the Director General of Taxation whose jurisdiction covers the residence or domicile of the taxpayer, and accordingly he/she is given a taxpayer code number.

(2) Any taxpayer as entrepreneur subject to taxes pursuant to the Value Added Tax Law of 1984 and its amendment shall report his/her business to the office of the Directorate General of Taxation whose jurisdiction covers the residence or domicile of the entrepreneur, and the business site for the purpose of validation as a taxable entrepreneur.

(3) The Director General of Taxation may appoint:

a. place of registration and/or place of reporting businesses other than those stipulated in paragraph (1) and paragraph (2);

b. place of registration at the office of the Director General of Taxation whose jurisdiction covers the business site, besides place of registration as referred to in paragraph (1), for certain individual taxpayers as entrepreneurs.

(4) The Director General of Taxation shall ex officio issue taxpayer code numbers and/or validated taxable entrepreneurs, if the taxpayers or taxable entrepreneurs fail to fulfill their obligations as referred to in paragraph (1) and/or paragraph (2).

(4a) Taxation obligations of taxpayer having issued by taxpayer code number and/or validated as taxable entrepreneurs ex officio as meant in paragraph (4) shall start from the moment when the taxpayers fulfill the subjective and objective requirements pursuant to the provisions of taxation legislation in not later than 5 (five) years before the issuance of taxpayer code number and/or validation as taxable entrepreneurs.

(5) The period of time for registration and reporting as well as procedures for registration and validation as referred to in paragraph (1), (2), (3) and (4) including the abolition of taxpayer code number and/or the revocation of the status as taxable entrepreneurs shall be regulated by or no the basis of a regulation of the Minister of Finance.

(6) The abolition of taxpayer code number shall be done by the Director General of Taxation if:

a. application for abolition of taxpayer code number is submitted by taxpayer and/or his/her heirs in case of the taxpayer not longer fulfilling the subjective and/or objective requirements in accordance with provisions of taxation legislation;

b. corporate taxpayer is liquidated because of business discontinuation or merger;

c. permanent-establishment taxpayer discontinues its business activity in Indonesia;

d. the Director General of Taxation deems it necessary to abolish taxpayer code number of taxpayer no longer fulfilling the subjective and/or objective requirements in accordance with provisions of taxation legislation.

(7) Following examination, the Director General of Taxation shall make decision on application for abolition of taxpayer code number in 6 (six) months in case of individual taxpayer or 12 (twelve) months in the case of corporate taxpayer, as from the date of receipt of complete application.

(8) The Director General of Taxation ex officio or on the basis of application of taxpayer can revoke validation of taxable entrepreneur.

(9) The Director General of Taxation, following examination, shall make decision on application for revocation of validation of taxable entrepreneur in 6 (six) months as from the date of receipt of complete application. "

3. A new article is supplemented between Article 2 and Article 3 to become Article 2A, which reads as follows:

"**Article 2A**

A tax period equivalent to one calendar month or other period of time regulated by a regulation of the Minister of Finance shall be 3 (three) calendar months at the maximum. "

4. The provision of Article 3 shall be amended so as to read as follows:

"**Article 3**

(1) Any taxpayer shall fill a tax return properly, completely and clearly in Indonesia language by using Latin letters, Arabic numbers, the rupiah currency, and sign and submit it to the office of the Directorate General of Taxation where the taxpayer is registered or validated or other places stipulated by the Director General of Taxation.

(1a) The taxpayer already securing a permit from the Minister of Finance to perform bookkeeping by using foreign language and currency other than the rupiah, shall submit a tax return in the Indonesian language and permitted currency other than the rupiah with the implementation here to regulated by or on the basis of regulation of the Minister of Finance;

(1b) The signing as meant in paragraph (1) can be done in an ordinary way, by stamp signature or electronic or digital signature, wholly having the same legality, with the technical procedures regulated by or on the basis of a regulation of the Minister of Finance.

(2) The taxpayer as referred to in paragraph (1) and (1a) shall pick up directly a tax return in the place appointed by the Director General of Taxation or by other methods whose

technical procedures are regulated by or on the basis of a regulation of the Minister of Finance.

(3) The deadline for the submission of tax return shall be:

a. for periodic tax return, no later than 20 (twenty) days after the end of the tax period;

b. for annual income tax return of individual taxpayer, no later than 3 (three) months after the end of the tax year;

c. annual income tax return of corporate taxpayer, no later than 4 (four) months after the end of the tax year.

(3a) Taxpayers belonging to certain criteria can report several tax periods in one tax return.

(3b) The taxpayers belonging to certain criteria and procedures for reporting as meant in paragraph (3a) shall be regulated by or on the basis of a regulation of the Minister of Finance.

(3c) The deadline and procedures for reporting the withholding or collection of tax by government treasurers and certain bodies shall be regulated by or on the basis of a regulation of the Minister of Finance.

(4) Taxpayers can extend the period of submission of the annual income tax return as meant in paragraph (3) to another period of 2 (two) months at the most by notification in writing or other methods to the Director General of Taxation with the provisions be regulated by or on the basis of a regulation of the Minister of Finance.

(5) The notification as referred to in paragraph (4) shall be accompanied by a letter of statement on the provisional calculation of tax due in 1 (one) tax year and tax payment form as evidence of the settlement of the remainder of tax due, with the provision here to be regulated by or on the basis of a regulation of the Minister of Finance.

(5a) If a tax return is not submitted in accordance with the deadline as referred to in paragraph (3) or the extended deadline for the submission of annual tax return as referred to in paragraph (4), a admonitory shall be issued.

(6) The model and content of tax return as well as information and/or documents, which must be attached to it shall be regulated by or on the basis of a regulation of the Minister of Finance.

(7) A tax return shall be considered not being submitted if:

a. the tax return is not signed as referred to in paragraph (1);

b. the tax return is not fully accompanied by information and/or documents as referred to in paragraph (6);

c. the tax return certifying overpayment is submitted after 3 (three) years, following the expiration of tax period, part of tax period or tax year and taxpayer had been reminded in writing.

(7a) If the tax return is considered not being submitted as referred to in paragraph (7), the Director General shall notify it to the taxpayer.

(8) Excepted from the obligation as referred to in paragraph (1) shall be certain income taxpayers regulated by or on the basis of a regulation of the Minister of Finance. "

5. The provision of Article 4 shall be amended so as to read as follows:

"**Article 4**

(1) Any taxpayer shall fill and submit a tax return in a correct, complete and clear way and sign it.

(2) If a taxpayer is a legal entity, a tax return shall be signed by the board of executives or the board of directors.

(3) If a taxpayer appoints a proxy by special power of attorney to fill and sign tax return, the special power of attorney shall be attached to the tax return.

(4) The annual income tax return filled by the taxpayer required to perform bookkeeping shall be accompanied by a financial statement in the form of balance sheet and profit/loss statement as well as other information needed to calculate the amount of taxable income.

(4a) The financial statement as referred to paragraph (4) shall be finance statement of the respective taxpayers.

(4b) If the financial statement as referred to in paragraph (4a) is audited by public accountant but not enclosed to tax return, the tax return shall be considered incomplete and unclear thus the tax return shall be considered being not submitted as referred to in Article 3 paragraph (7) letter b.

(5) Procedures of accepting and processing tax returns shall be regulated by on the basis of a regulation of the Minister of Finance. "

6. The provision of Article 6 shall be amended so as to read as follows:

"**Article 6**

(1) The tax return directly submitted by a taxpayer to the office of the Director General of Taxation shall be given the date of receipt by the official appointed to that effect, while the annual tax return shall also be given proof of receipt.

(2) A tax return can be sent by mail with evidence of sending of the letter or other ways regulated by or on basis of a regulation of the Minister of Finance.

(3) The proof and date of sending the tax return as referred to in paragraph (2), provided that the tax return is already complete, shall be regarded as proof and date of receipt. "

7. The provision of Article 7 shall be amended so as to read as follows:

"**Article 7**

(1) If a tax return is not submitted within the period of time as referred to in Article 3 paragraph (3) or prior to the extended deadline for the submission of tax return as referred to in Article 3 paragraph (4), the taxpayer shall be subject to administrative sanction in the form of

fine as much as Rp 500,000.00 (five hundred thousand rupiah) in the case of periodic value-added tax return and Rp 100,000.00 (one hundred thousand rupiah) in the case of other periodic tax returns and Rp 1,000,000.00 (one million rupiah) in the case of annual income tax return of corporate taxpayer as well as Rp 100,000.00 (one hundred thousand rupiah) in the case of annual income tax return of individual taxpayer.

(2) The administrative sanction in the form of fine as referred to in paragraph (1) shall not be imposed on:

a. individual taxpayers already passed away;

b. individual taxpayers no longer undertaking independent business activity or job;

c. individual taxpayers having the status of foreign citizens who have not lived in Indonesia anymore;

d. permanent establishment no longer undertaking activity in Indonesia;

e. corporate taxpayers no longer undertaking business activity but not yet dissolved in accordance with the provisions in force;

f. treasurers no longer conducting payment;

g. taxpayers affected by disaster, with the provisions here to ruled by a regulation of the Minister of Finance; or

h. other taxpayers ruled by or on the basis of a regulation of the Minister of Finance."

8. The provision of Article 8 shall be amended so as to read as follows:

"Article 8

(1) A taxpayer, at his/her own will, can rectify the already-submitted tax return by submitting a written statement, on condition that the Director General of Taxation has not conducted an audit.

(1a) If the rectification of the tax return as referred to in paragraph (1) certifies loss or overpayment, the rectification of tax return shall be submitted in not later 2 (two) years before the expiration of stipulation.

(2) If the taxpayer himself/herself rectifies tax return causing the amount of tax debt to become larger, he/she shall be subject to administrative sanction in the form of interest as much as 2% (two percent) of the underpaid tax per month, starting from the expiration of the deadline for the submission of tax return to the date of payment and part of month shall be rounded up to one month;

(2a) If the taxpayer himself/herself rectifies tax return causing the amount of tax debt to become larger, he/she shall be subject to administrative sanction in the form of interest as much as 2% (two percent) of the underpaid tax per month, starting from the maturity of payment to the date of payment and part of month shall be rounded up to one month.

(3) Even though audit has been conducted, so long as investigation into irregularities made by the taxpayer as referred to in Article 38 has not been conducted, the irregularities shall not be subject to investigation, if the taxpayer, at his/her own will, discloses the irregularities by accompanying evidence of the settlement of the remainder of the tax due and paying administrative sanction in the form of fine as much as 150% (one hundred and fifty percent) of the amount of underpaid tax.

(4) Even if the Director General of Taxation conducted audit, on condition that the Director General of Taxation has not issued tax assessment, the taxpayer, at his/her own awareness, can disclose in a separate report that the submitted tax return is not filled in accordance with the actual condition thus being potential to use:

a. the amount of taxes yet to be paid to become larger or smaller; or

b. the amount of losses based on the tax provisions to become larger or smaller; or

c. the value of assets to become larger or smaller; or

d. the value of capital to become larger or smaller and audit still continues.

(5) The underpaid tax resulting from the disclosure of irregularities in filling the tax return as referred to in paragraph (4) as well as the administrative sanction in the form of fine as much as 50% (fifty percent) of the underpaid tax, shall be settled by the taxpayer himself/herself prior to the submission of the separate report.

(6) A taxpayer can correct annual tax return already submitted in the event that the taxpayer receives tax assessment, decision on objection, decision on rectification, decision on appeal or decision of judicial review of the previous tax year or previous tax years, which certifies that the fiscal loss is different from the fiscal loss already compensated in the would-be corrected annual tax return, in a period of 3 (three) months after receiving the tax assessment, decision on objection, decision on rectification, decision on appeal or decision of judicial review on condition that the Director General of Taxation has not conducted audit. "

9. The provision of Article 9 shall be amended so as to read as follows:

"Article 9

(1) The Minister of Finance shall set the maturity date of the payment and remittance of tax due in a certain time or tax period for each type of tax, no later than 15 (fifteen) days after the time when the tax becomes due or the tax period has expired.

(2) The remainder of tax due based on the annual income tax return shall be settled, prior to the submission of the annual income tax return.

a. if the payment or remittance of tax as referred to in paragraph (1) is made after the maturity date of the payment or remittance of tax, the taxpayer shall be subject to administrative sanction in the form of interest as much as 2% (two percent) per month, calculated as from the maturity date of payment to the date of payment and part of the month is rounded up to 1 (one) month;

b. the payment or remittance of tax as referred to in paragraph (2), which is realized after the deadline for the submission of annual tax return shall be subject to administrative sanction in the form of interest as much as 2% (two percent) per month, calculated as from the expiration of the deadline for the submission of annual tax return to the date of payment and part of the month is rounded up to 1 (one) month.

(3) If the amount of tax still has to be paid becomes larger in tax collection form, underpaid tax assessment, additional underpaid tax assessment, decision on rectification, decision objection, and decision on appeal, it shall be settled within a period of 1 (one) month after the date of issuance.

(3a) In the case of taxpayers being categorized as small-scale businesses and taxpayers living in certain regions, the settlement period as referred to in paragraph (3) can be extended to another term of 2 (two) months at the most with the provisions hereto is to be regulated by or on the basis of a regulation of the Minister of Finance.

(4) The Director General of Taxation, at the request of a taxpayer, can give approval to pay by installments on or postpone the payment of tax including the remainder of tax due as referred to in paragraph (2) no later than 12 (twelve) months, the procedure hereof is to be regulated by or on the basis of a regulation of the Minister of Finance. "

10. The provision of Article 10 shall be amended so as to read as follows:

"Article 10

(1) Any taxpayer shall pay or remit tax due by using tax payment form to the state cash through places of payment ruled by or on the basis of a regulation of the Minister of Finance.

(1a) The tax payment form as referred to in paragraph (1) shall function as a proof of tax payment if it has been legalized by authorized official of payment receiving office or has been validated, with the provision hereof regulated by or on the basis of a regulation of the Minister of Finance.

(2) Procedures for paying, remitting and reporting taxes, as well as procedures for paying by installments on or postponing the payment of taxes shall be ruled by or on the basis of a regulation of the Minister of Finance. "

11. The provision of Article 11 shall be amended so as to read as follows:

"Article 11

(1) At the request of a taxpayer, the excess of tax payments as referred to in Article 17, Article 17B, or Article 17C shall be returned, but it shall first be deducted from the tax debt if

the taxpayer still has tax debt.

(1a) The excess of tax payments attributable to the issuance of decision on objection, decision on rectification, decision on reduction of administrative sanction, decision on abolition of administrative sanction, decision on reduction of tax assessment, decision of nullification of tax assessment and decision on appeal or decision on review as well as decision on the granting of interest compensation shall be returned to the taxpayer but it shall be included directly first to settle tax due if the taxpayer still has tax due.

(2) The excess of tax payments as referred to in paragraph (1) and paragraph (1a) shall be refunded no later than one month after the request for restitution of the excess of tax payments has been received in connection with the issuance of the overpaid tax assessment as referred to in Article 17 paragraph (1), or as from the date of issuance of the decision on preliminary restitution of overpaid tax as referred to in Article 17 paragraph (2) and Article 17B or the decision on preliminary restitution of overpaid tax as referred to in Article 17C or Article 17D or the date of issuance of decision on objection, decision on rectification, decision on reduction of administrative sanction, decision on abolition of administrative sanction, decision on reduction of nullification of tax assessment or decision on the granting of interest compensation or as from the date of receipt of decision on appeal or decision on review, which causes overpaid tax.

(3) If the excess of tax payment is refunded after a period of one month, the government shall give an interest compensation as much as 2% (two percent) per month due to lateness in the restitution of overpaid tax, calculated as from the deadline as referred to in paragraph (2) to the date when the excess of tax payments is paid.

(4) Procedures for calculating and restituting the excess of tax payments shall be ruled by or on the basis of regulation of the Minister of Finance. "

12. The provision of Article 12 shall be amended so as to read as follows:

"Article 12

(1) Any taxpayer shall pay tax due in accordance with taxation legislation, without relying on the existence of tax assessment form.

(2) The amount of the tax due based on the tax return submitted by the taxpayer shall be the amount of tax due according to taxation legislation.

(3) If the Director General of Taxation has evidence that the amount of tax due based on the tax return as referred to in paragraph (2) is untrue, the Director General of Taxation shall stipulate the amount of tax due. "

13. The provision of Article 13 shall be amended by supplementing one paragraph to become paragraph (6) so that the article entirely reads as follows:

"Article 13

(1) In five years after the moment when the tax becomes due or tax period, part of tax year or tax year ends, the Director General of Taxation can issue Underpaid Tax Assessment in the following cases:

a. based on results of audit or other information, the amount of tax due is unpaid or underpaid;

b. the tax return is not conveyed in the period as referred to in Article 3 paragraph (3) and, following the issuance of reminder in writing, is not conveyed in the period as stipulated in the letter of reminder;

c. based on results of audit, Value Added Tax on Goods and Services and Sales Tax on luxury goods should not be compensated for the positive difference of tax, should not be subjected to a tariff of 0% (nil percent);

d. the obligation as referred to in Article 28 and Article 29 is not fulfilled thus the amount of tax due cannot be ascertained.

e. taxpayer is provided ex officio with taxpayer code number and/or validated as taxable entrepreneur as referred to in Article 2 paragraph (4a).

(2) The amount of underpaid tax in the Tax Assessment as referred to in paragraph (1) letter a and letter e shall be supplemented by administrative sanction in the form of interest compensation as high as 2% (two percent) per month for 24 (twenty-four) months at the maximum, starting from the moment when the tax becomes due or tax period, part of tax year or tax year ends to the date of issuance of the Underpaid Tax Assessment.

(3) The amount of tax in the Tax Assessment as referred to in paragraph (1) letter b, c, and d shall be supplemented by administrative sanction in the form of an increase as high as:

a. 50% (fifty percent) of the underpaid or unpaid Income Tax in one tax year;

b. 100% (one hundred percent) of the unwithheld or under withheld, uncollected or under collected, unremitted or under remitted and withheld or collected but unremitted or under remitted Income Tax;

c. 100% (one hundred percent) of the unpaid or underpaid Value Added Tax on Goods and Services and Sales Tax on Luxury Goods.

(4) The amount of Income Tax notified by taxpayer in a tax return shall be fixed in accordance with the provisions of taxation legislation if tax assessment is not issued in the five-year period as referred to in paragraph (1), after the moment when the tax becomes due or tax period, part of tax period or tax year ends.

(5) Even though the five-year period as referred to in paragraph (1) elapsed, underpaid tax assessment still can be issued plus administrative sanction in the form of interest as high as 48% (forty-eight percent) of the amount of the unpaid or underpaid tax if the taxpayer, after the

period, is sentenced for committing criminal offence in the taxation sector or other criminal offences potential to inflict loss on the state income on the basis of a legally fixed court decision.

(6) Procedures for issuing the underpaid tax assessment as referred to in paragraph (5) shall be regulated by or on the basis of a regulation of the Minister of Finance. "

14. A new article shall be supplemented between Article 13 and Article 14 to become Article 13A, which reads as follows:

" **Article 13A**

A taxpayer, due to his/her negligence, not conveying tax return or conveying tax return but the content is untrue or incomplete or enclosing information with untrue content thus being potential to inflict loss on the state income shall not be subject to penalty if the taxpayer committed the negligence for the first time and the taxpayer shall settle the remainder of tax due and administrative sanction in the form of an increase as high as 200% (two hundred percent) of the amount of underpaid tax stipulated through the issuance of underpaid tax assessment. "

15. The provision of Article 14 shall be amended so as to read as follows:

" **Article 14**

(1) The Director General of Taxation can issue a tax collection form if:

a. income tax in the current year is not paid or is underpaid;

b. based on the result of the verification of tax return there is a shortage of tax payment as a result of miswriting and/or miscalculation;

c. the taxpayer is subject to administrative sanction in the form of fine and/or interest;

d. the entrepreneur has been validated as taxable entrepreneur but does not make tax invoice or makes tax invoice not punctually;

e. the entrepreneur has been validated as taxable entrepreneur not filling tax invoice completely as referred to in Article 13 paragraph (5) of the Value Added Tax Law of 1984 and its amendment, other than:

① The identity of buyer as referred to in Article 13 paragraph (5) letter b of the Value Added Tax Law of 1984 and its amendments;

② The identity of buyer as well as name and signature as referred to in Article 13 paragraph (5) letter b and letter g of the Value Added Tax law of 1984 and its amendments, in the case of the delivery being realized by taxable entrepreneur categorized as retailer;

f. the entrepreneur reports tax invoice not suitable to the period of issuance of tax invoice; or

g. the taxable entrepreneur failed to produce and has been given restitution of input tax as meant in Article 9 paragraph (6a) of the Value Added Tax Law of 1984 and its amendments.

(2) The tax collection form as referred to in paragraph (1) shall have the same legal force as tax assessment.

(3) The remainder of tax due in the tax collection form as referred to in paragraph (1) letter a and letter b, plus administrative sanction in the form of interest as much as 2% (two percent) per month for 24 (twenty-four) months at the most, shall be calculated as from the date when the tax becomes due or the expiration of tax period, part of tax year or tax year to the issuance of tax collection form.

(4) The entrepreneur or the taxable entrepreneurs as referred to in paragraph (1) letter d, e and f shall respectively be subject to administrative sanction in the form of fine as much as 2% (two percent) of tax base.

(5) The taxable entrepreneur as referred to in paragraph (1) letter g shall be subject to administrative sanction in the form of fine as much as 2% (two percent) of the amount of re-collected tax, which is counted as from the date of issuance of decision on restitution of overpaid tax to the date of issuance of tax collection form and part of the month is rounded up to one month.

(6) Procedures for issuing the tax collection form shall be ruled by or on the basis of a regulation of the Minister of Finance. "

16. The provision of Article 15 shall be amended so as to read as follows:

"**Article 15**

(1) The Director General of Taxation can issue additional underpaid tax assessment within a period of 10 (ten) years after the time when tax has become due, the tax period, part of tax year or tax year has terminated if the finding of new data add the amount of tax due after auditing is executed in the framework of issuing the additional underpaid tax assessment.

(2) The remainder of tax due in the additional underpaid tax assessment shall be added by administrative sanction in the form of a 100% (one hundred percent) increase from the remainder of tax due.

(3) The increase as referred to in paragraph (2) shall not be applied if the additional underpaid tax assessment is issued on the basis of written information from the taxpayer on his/her own will, on condition that the Director General of Taxation has not started conducting audit in the framework of issuing the additional underpaid tax assessment.

(4) If after the period of 5 (five) years as referred to in paragraph (1) has elapsed, the additional underpaid tax assessment can constantly be issued by imposing administrative sanction in the form of interest as much as 48% (forty-eight percent) of the amount of unpaid or underpaid tax, in case the taxpayer after the period of 5 (five) years has been sentenced for committing a criminal offence in the taxation field or other criminal offence potential to inflict loss on the state income on the basis of a legally fixed court decision.

(5) Procedures for issuing the additional underpaid tax assessment as meant in paragraph

(4) shall be regulated by or on the basis of a regulation of the Minister of Finance. "

17. The provision of Article 16 shall be amended so as to read as follows:

"Article 16

(1) The Director General of Taxation shall ex officio or at the request of a taxpayer can rectify tax assessment, tax collection form, decision on objection, decision on the reduction of administrative sanction, decision on abolition of administrative sanction, decision on the reduction of tax assessment, decision on the nullification of tax assessment, decision on the preliminary restitution of overpaid tax or decision on the granting of interest compensation, which, in the issuance, contains miswriting, miscalculation and/or mistakes in the application of certain provisions in taxation legislation.

(2) The Director General of Taxation shall, within a period of 6 (six) months after the request has been received, issue a decision with regard to the application for restitution submitted the taxpayer as referred to in paragraph (1).

(3) If after the period as referred to in paragraph (2) elapsed but the Director General of Taxation does not issue any decision, the application for restitution shall be considered approved.

(4) If a taxpayer request, the Director General of Taxation shall provide information in writing about matters becoming the basis for rejection of approval of part of the application of taxpayer as referred to in paragraph (1). "

18. The provision of Article 17 shall be amended so as to read as follows:

"Article 17

(1) After auditing, the Director General of Taxation shall issue overpaid tax assessment if the amount of tax credit or the paid tax is bigger than the amount of tax due.

(2) Based on application of taxpayer, the Director General of Taxation, after examining the truth of tax payments, shall issue overpaid tax assessment taxes should not become due, with the provision hereof ruled by or on the basis of a regulation of the Minister of Finance.

(3) Overpaid tax assessment shall remain possible to issue if the overpaid taxes, based on results of audit and/or new data, is bigger than the excess for tax payments already stipulated. "

19. The provision of Article 17A shall be amended so as to read as follows:

"Article 17A

(1) The Director General of Taxation, after auditing, shall issue nil tax assessment if the amount of tax credits or paid taxes is the same as the amount of tax due or tax does not become due or there is no tax credit or tax payment.

（2）Procedures for issuing nil tax assessment shall be ruled by or on the basis of a regulation of the Minister of Finance. "

20. The provision of Article 17B shall be amended so as to read as follows:

"Article 17B

（1）The Director General of Taxation, after auditing the application for restitution of overpaid tax other than the application for restitution of overpaid tax from taxpayer with certain criteria as referred to in Article 17C and taxpayers as referred to in Article 17D shall issue tax assessment no later than 12 (twelve) months after the date of receipt of complete application.

（1a）The provision as referred to in paragraph（1）shall not apply to taxpayers in the course of audit of initial evidence of criminal offence in the taxation field, with the provisions hereof ruled by or on the basis of a regulation of the Minister of Finance.

（2）If after the period of time as referred to in paragraph（1）has passed but the Director General of Taxation does not issue any decision, the application for restitution of overpaid tax shall be considered approved and accordingly, overpaid tax assessment shall be issued no later than one month after the period of time has passed.

（3）If the overpaid tax assessment is issued behind the period of time as referred to in paragraph（2）, the taxpayer shall deserve to interest as much as 2% (two percent) per month, calculated as from the date when the period of time as referred to in paragraph（2）has expired to the time when the overpaid tax assessment is issued.

（4）If the audit of initial evidence of criminal offence in the taxation field as referred to in paragraph（1a）is not continued by investigation; is continued by investigation but not continued by prosecution against criminal offence in the taxation field; or continued by investigation and prosecution against criminal offence in the taxation field but ruled not guilty or free from all legal charges on the basis of a legally fixed court verdict and overpaid tax assessment is issued to taxpayer, the taxpayer shall be given interest compensation as much as 2% (two percent) per month for a period of 24 (twenty-four) months at the maximum, starting from the date of expiration of the 12 (twelve) month period as referred to in paragraph（1）to the moment when the overpaid tax assessment is issued and part of month is rounded up to one month. "

21. The provision of Article 17C shall be amended so as to read as follows:

"Article 17C

（1）The Director General of taxation, after examining the application for restitution of overpaid tax from the taxpayer under certain criteria, shall issue a decision on the initial restitution of overpaid tax no later than 3 (three) months after the application has been received in the case of income tax and no later than 1 (one) month after the request has been received in the case of value added tax.

(2) The certain criteria as referred to in paragraph (1) shall include:

a. conveying tax return on time;

b. not having tax arrear of all types of taxes, except tax arrears already securing license to pay by installments or postpone the payment of taxes;

c. financial statement audited by public accountant or the government financial supervisory institution with unqualified for 3 (three) years consecutively;

d. having never sentenced for committing criminal offence in the taxation field on the basis of a legally fixed court verdict in the last 5 (five) years.

(3) The taxpayer under the certain criteria as referred to in paragraph (2) shall be stipulated by a decision of the Director General of Taxation.

(4) The Director General of Taxation can audit the taxpayer as referred to in paragraph (1), and issue a tax assessment after realizing initial restitution of overpaid tax.

(5) If based on the result of the audit as referred to in paragraph (4), the Director General of Taxation issues underpaid tax assessment, the amount of underpaid tax shall be added by administrative sanction in the form of a 100% (one hundred percent) increase of the amount of underpaid tax.

(6) The taxpayer as referred to in paragraph (1) shall not be entitled to initial restitution of overpaid tax if:

a. the taxpayer is subject to investigation into criminal offence in the taxation field;

b. the taxpayer is late in conveying periodic tax return of certain type of tax for 2 (two) tax periods consecutively;

c. the taxpayer is late in conveying periodic tax return of a certain type of tax for 3 (three) tax periods in one calendar year; or

d. the taxpayer is late in conveying annual tax return.

(7) Procedures for stipulating taxpayer under certain criteria shall be regulated by or on the basis of a regulation of the Minister of Finance. "

22. Two articles shall be supplemented between Article 17C and Article 18 to become Article 17D and Article 17E, which read as follows:

"**Article 17D**

(1) The Director General of Taxation after examining the application for restitution of overpaid tax from taxpayer fulfilling certain criteria shall issue decision on the preliminary restitution of overpaid tax in not later than 3 (three) months as from the date of receipt of complete application in the case of income tax and not later than one month as from the date of receipt of complete application in the case of value added tax.

(2) The taxpayer as referred to in paragraph (1) entitled to the preliminary restitution of overpaid tax shall be:

a. individual taxpayer not undertaking independent business or job;

b. individual taxpayer undertaking independent business or job with the amount of turnover or overpayment up to certain amount;

c. corporate taxpayer with the amount of turnover or overpayment up to certain amount;

d. taxable entrepreneur conveying periodic value added tax return with the amount of delivery and overpayment up to certain amount.

(3) The limit of the amount of turnover, delivery and overpayment as referred to in paragraph (2) shall be regulated by or on the basis of a regulation of the Minister of Finance.

(4) The Director General of Taxation can audit the taxpayer as referred to in paragraph (1) and issue tax assessment after realizing preliminary restitution of overpaid tax.

(5) If based on results of the audit as referred to in paragraph (4), the Director General of Taxation shall issue underpaid tax assessment, the amount of the underpaid tax shall be supplemented by administrative sanction in the form of an increase of 100% (one hundred percent) . "

23. The provision of Article 18 shall be amended so as to read as follows:

"**Article 18**

(1) Tax collection form, underpaid tax assessment, additional underpaid tax assessment and decision on rectification, decision on objection, decision on appeal as well as decision on judicial review, which cause the amount of tax yet to be paid to increase, shall serve as the basis for the collection of taxes.

(2) Abolished. "

24. The provision of Article 19 shall be amended so as to read as follows:

"**Article 19**

(1) If the underpaid tax assessment or additional underpaid tax assessment as well as decision on rectification, decision on objection, decision on appeal or decision on judicial review causes the amount of tax yet to be paid to increase, at the time of maturity, not paid or underpaid, the amount of tax, which is not paid or is underpaid shall be subject to administrative sanction in the form of interest as much as 2% (two percent) per month for all periods, calculated as from the date of maturity to the date of payment or the date of issuance of the tax collection form and part of the month is rounded up to one full month.

(2) The taxpayer allowed to pay tax by installments or defer tax payments shall also be subject to interest as much as 2% (two percent) per month of the amount of taxes yet to be paid

and part of the month is rounded up to one full month.

(3) If the taxpayer is allowed to postpone the submission of tax return and based on the provisional calculation, the tax due as referred to in Article 3 paragraph (5) is lower than the actual amount of tax due, the remainder of tax due shall be subject to interest as much as 2% (two percent) per month, calculated as from the expiry date of the deadline for the submission of the tax return as referred to in Article 3 paragraph (3) letter b or c to the date when the remainder of tax due is paid and part of the month is rounded up to one full month. "

25. The provision of Article 20 shall be amended so as to read as follows:

"**Article 20**

(1) If the amount of tax due based on the tax collection, underpaid tax assessment, additional underpaid tax assessment and decision on rectification, decision on objection, decision on appeal as well as decision judicial review that increases the amount of taxes yet to be paid by the tax guarantor in accordance with the period of time as referred to in Article 9 paragraph (3) or (3a), the tax due shall be collected by distress warrant in accordance with the provisions of taxation legislation.

(2) Excepted from the provisions in paragraph (1), the instant and lump sum collection shall be done in case:

a. the tax guarantor will leave Indonesia forever or intends to do so;

b. the tax guarantor transfers the goods he/she possesses or controls to somebody else in an attempt to stop or scale down the company's activities, or the job he/she does in Indonesia;

c. there are signs that the tax guarantor will dissolve his/her corporate body, or merge his/her businesses, or expand his/her businesses, or transfer the company he/she possesses or controls to somebody else, or change the company into other form;

d. the state will dissolve the corporate body; or

e. the confiscation of the tax guarantor's possessions by a third party or there are signs of bankruptcy.

(3) The collection of tax by distress warrant shall be done pursuant to the provisions of taxation legislation. "

26. The provision of Article 21 shall be amended so that it entirely reads as follows:

"**Article 21**

(1) The state shall have preemptive rights to tax claims over goods belonging to a tax guarantor.

(2) Provisions on the preemptive rights as referred to in paragraph (1) shall cover tax principal, administrative sanction in the form of interest, fine, increase and tax collection

expenses.

(3) The preemptive rights to tax claims shall be above all other preemptive rights, except for:

a. court fees merely as a result of punishment to auction movables and/or immovable;

b. expenses spent on rescuing the goods in rescuing the goods in question;

c. court fees merely as a result of auction and settlement of heritage.

(3a) In the case of the taxpayer being declared bankrupt or liquidated, curator, liquidator or person or body assigned to settle the case shall be prohibited from sharing assets of the taxpayer in bankruptcy, dissolution or liquidation to other shareholders or creditors before using the assets for paying tax due of the taxpayer.

(4) The preemptive rights shall disappear after it has passed a period of 2 (two) years since the issuance date of tax collection form, underpaid tax assessment, additional underpaid tax assessment, decision on rectification, decision on objection, decision on appeal or decision on judicial review that increases the amount of taxes yet to be paid.

(5) The calculation of the period of preemptive rights shall be stipulated as follows:

a. if the warrant to pay is officially announced, the period of 5 (five) years as referred to in paragraph (4) is calculated as from the notification date of the warrant; or

b. in the case of deferral of payment or approval of payments by installments being given, the period of 5 (five) years is counted as from the expiration of the deferral period. "

27. The provision of Article 22 shall be amended so that it entirely reads as follows:

" Article 22

(1) The right to collect tax, including interest, fine. Increase and tax collection expenses shall expire after it has passed a period of 5 (five) years, starting from the date of issuance of tax collection form, underpaid tax assessment, as well as additional underpaid tax assessment and decision on rectification, decision on objection, decision on appeal as well as decision on judicial review.

(2) The expiry date of tax collection as referred to in paragraph (1) shall be deferred if:

a. warrant is issued;

b. there is acknowledgment of tax debt by the taxpayer, either directly or indirectly;

c. the underpaid tax assessment as referred to in Article 13 paragraph (5) or additional underpaid tax assessment form as referred to in Article 15 paragraph (4) is issued;

d. investigation into criminal offence in the taxation field is executed.

28. The provision of Article 23 shall be amended so that the article reads as follows:

"Article 23

(1) Abolished.

(2) Lawsuit by a taxpayer or a tax guarantor against:

a. the execution of warrant, order for confiscation, or auction notification;

b. the decision on prevention in the framework of tax collection;

c. the decision related to the execution of tax decision, other than those provided for in Article 25 paragraph (1) and Article 26;

d. the issuance of tax assessment or decision on objection not suitable to procedures and mechanisms already ruled in the provisions of taxation legislation, can only be filed to the tax court.

(3) Abolished.

29. The provision of Article 24 shall be amended so that it entirely reads as follows:

"Article 24

Procedures for writing off tax claims and stipulating the amount of tax claims to be written off shall be ruled by or on the basis of a regulation of the Minister of Finance. "

30. The provision of Article 25 shall be amended so that it entirely reads as follows:

"Article 25

(1) Any taxpayer can file objections only with the Director General of Taxation to:

a. underpaid tax assessment;

b. additional underpaid tax assessment;

c. overpaid tax assessment;

d. nil tax assessment;

e. the withholding or collection of tax by a third party pursuant to the provisions of taxation legislation.

(2) The objections shall be filed in writing in the Indonesian language by mentioning the amount of tax due or the amount of taxes already withheld or collected or the amount of losses according to the calculation by the taxpayer by providing reasons becoming the basis for the calculation.

(3) The objections shall be filed within a period of 3 (three) months as from the date of sending of tax assessment or as from the date of tax withholding or collection as referred to in paragraph (1), except if the taxpayer can prove that the period of time cannot be fulfilled because of force majeure.

(3a) In the case of a taxpayer raising objection to tax assessment, the taxpayer shall settle taxes be paid minimally as much as the amount already approved by the taxpayer in closing conference of audit result, before the letter of objection is submitted.

(4) The objections not complying with the conditions as referred to in paragraph (1), paragraph (2), paragraph (3) or paragraph (3a) shall not be regarded as objections so that they will not be taken into consideration.

(5) Evidence of the receipt of objection given by the official of the Director General of Taxation assigned to that effect or evidence of the sending of objection by recorded mail or other methods ruled by or on the basis of a regulation of the Minister of Finance shall serve as evidence of the receipt of objection.

(6) If requested by the taxpayer for the purpose of filing an objection, the Director General of Taxation shall give information in writing about matters serving as the basis for the imposition of tax, the calculation of losses, the withholding or collection of taxes.

(7) If a taxpayer files objection, the period of settlement of taxes as referred to in Article 9 paragraph (3) or paragraph (3a) for the taxes not yet paid upon the submission of the objection shall be deferred up to one month as from the date of issuance of tax assessment;

(8) The amount of taxes not yet paid upon the submission of the objection as referred to in paragraph (7) shall exclude the tax due as referred to in Article 11 paragraph (1) and paragraph (1a).

(9) If the objection of taxpayer is rejected or approved partly, the taxpayer shall be subject to administrative sanction in the form of a fine as much as 50% (fifty percent) of the amount of taxes based on the decision on objection, subtracted by the amount of taxes already paid before filling the objection.

(10) If the taxpayer files application for appeal, the administrative sanction in the form of a fine as much as 50% (fifty percent) as referred to in paragraph (9) shall not be imposed. "

31. The provision of Article 26 shall be amended so as to read as follows:

"Article 26

(1) In not later than twelve months as from the date of receipt of the objection, the Director General of Taxation shall make decision on the submitted objection.

(2) Before the decision is issued, taxpayers can convey additional reasons or written explanation.

(3) Decision of the Director General of Taxation on the objection can be accepting wholly or partly, denying or supplementing the amount of tax due.

(4) In the case of taxpayers submitting objection to the tax assessment stipulated in Article 13 paragraph (1) letter b and letter d, the taxpayers shall be able to prove the untruth of the tax assessment.

(5) In the case of the period as meant in paragraph (1) elapsing and the Director General of Taxation not making a decision, the submitted objection shall be deemed acceptable. "

32. A new article shall be supplemented between Article 26 and Article 27 to become Article 26A, which reads as follows:

"**Article 26A**

(1) Procedures for submitting and settling the objection shall be regulated by or on the basis of a regulation of the Minister of Finance.

(2) The procedures for submitting and settling the objection as referred to in paragraph (1) shall rule, among others, the granting of right to taxpayers to appear for testifying or obtaining explanation about their objection.

(3) In the case of the taxpayers not exercising the tight as referred to in paragraph (2), the settlement of the objection shall continue.

(4) In the event that taxpayers disclose bookkeeping, records, data, information or other remarks in the settlement of the objection, which has not been obtained by the taxpayers from the third party upon the audit, the bookkeeping, records, data, information or other remarks shall not be considered in the settlement of objection. "

33. The provision of Article 27 shall be amended so that the article entirely reads as follows:

"**Article 27**

(1) Any taxpayer can file an application for appeal only with the tax court against the decision on objection as referred to in Article 26 paragraph (1).

(2) The decision of the tax court shall be a decision of special court within the state administration court.

(3) The application as referred to in paragraph (1) shall be filed in writing in the Indonesia language by mentioning clear reasons in not later than 3 (three) month as from the date of receipt of decision on objection and enclosed by copy of the decision on objection.

(4) Abolished.

(4a) If requested by taxpayer of the purpose of submission of application for appeal, the Director General of Taxation shall give information in writing about the matters becoming the basis for the issued decision on objection.

(5) Abolished.

(5a) If a taxpayer files appeal, the period of settlement of the taxes as referred to in Article 9 paragraph (3), paragraph (3a) or Article 25 paragraph submitting objection, shall be deferred up to one month as from the date of issuance of decision on appeal.

(5b) The amount of taxes not yet paid upon submitting application for appeal as referred to in paragraph （5a） shall exclude the tax due as referred to in Article 11 paragraph （1） and paragraph （1a） .

（5c） The amount of taxes not yet pad upon submitting the application for appeal shall not become tax due until decision on appeal is issued.

（5d） In the case of application for appeal being rejected or approved partly， the taxpayer shall be subject to administrative sanction in the form of a fine as much as 100% （one hundred percent） of the amount of taxes based the decision on appeal， subtracted by amount of taxes already paid before submitting the objection.

（6） The tax court as referred to in paragraph （1） and Article 23 paragraph （2） shall be regulated by a law. ”

34. The provision of Article 27A shall be amended so as to read as follows：

“Article 27A

（1） If the objection or application for appeal is accepted partially or wholly， provided that the tax debt as referred to in the underpaid tax assessment， additional underpaid tax assessment， nil tax assessment and overpaid tax assessment already paid has already been paid and resulted in overpaid tax， the access of tax payments shall be refunded， plus interest compensation as much as 2% （two percent） per month for a maximum of 24 （twenty-four） months with the provision as follows：

a. in the case underpaid tax assessment and additional underpaid tax assessment， starting， from the date of payment causing the over payment to the date of issuance of decision on objection， decision on appeal or decision on judicial review；

b. in the case of nil tax assessment and overpaid tax assessment， starting from the date of issuance of decision of the tax assessment to the date of issuance of decision on objection， decision on appeal or decision on judicial review.

（1a） The interest compensation as meant in paragraph （1） also shall be granted due to decision on rectification， decision on reduction of tax assessment， which is approved partly or wholly and results in overpayments with the provision as follows：

a. in the case of underpaid tax assessment and additional underpaid tax assessment， starting from the date of payment causing the access of tax payment to the date of decision on rectification， decision on reduction of tax assessment or decision on nullification of tax assessment；

b. in the case of nil tax assessment and overpaid tax assessment， starting from the date of issuance of tax assessment to the date of issuance of decision on rectification， decision on reduction of tax assessment or decision on nullification of tax assessment；

c. in the case of tax collection form， starting from the date payment causing the access of tax payment to the date of issuance of decision on rectification， decision on reduction of tax assessment or decision on nullification of tax assessment.

(2) the interest compensation as referred to in paragraph (1) shall also apply to the overpayment of administrative sanction in the form of fine as referred to in Article 14 paragraph (4) and/or interest as referred to in Article 19 paragraph (1) based on the decision on reduction or abolition of administrative sanction, as a result of the issuance of the decision on objection, decision on appeal or decision on judicial review approving the application from the tax payer partially or wholly.

(3) Procedures for calculating the restitution of overpaid taxes and providing interest compensation shall be ruled by or on the basis of a regulation of the Minister of Finance. "

35. The provision of Article 28 shall be amended so as to read as follows:

"Article 28

(1) Any individual tax payer who carries out independent business activity or job and any corporate taxpayer in Indonesia shall perform bookkeeping.

(2) Excepted from the obligation to perform bookkeeping as referred to in paragraph (1) but still required to make records shall be an individual taxpayer carrying out independent business activity job, who is under taxation legislation permitted to calculate net income by using net income calculation norms and an individual taxpayer, who does not carry out independent business activity or job.

(3) The bookkeeping or recording shall be conducted by paying attention to goodwill and reflection the actual conditions or business activities.

(4) The bookkeeping or recording shall be conducted in Indonesia by using Latin alphabet, Arabic number, rupiah currency and the Indonesian language or foreign language permitted by the Minister of Finance.

(5) The bookkeeping shall be conducted under the principles of consistency and accrual or cash system.

(6) Any change the bookkeeping method and/or accounting year shall secure approval from the Director General of Taxation.

(7) The bookkeeping shall at least consist of records on assets, liabilities, capital, income and cost, as well as sales and purchase, so that the amount of tax due can be calculated.

(8) The bookkeeping using foreign language and currency other than the rupiah can be conducted by a taxpayer after securing a permit from the Minister of Finance.

(9) The recording as referred to in paragraph (2) shall consist of data gathered in a regularly way on the gross turnover or revenue and/or gross income as the basis for the calculation of tax due, including non-tax object income and/or income subject to final tax.

(10) Abolished.

（11）Books, records and document serving as the basis for bookkeeping or recording as well as other document shall be kept for 10 (ten) years in Indonesia, namely in business site or residence of the individual taxpayer or in the domicile of the corporate taxpayer.

（12）Model and procedures for recording as referred to in paragraph （2） shall be regulated by or on the basis of a regulation of the Minister of Finance. ”

36. The provision of Article 29 shall be amended so that it entirely reads as follows：

“Article 29

（1） The Director General of Taxation shall be authorized to conduct audit to assess compliance with tax obligations of taxpayers and to achieve other goals in the framework of implementing the provision of taxation legislation.

（2） For the purpose of audit, auditors shall possess auditors identify cards and audit orders and show them to the taxpayer to be audited.

（3） The audited taxpayer shall：

a. show and/or lend books or records, documents serving as the basis for the audit and other documents related to the earned income business activities, independent job of the taxpayer, or object subject to tax；

b. give a change to enter places or rooms considered necessary and give assistance to ensure that the audit can be conducted smoothly and/or provide other necessary information.

（3a） The books, records and document as well as data and other information as referred in paragraph （3） shall be provided by taxpayer in not later that one month as from the date of submission of the request.

（3b） If an individual taxpayer conducting independent business activity or job does not fulfill the provision as referred to in paragraph （3） thus the amount of taxable income cannot be counted, the taxable income can be counted ex officio in accordance with the provision of taxation legislation.

（4） If in disclosing bookkeeping, record or documents and information request, the taxpayer is bound to the obligation to keep them in secrecy, the obligation shall be abolished by the request for the purpose of the audit as referred to in paragraph （1）. ”

37. A new article shall be supplemented between Article 29 and Article 30 to become Article 29A, which reads as follows：

“Article 29A

Corporate taxpayers having their share-listing statements already declared effective by the capital market supervisory board and conveying tax returns accompanied by public accountants with unqualified opinion, of which：

a. annual tax returns certify the overpayment as referred to in Article 17B;

b. is selected for auditing on the basis of risk analysis;

c. can be audited through office audit. "

38. The provision of Article 30 shall be amended so as to read as follows:

"Article 30

(1) The Director General shall be authorized to seal certain places or rooms as well as movable and/or immovable goods in the case of taxpayers failing to fulfill the obligation as referred to in article 29 paragraph (3) letter b.

(2) Procedures for the sealing as referred to in paragraph (1) shall be ruled by or on the basis of a regulation of the minister of finance. "

39. The provision of Article 31 shall be amended so that it entirely reads as follows:

"Article 31

(1) Procedures for auditing shall be ruled by or on the basis of a regulation of the Minister of Finance.

(2) The auditing procedures as referred to in paragraph (1) shall rule, among others, reaudit, audit period, obligation to convey notification about audit result to taxpayers and right of taxpayers to appear in closing conference of audit result in a specified period.

(3) Unless taxpayers fulfill the obligation as referred to in Article 29 paragraph (3) in the implementation of audit thus the taxable income is calculated ex officio, the Director of Taxation shall convey notification about audit result to the taxpayers and provide the taxpayers with a tight to appear in closing conference of audit result in a specified period. "

40. The provision of Article 32 shall be amended so as to read as follows:

"Article 32

(1) In exercising right and fulfilling obligations pursuant to taxation legislation, a taxpayer shall be represented in the case of:

a. body, by the executive board;

b. body declared bankrupt, by the curator;

c. body in the course of dissolution, by the individual or board assigned to take care;

d. body in liquidation, by the liquidator;

e. undivided heritage, by one of the heir executing testament or the person taking care of inherited wealth;

f. immature children or persons under guardianship, by the proxy or guardian.

(2) The proxies as referred to in paragraph (1) shall individually and/or collectively be responsible for paying tax due, except if they can prove and convince the Director General of Taxation that their position will truly make it impossible for them to be responsible for paying the tax due.

(3) An individual or body can appoint a proxy by means of a special power of attorney exercise rights and fulfill obligations pursuant to taxation legislation.

(3a) The proxy as referred to in paragraph (3) shall meet requirements set by or on the basis of a regulation of the Minister of Finance.

(4) The definition of executive board as referred to in paragraph (1) letter a shall include persons who really have the authority to take part in making policies and/or decisions in running the company. "

41. The provision of Article 33 shall be abolished.

42. The provision of Article 34 shall be amended so as to read as follows:

"Article 34

(1) Any official shall be banned from informing other party of everything he/she knows or being informed by the taxpayer within the frame of his/her position or job to implement provisions in taxation legislation.

(2) The ban as referred to in paragraph (1) shall also be applicable to experts appointed by the Director General of Taxation to assist in implementing the provisions of taxation legislation.

(2a) Excepted from the provisions as referred to in paragraph (1) and paragraph (2) shall be:

a. officials and experts acting as witnesses or expert witnesses in court proceedings;

b. officials and experts stipulated by the Minister of Finance to give testimonies to other officials of state institutions authorized to undertake audit in the state finance field.

(3) In the interests of the state, the Minister of Finance shall have the authority to issue written evidence from or about the taxpayer to the party appointed.

(4) For the purpose of conducting investigation into criminal offences or civil offences in the court at the request of the judge pursuant to the Criminal Code and the Civil Code, the Minister of Finance can issue a written permit to the officials as referred to in paragraph (1) and the experts as referred to in paragraph (2) to ask for written evidence and information available to them about the taxpayer.

(5) The judge's request as referred to in paragraph (4) shall mention the name of suspect or defendant, information requested and the linkage between the relevant criminal or civil case and the information requested. "

43. The provision of Article 35 shall be amended so as to read as follows:

"Article 35

(1) If information or evidence from bank, public accountant, notary, tax consultant, administrative office and/or the third party having relations to the audited taxpayers is needed in executing the provisions of taxation legislation, based on a request form the Director General of Taxation, the parties shall give up the requested information or evidence.

(2) In the case of the third party as referred to in paragraph (1) being bound by an obligation to keep it in secrecy, for the purpose of audit, tax collection or investigation into criminal offence in the taxation field, the obligation to keep it in secrecy shall be abolished, except for bank wherein the obligation to kept it in secrecy shall be abolished on the basis of written request from the Minister of Finance.

(3) Procedures for requesting information or evidence from the parties bound by the obligation to keep it in secrecy as referred to in paragraph (2) shall be ruled by or on the basis of a regulation of the Minister of Finance. "

44. A new article shall be supplemented between Article 35 and Article 36 to become Article 35A, which reads as follows:

"Article 35A

(1) Every government agency, institution, association, and other party shall give up taxation-related data and information to the Director General of Taxation with the provision here of regulated under government regulated by observing the provision as referred to in Article 35 paragraph (2) .

(2) In the case of the data and information as referred to in paragraph (1) being not sufficient, the Director General of Taxation shall be authorized to gather data and information in the interest of the State revenue with the provision here of regulated under a government regulation by observing the provision as referred to in Article 35 paragraph (2) . "

45. The provision of Article 36 shall be amended so as to read as follows:

"Article 36

(1) The Director General of Taxation can:

a. reduce or abolish administrative sanction in the form of interest, fine and increase which become due pursuant to taxation legislation if the sanction is imposed due to ignorance of taxpayers or non-mistake of taxpayers;

b. reduce or nullify untrue tax assessment;

c. reduce or nullify the tax collection form as referred to in Article 14, which is untrue; or

d. nullify result of tax audit or tax assessment resulting from tax audit, which is implemented without:

① conveying notification about audit result; or

② disclosing conference of audit result with taxpayers.

(1a) The application for the matter as referred to in paragraph (1) letter a, letter b and letter c only can be submitted by taxpayers twice at the maximum.

(1b) The application for the matter as referred to in paragraph (1) letter d only can be submitted by taxpayers once.

(1c) The Director General of Taxation in no later than 6 (six) months as from the date of receipt of the application as referred to in paragraph (1) shall make a decision on the submitted application.

(1d) In the case of the period as referred to paragraph (1c) elapsing but the Director General of Taxation not making a decision, the application of the taxpayers as referred to paragraph (1) shall be deemed acceptable.

(1e) If taxpayers request, the Director General of Taxation shall give up information in writing about the matters becoming the basis for rejecting or approving partly the application of taxpayers as referred to in paragraph (1c).

(2) Technical directives for the provisions of paragraph (1), paragraph (1a), paragraph (1b), paragraph (1c), paragraph (1d) and paragraph (1e) shall be ruled by or on the basis of a regulation of the Minister of Finance.

46. The provision of Article 36A shall be amended so as to read as follows:

"**Article 36A**

(1) Tax officers due to whose negligence or intentionally calculating or stipulating tax in a way contravening the provision of taxation legislation shall be subject to sanction pursuant to the provisions of legislation.

(2) Tax officers who in executing their tasks internationally act beyond their authority ruled in the provisions of taxation legislation can be complained to an internal unit of the Minister of Finance, which is authorized to audit and investigate and if the tax officers are proven committing the action, sanction shall be imposed in accordance with the provision of legislation.

(3) Tax officers who in executing their tasks are proven extorting and threatening taxpayers to favor themselves unlawfully shall be charged with the penalty as referred to in Article 268 of the Criminal Code.

(4) Tax officers intending to favor themselves unlawfully by abusing their power to force someone to give something, pay or receive payment or to work something for themselves shall be charged with the penalty as referred to in Article 12 of Law Number 31 Year 1999 regarding Anti-

corruption and its amendments.

(5) Tax officers shall not be liable to criminal and civil charge if the tax officers execute their tasks on the basis of goodwill and in accordance with the provision of taxation legislation. "

47. Three articles shall be supplemented between Article 36A and Article 37 to become Article 36B, Article 36C and Article 36D, which read as follows:

"Article 36B

(1) The Minister of Finance shall be obligated to prepare code of conduct of employees of the Director General of Taxation.

(2) The employees of the Director General of Taxation shall abide by the code of conduct of employees of the Director General of Taxation.

(3) Supervision over the implementation and accommodation of complaints about violation of code of conduct of employees of the Director General of Taxation shall be done by committee for code of conduct with the provision here of ruled by or on the basis of a regulation of the Minister of Finance.

Article 36C

The Minister of Finance shall set up a taxation supervisory committee with the provisions hereof ruled by or on the basis of a regulation of the Minister of Finance.

Article 36D

(1) The Director General of Taxation can be given incentives on the basis of accomplishment of certain performance.

(2) The granting of the of the incentives as referred to in paragraph (1) shall be stipulated through the state budget of revenue and expenditure.

(3) Procedures for granting and utilizing the incentives as referred to in paragraph (1) shall be ruled by or on the basis of a regulation of the Minister of Finance. "

48. A new article shall be supplemented between Article 37 and Article 38 to become Article 37A, which reads as follows:

"Article 37A

(1) Taxpayers conveying rectification of annual income tax returns before Tax Year 2007, which cause the amount of taxes yet to be paid to become bigger and are realized in not later than one year after the enforcement of this law, can be given deduction or abolition of administrative sanction in the form of interest due to lateness in the settlement of the shortage of tax payments with the provision hereof ruled by or the basis of a regulation of the Minister of Finance.

(2) Individual taxpayers voluntarily registering themselves to obtain taxpayers code number in not later than one year after the enforcement of this law shall be given abolition of administrative sanction against the unpaid or underpaid taxes for the tax years before the taxpayer code number in obtained and tax audit shall not be executed unless otherwise data or information certify that the annual tax returns conveyed by the taxpayers are untrue or overpaid. "

49. The provision of Article 38 shall be amended so that it entirely reads as follows:

"Article 38

Anybody who because of his/her act of negligence:

a. fails to submit a tax return; or

b. submits a tax return but its content is not true or complete, or attaches false information so that it can inflict a loss on the state revenue and the action constitutes action after the first-time action as referred to in Article 13A,

shall be subject to a fine as much as the amount of the unpaid or underpaid tax at the minimum and twice the amount of unpaid or underpaid tax at the maximum or sentenced to imprisonment for 3 (three) months at the minimum or one year at the minimum. "

50. The provision of Article 39 shall be amended so that it entirely reads as follows:

"Article 39

(1) Anybody who deliberately:

a. does not register to be given taxpayer code number or does not report his/her business for validation as taxable entrepreneur;

b. abuses or illegally uses the taxpayer code number or taxable entrepreneur validation;

c. does not submit a tax return;

d. submits an incorrect or incomplete tax return and/or information; or

e. denies the audit as referred to in Article 29; or

f. shows false or falsified bookkeeping, records, or other document thus seeming true or not describing the actual condition; or

g. does not perform bookkeeping or recording, does not show or lend books, record, or other documents; or

h. does not keep books, records or documents becoming the basis for bookkeeping or recording and other documents, including results of processing of data from bookkeeping managed electronically or executed by on line application in Indonesia as referred to in Article 28 paragraph (11); or

i. does not remit the withheld or collected taxes,

thus being potential to inflict a loss on the State revenue, shall be sentenced to imprisonment for 6 (six) years at the minimum and 6 (six) years at the maximum and a fine as much as twice of the amount of the unpaid or underpaid taxes or 4 (four) times the amount of unpaid or underpaid taxes at the maximum.

(2) The sentence as referred to in paragraph (1) shall be doubled if the person concerned commits another criminal offence in the taxation field before a period of 1 (one) year has passed, starting from the date after he/she has completed his/her jail term.

(3) Anybody who attempts to commit a criminal offence:

a. by misusing or illegally using the taxpayer code number or taxable entrepreneur validation as referred to in paragraph (1) letter b; or

b. by submitting an incorrect or incomplete tax return and/or information as referred to in paragraph (1) letter d within the frame of applying for restitution or compensating tax or crediting tax, shall be sentenced to imprisonment for 6 (six) month at the minimum and subject to a fine as much as twice of the amount of the requested restitution and/or compensation or credit at the maximum. "

51. A new article shall be supplemented between Article 39 and Article 40 to become Article 39A, which reads as follows:

" **Article 39A**

Anybody who intentionally:

a. issues and/or uses tax invoice, tax collection form, tax withholding form and/or tax payment form, which is not based on the actual transaction; or

b. issues tax invoice but not yet validated as taxable entrepreneur,
shall be sentenced to imprisonment for 2 (two) years at the minimum and 6 (six) years at the maximum as well as subject to a fine as much as twice of the amount of taxes in the tax invoice, tax collection form, tax withholding form and/or tax payment form at the minimum and 6 (six) times of the amount of the taxes in the invoice, tax collection form, tax withholding form and/or tax payment form at the maximum. "

52. The provision of Article 41 shall be amended so that it entirely reads as follows:

" **Article 41**

(1) The official who fails to keep the secret of the matter as referred to in Article 34 due to his/her negligence, shall be sentenced to a maximum of 1 (one) year in jail and fined a maximum of Rp 25,000,000.00 (twenty-five million rupiah).

(2) The official who deliberately fails to meet his/her obligations or the individual who makes the official as referred to in Article 34 failing to meet his/her obligations, shall be sentenced to a maximum of 2 (two) years in jail and fined a maximum of Rp 50,000,000.00 (fifty million rupiah) .

（3）The indictment against the criminal offences as referred to in paragraph （1）and paragraph （2）shall only be conducted on the basis of a complaint from the individual whose privacy is violated. "

53. The provision of Article 41A shall be amended so that it entirely reads as follows:

"Article 41A

Anybody who pursuant to Article 35 of this law is required to provide information or evidence requested but deliberately fails to do so, or provide incorrect information or evidence, shall be sentenced to a maximum of 1 （one） year in jail and fined a maximum of Rp 25,000,000.00 （twenty-five million rupiah）. "

54. The provision of Article 41B shall be amended so that it entirely reads as follows:

"Article 41B

Anybody who deliberately hampers or obstructs investigation into criminal offence in the taxation field shall be sentenced to a maximum of 3 （three） years in jail and fined a maximum of Rp 75,000,000 （seventy-five million rupiah）. "

55. A new article shall be supplemented between Article 41B and Article 42 to become Article 41C, which reads as follows:

"Article 41C

（1）Anybody who intentionally does not fulfill the obligation as referred to in Article 35A paragraph （1） shall be sentenced to a maximum of one year in jail and fined a maximum of Rp 1,000,000,000.00 （one billion rupiah）.

（2）Anybody who intentionally makes the official or other party unable to fulfill the obligation as referred to in Article 35A paragraph （1） shall be sentenced to a maximum of 10 （ten） years in jail and fined a maximum of Rp 800,000,000.00 （eight hundred million rupiah）.

（3）Anybody who intentionally not gives data and information requested by the Director General of Taxation as referred to in Article 35A paragraph （2） shall be sentenced to a maximum of 10 （ten） years in jail and fined a maximum of Rp 800,000,000.00 （eight hundred million rupiah）.

（4）Anybody who intentionally misuses taxation data and information thus inflicting loss on the state shall be sentenced to a maximum of one year in jail and fined a maximum of Rp 500,000,000.00 （five hundred million rupiah）. "

56. The provision of Article 43 shall be amended so that it entirely reads as follows:

"**Article 43**

(1) The provisions as referred to in Article 39 and Article 39A shall also apply to representative, proxy, employee of taxpayer or other parties ordering to do so, taking part in committing it, suggesting or helping commit criminal offence in the taxation field. "

(2) The provisions as referred to in Article 41A and Article 41B shall also apply to parties ordering, suggesting or helping commit criminal offense in the taxation field. "

57. Before Article 44 in CHAPTER IX, a new article shall be supplemented to become Article 43A, which reads as follows:

"**Article 43A**

(1) Based on information, data, report and complaint, the Director General of Taxation shall be authorized to examine initial evidence before investigation into criminal offense in the taxation field is executed.

(2) If there is an indication of involvement of officers of the Director General of Taxation in criminal offense in the taxation field, the Minister of Finance can assign the internal auditing unit within the Ministry of Finance to examine initial evidence.

(3) In the case of substance of corruption being found from the initial evidence, the implicated employee of the Director General of Taxation shall be processed pursuant to the provisions of the anticorruption law.

(4) Procedures for examining the initial evidence of criminal offence in the taxation field as referred to in paragraph (1) and paragraph (2) shall be ruled by or on the basis of a regulation of the Minister of Finance. "

58. The provision of Article 44 shall be amended so that it entirely reads as follows:

"**Article 44**

(1) Criminal offences in the taxation sector only can be investigated by certain state civilian officials at the Director General of taxation, who are given special authority to act as investigators of criminal offences in the taxation sector, as referred to the Penal Code in force.

(2) The investigators' authority as referred to in paragraph (1) shall be:

a. receiving, searching, gathering, and examining information or reports related to criminal offences in the taxation sector to make the information or reports more complete and clearer;

b. examining, searching and gathering information on individuals or bodies to ascertain the truth of actions taken in connection with criminal offences in the taxation sector;

c. asking for information and evidence from individuals or bodies in connection with criminal offences in the taxation sector;

d. examining books, records and other documents related to criminal offences in the taxation sector;

e. ransacking places to obtain evidence of bookkeeping, recording and other documents, and confiscating the evidence;

f. asking for help from experts to conduct investigation into criminal offences in the taxation sector;

g. ordering an individual to stop and/or banning an individual from leaving a room or place at the time when an audit is underway and check the identity of the individual and/or documents brought as referred to in letter e;

h. taking a picture of the individual implicated in the criminal offence in the taxation sector;

i. summoning an individual to get his/her testimonies or to interrogate him/her as suspect or witness;

j. stopping investigation;

k. taking other actions needed to ensure the smooth investigation of criminal offences in the taxation sector pursuant to the responsible law.

(3) The investigators as referred to in paragraph (1) shall notify the commencement of investigation and report the results of investigation to the public prosecutors through investigators of the Indonesian Police, pursuant to the Penal Code in force.

(4) In implementing the investigation authority as referred to in paragraph (1), the investigators can seek assistance from other law enforcement apparatuses. "

59. The provision of Article 44B shall be amended so that it entirely reads as follows:

"Article 44B

(1) In the interest of state revenue, based on a request from the Minister of Finance, the Attorney General can discontinue investigation into criminal offences in the taxation sector in not later than 6 (six) months as from the date of the request.

(2) The discontinuation of investigation into criminal offences in the taxation sector as referred to in paragraph (1) only can be realized after taxpayers settle tax due which is not paid or underpaid or should not deserve to restitution plus administrative sanction in the form of a fine as much as 4 (four) times of the amount of tax, which is not paid or underpaid or should not deserve to restitution. "

Article 2

1. The provisions of Law Number 6 of 1983 regarding Taxation General Provisions and Procedures, as already amended several times and the latest by Law Number 16 of 2000 shall

apply to all taxation rights and obligations from Tax Year 2001 to Tax Year 2007, which have not been settled.

2. Except for the provision as referred to in point 1, stipulation for Tax Period, Part of Tax Year or Tax Year 2000 and previously, other than stipulation as referred to in Article 13 paragraph (5) or Article 15 paragraph (4) shall expire in no later than Tax Year 2013.

3. The law shall come into force as from January 1, 2008. For public cognizance, this law shall be promulgated by placing it in the Statute Book of the Republic of Indonesia.

印度尼西亚共和国 1983 年第 6 号
税法通则第 3 次修正案

（2007 年 7 月 17 日第 28 号法案）

鉴于：

　　a. 为提供公平正义，加强对纳税人的服务，并更好地提供法律稳定性以及促进信息产业发展和税收领域的物资供应发展，有必要对 1983 年第 6 号税法通则进行修正，此法业经 2000 年第 16 号法修正；

　　b. 基于 a 项所述的考虑，需要就 1983 年第 6 号税法通则第 3 次之修正制定法律。

参照：

　　1. 1945 年宪法第 5 条第（1）款、第 20 条和第 23 条。

　　2. 1983 年第 6 号税法通则（印度尼西亚共和国 1983 年第 49 号法令汇编，3262 号法令全书增刊）业经数次修改且最近一次为 2000 年 16 号法案（印度尼西亚共和国 2000 年第 126 号法令汇编，第 3984 号法令全书增刊）所修正。

经印度尼西亚共和国众议院批准决定：

特制定：

　　1983 年第 6 号税法通则第 3 次修正案法案。

第 1 条

　　经数次修改且最近一次为 2000 年 16 号法案（印度尼西亚共和国 2000 年第 126 号法令汇编，第 3984 号法令全书增刊）所修正的 1983 年第 6 号税法通则（印度尼西亚共和国 1983 年第 49 号法令汇编，3262 号法令全书增刊）中的数项条款应做如下修正：

　　1. 第 1 条之规定应修正为：

"**第 1 条**

　　1. 税是对国家的一种强制性义务，由个人或团体依法缴纳，无直接赔偿，并最大限度地用于国家需要和人民之福祉。

　　2. 纳税机构应为个人或团体，包括纳税人、税款代扣人和按照税收法律规定拥有税收权利和义务的税收官。

　　3. 团体为不可分割的且无论开展业务与否的一组个人和/或资本，包括国家有限责任公司，有限合伙制、其他有限责任公司，或任何名头和形式的国营或地企、商号、商业联合体、合作社、养老基金、联盟、关联公司、基金会、群众团体、社会政治组织及诸如此类组织、机构、常设机构以及其他形式的团体。

4. 企业家指任何形式的个人或团体，在其业务活动或工作当中生产商品、进口商品、出口商品、进行贸易，从关税区外获利于无形资产，提供服务或从源自关税区外的服务中获益。

5. 应纳税雇主是指交付应纳税商品和/或提供应纳税服务的企业家，其应按 1984 年增值税法及其修正案进行纳税。

6. 纳税人编码是作为一种税收管理手段而给予纳税人的号码，当纳税人行使其纳税权利和义务时，用于个人识别或用作纳税人的识别符。

7. 纳税期为纳税人按照法律规定在特定时间内计算，汇出和申报到期税款的基础时间段。

8. 纳税年度为一个日历年期间，纳税人使用异于日历年的财务年度的除外。

9. 部分纳税年度为一个纳税年度期间的一部分。

10. 应纳税额指必须在纳税时段、纳税年度或部分纳税度期间的某一时间点依法必须缴付的税款。

11. 纳税申报单指纳税人依照税法在申报其税收计算和/或支付，纳税对象和/或非纳税对象和/或资产和负债时所使用的说明书。

12. 定期纳税申报单指某一时间段的纳税申报单。

13. 年度纳税申报单指纳税年度或部分纳税年度的申报单。

14. 税款单指支付税款的一种证据，它通过使用表格或其他方法来证明现金已打到财长指定的支付地点之方法加以完成。

15. 税收评估书为一种契约书，它包含欠缴税款评估、额外欠缴税额评估、无纳税评估单或超额纳税评估单。

16. 欠缴税款评估为确定了纳税本金额、纳税抵免额、欠缴税款评估本金额、行政处罚额和仍需缴纳的税额的税收评估书。

17. 额外欠缴税款评估单指规定了对已经确定的纳税额进行追加的税款评估书。

18. 无纳税评估单是一种纳税评估书，它规定纳税本金与纳税抵免额相同或税额非为应付和税收抵免为零。

19. 超额纳税评估单为一种纳税评估书，它规定了由于纳税抵免大于应缴税款或非应付税款时产生的税款多余量。

20. 税收认缴单指用来征税和/或以利息和/或罚金形式进行行政处罚的证明单。

21. 扣押令是指经签发后用于交纳应付税款和税款征收费用的指令。

22. 所得税抵免是指纳税人直接缴纳的税款，及因近年欠缴或少缴的征税单中应付的正税，加上代扣或代征的税额，加上境外已付或未付的所得税，减去从应付税款中扣除的超额税款初步返还额。

23. 增值税抵免为进项税，在扣除超额税款或已偿税款后可进行抵免，从应付税款中扣除。

24. 独立工作指个人完成的工作，该个人通过特殊技能获取收入而不受劳资关系制约。

25. 审计是指一系列用于收集和处理数据、信息和/或证据的活动，在审计标准的基础上，客观地和专业地评估纳税人的合规性和/或在执行税收立法的框架内达成其他目的。

26. 初始证据是指以消息、书面或材料之形式表露的情况、行为和/或证据，用于指控任何人所进行的可能有损于国家税收的纳税犯罪行为，无论该行为正在实施或已实施完毕。

27. 初始证据的审计是指已开始执行的用于获得与纳税犯罪业已实施的指控相关的初始证据。

28. 纳税担保人指有义务依照纳税立法进行纳税的个人或公司，包括代行权利与义务的代理人。

29. 记账是指定期收集金融数据和信息的记录过程，包括资产、负债、资金、收入与支出以及商品与服务的获取和交割价格，最后以该记录过程被制成该财务年度的资产负债表和损益表等财务报表而结束。

30. 审查是指对纳税单及其附件是否填写而进行评估的一系列活动，包括评定书写和计算是否正确。

31. 税收领域的犯罪调查指调查员为寻找和收集证据以揭露税收领域的犯罪行为以及锁定嫌疑犯而进行的一系列活动。

32. 整改决议是指发布的关于改正笔误、误算和/或在执行立法条文过程中出现的错误的决定，上述错误之出处包括：税务评估单、征税单、整改决议、发对决议、减轻或废除行政处罚决议、降低征税评估决议、取消评估决议、初步返还超额纳税决议或权益授予决议。

33. 上诉判决是指税务法院签发的针对纳税人的上诉做出的裁决。

34. 异议决议是指纳税人在对税务评估、预提税或第三方代征产生异议时提交的决议。

35. 上诉判决是税务法院针对纳税人之异议上诉做出的判决。

36. 诉讼判决是税务法院针对依据税务立法规定而提起的诉讼事项所签发的判决。

37. 司法审查判决是指最高法院针对纳税人或税务总干事就税务法院所做裁决，要求进行司法审查的申请而签发的裁决。

38. 初步归还多缴税款的决定包含对某些纳税人的超额税款进行首次退款的额度。

39. 给予利益赔偿决定指确定给予纳税人利益赔偿数额的决议。

40. 发出日期指邮戳日期、传真日期，或直接发出的信件或裁决中所著的日期。

41. 接收日期指邮戳日期、传真日期，或直接发出的信件或裁决中所著的日期。"

2. 第 2 条修正如下：
"**第 2 条**
（1）任何按照立法规定满足主客观条件的纳税人应在对其住所拥有管辖权的税务总局进行登记，并相应地获得纳税人代码。

（2）任何按照 1984 年增值税法及其修正案应纳税的企业主应向对其住所及业务场所拥有管辖权的税务总局申报其业务，以确认成为纳税企业主。

（3）税务总干事可指定：

a. 除第（1）款和第（2）款规定之外的登记地点和/或业务申报地点；

b. 除第（1）款规定的登记地点之外，位于税务总局办公地点的登记场所。

（4）如果纳税人或应纳税企业主未能履行第（1）款和/或第（2）款中规定的义务，则税务总干事可按职权签发纳税人代码或对纳税企业主进行确认。

（4a）已按规定获得纳税人代码的纳税人或已获确认的纳税企业主，应在按照税务法规已满足主客观要求时起 5 年内实施纳税义务。

（5）登记及申报时限以及第（1）款、第（2）款、第（3）款、第（4）款所述登记程序（包括纳税代码的废止和纳税实体地位的废除）应由财政部部长管控。

（6）在下列情况下，纳税代码的废止工作由税务总干事负责：

a. 申请纳税人不再满足税法规定的主客观要求，纳税人和/或其继承人申请废止纳税代码；

b. 企业纳税人已因业务中断或兼并而进行清算；

c. 常设机构纳税人中断在印尼的业务活动；

d. 税务总干事认为有必要废止不再满足税法规定的主客观要求的纳税人之纳税代码。

（7）在接到个人纳税人提出废止纳税人代码 6 个月内或接到企业纳税人之申请 12 个月内，在审验之后，税务总干事应做出决定。

（8）税务总干事可依职权或接到纳税人申请后，取消纳税企业主的有效资格。

（9）税务总干事在收到纳税企业主撤销纳税资格的申请后，经审验，应在 6 个月内就上述申请做出决定。"

3. 在第 2 条和第 3 条之间增加第 2A 条如下：

"第 2A 条

征税期时长为一个月或由财政部部长规定的其他时间段内最长为 3 个月的时期。"

4. 第 3 条修正如下：

"第 3 条

（1）所有纳税人均应使用拉丁字母、阿拉伯数字的印尼语，采用卢比作为货币单位，恰当、完整和清晰地填写纳税申报单，签署后提交至纳税人辖区的税务总局或税务总干事指定之地点。

（1a）已从财长处获得许可，使用非印尼语和卢比以外货币从事簿记的纳税人，应提交印尼语的和以获准的非卢比货币填写的纳税申报单，并受财政部部长管控。

（1b）第（1）款中的签字可以采用普通方式，比如盖章，电子签或数字签，均有同等法律效力，技术程序由财政部部长管控。

（2）第（1）款和第（1a）款所规定的纳税人可直接从税务总干事指定的地点拿取纳税申报单或按财政部部长规定的手续获取。

（3）提交纳税申报单的最后期限为：

a. 如为阶段性纳税单，则不得晚于纳税期限结束后 20 日；

b. 如为个人年度所得税单，则不得晚于纳税年度后 3 个月；

c. 企业纳税人的申报不得晚于纳税年度后 4 个月。

（3a）属于某些特殊标准的纳税人在一份纳税单中可申报数个纳税期。

（3b）属于某些特殊标准和第（3a）款申报手续的纳税人应受财政部部长管控。

（3c）政府财务部门以及某些机构申报代扣或代征的最后期限和程序应受财政部部长管控。

（4）纳税人可通过书面通知或其他形式向税务总干事要求延迟提交年所得税纳税单，但最长不得超过 2 个月。

（5）在发出书面通知时，应随附一份关于一个纳税年度临时应付税额的声明以及一份缴税表，作为应付余额的结算证明。

（5a）如未能在第（3）款规定的最后期限前或第（4）款规定的延长期之前提交纳税单，则应提出告诫。

（6）纳税单的模式和内容，以及随附的数据或单据，应由财政部部长管控。

（7）在下列情况下，纳税单视为未予提交：

a. 纳税单未签字；

b. 未能随附第（6）款规定的信息或文件；

c. 超额纳税申报单在纳税期，部分纳税期或纳税年度过后 3 年才提交，且已对纳税人进行过书面通知的。

（7a）如第（7）款所述纳税申报单视为未提交的，税务总干事应通知纳税人。

（8）除第（1）款规定的义务外，某些所得税纳税人应受财政部部长管控。"

5. 第 4 条修正如下：

"第 4 条

（1）所有纳税人应正确、完整且清楚地填写并提交纳税单并签署之。

（2）如纳税人为实体，则纳税单应由董事会签署。

（3）如纳税人指派代理人填写并签署纳税单，则应提供授权书。

（4）纳税人在提交用于簿记的年所得税纳税单时应随附财务报表，如资产负债表、损益表以及其他数据，用来计算应纳税收入额。

（4a）第（4）款所述的财务报表应分别为各纳税人的报表。

（4b）如第（4a）中规定的财务报表虽经会计师事务所审计但未能和纳税单同时提交，则该纳税单视为不完整和不清晰，因此该纳税单将视同第 3 条第（7）款 b 项所规定的未予提交。

（5）验收和处理纳税单的程序由财政部部长管控。"

6. 第 6 条修正如下：

"第 6 条

（1）纳税人直接向税务总局提交的纳税申报单的时间应由负责该事的指定官员规定，而年度纳税单亦应出具接收证据。

（2）纳税单亦可采用邮寄形式，但应出具邮寄证明，亦可采用财政部部长管控的其他形式。

（3）第（2）款中规定的证明和日期，在纳税单已完备的情况下，应视同接收证明及日期。"

7. 第 7 条修正如下：

"第 7 条

（1）如纳税单未能按第 3 条第（3）款规定的日期或按第 3 条第（4）款规定的延长期结束之前提交，纳税人应接受行政处罚，罚金如下：如为定期的增值税纳税单，则处罚 500 000.00 卢比；如为其他定期纳税单，则处罚 100 000.00 卢比；如为企业纳税人的年度所得税纳税单，处罚 1 000 000.00 卢比；如为个人纳税人的年度所得税纳税单，处罚 100 000.00 卢比。

（2）上述行政处罚金不适用于以下情况：

a. 过世的个人纳税人；

b. 不再从事独立经营活动或工作的个人纳税人；

c. 拥有外国公民身份的不再居住于印尼的个人纳税人；

d. 不再印尼从事活动的常设机构；

e. 不再从事经营活动但按现行法律规定仍未解散的企业纳税人；

f. 不再进行付款的财务人员；

g. 按财政部部长的规定，遭受灾难的纳税人；

h. 其他受财政部部长调整的纳税人。"

8. 第 8 条修正如下：

"第 8 条

（1）在税务总干事尚未进行审计的情况下，纳税人可自愿提交一份书面说明，要求对已提交的纳税单进行整改。

（1a）如果第（1）款所述的整改证实存在漏报或超额纳税，则整改结果应在规定期满前 2 年内提交。

（2）如纳税人由于自身整改而导致所欠税款增多，则其应受到行政处罚，以每月相当于欠缴税款 2% 的利息的形式进行，开始时间为交纳税单的最后期限期满日，至付款日止，不满一个月的以一个月计。

（2a）如纳税人由于自身整改而导致欠税变大，则其应受到行政处罚，即处以每月相当于欠缴税款 2% 的利息的罚款，处罚自付款到期之日起，至实际付款日止，不足一个月的以一个月计。

（3）即使审计过，如第 38 条规定的对纳税人不规范申报所进行的调查尚未进行，在纳税人自愿披露其在申报中的违规行为，并提供随附文件证明已缴纳应付税款余额及已上缴欠缴税额的 150% 作为行政处罚金的情况下，则无须对此不规范性再进行调查。

（4）即使税务总干事已进行审计，只要其尚未签发税收评估书，则纳税人可自愿在另外的报告中公开披露已提交的纳税单未能按实际情况填报，因此可作备用：

　　a. 已缴纳税额增加还是减少；

　　b. 基于税法规定的亏损额增加还是减少；

　　c. 资产额增加还是减少；

　　d. 资本额增加还是减少，且审计仍在进行中。

　　（5）如第（4）款规定所提由纳税单填报不规范导致的欠缴税额以及征收的相当于欠缴税额 50% 的行政处罚金，应由纳税人自身在提交另外报告之前进行结算。

　　（6）如纳税人收到税收评估书、反对决议、整改决议、诉讼决议或关于近年的纳税年度的司法审查决议，且上述文件证实该经济损失不同于即将更正的年度纳税单中已赔付的经济损失，则在税务总干事尚未进行审计的情况下，纳税人可在接到上述文件后 3 个月内修正年度纳税单。"

　　9. 第 9 条修正如下：

　　"第 9 条

　　（1）财政部部长须确定某一时期内应付税款或纳税款项支付的到期之日，时间不得晚于纳税期满后 15 天。

　　（2）基于年度所得税纳税单的应缴税额之差数，应在提交年度所得税纳税单之前进行结算。

　　a. 如第（1）款规定的税款之汇付是在纳税期满日之后进行的，则纳税人应缴纳行政处罚金，采用每月缴纳 2% 的利息的形式处罚，计算时间自纳税期满日起至税款支付日，不足一个月的以一个月计；

　　b. 如第（2）款规定的税款之汇付是在年纳税申报单规定提交的最后期限之后进行的，则纳税人应缴纳行政处罚金，采用的形式为每月缴纳 2% 的利息的形式处罚，计算时间自最后期限到期日起至税款支付日，不满一个月的以一个月计。

　　（3）如在征税单、欠缴税额评估书、额外欠缴税额评估书、整改决议、反对决议以及上诉决议等文件中仍须缴纳的税额变大，则其应在上述文件签发后一个月内结算完毕。

　　（3a）如纳税人属于小型企业并居住在某些特定地区，则第（3）款所述的结算期限可最多可延长 2 个月，具体规定受财政部部长之管控。

　　（4）应纳税人之要求，税务总干事可准许纳税人分期纳税或推迟纳税，包括第（2）款规定的应付纳税余额，但最长不得超过 12 个月，其具体步骤受财政部部长之管控。"

　　10. 第 10 条修正如下：

　　"第 10 条

　　（1）所有纳税人应使用纳税支付单向国库支付税款，支付地点以财政部部长规定为准。

　　（1a）当付款接收处的授权代表对上述纳税支付单进行法律认证后，或按财政部部长之规定对其获得确认后，此单即可作为税讫之证据。

（2）税款之支付，汇付及申报之程序，以及分期缴纳或延期缴纳之程序，均受财政部部长之监控。"

11. 第 11 条修正如下：

"**第 11 条**

（1）如纳税人提出要求，则第 17 条、第 17B 条或第 17C 条提及的超额税款应予退还，但纳税人尚有欠税情形的，应先扣除所欠税额。

（1a）由于签发下列文件而造成的超额税款应退还纳税人，但纳税人尚有未支付的应付税款除外：反对决议、整改决议、降低行政处罚决议、废除行政处罚决议、降低税收评估值决议、取消税收评估决议、上诉决议，审查决议及准予利息补偿决议。

（2）在下列情况下，当收到纳税人要求退还差额税款时，则第（1）款及第（1a）款中所述的超额税款应在一个月内退还纳税人：由于签发第 17 条第（1）款所述的超额纳税评估单；从签发第 17 条（2）和第 17B 条所述的超额税款初步归还决议之日起；从签发第 17C 条和第 17D 条所述的超额税款初步归还决议之日起；从签发反对决议、整改决议、降低行政处罚决议、废除行政处罚决议、降低或取消税收评估值决议及准予利息补偿决议；从接到造成超额纳税的上诉决议或审查决议之日起。

（3）如第（2）款所述超额税款的退还日期迟于一个月，则政府应因其迟退行为给予纳税人每月 2% 的利息补偿，计算时间从第（2）款规定的最后期限起至超额税款退还之日止。

（4）超额税款的计算和退还程序应由财政部部长管控。"

12. 第 12 条修正如下：

"**第 12 条**

（1）无论是否存在纳税评估单，纳税人均应依据税法缴纳应付税款。

（2）纳税人提交的纳税申报单中的应付税额应与税法规定的应付税额相一致。

（3）如税务总干事有证据证明第（2）款所述的纳税单中的纳税金额不真实，则其可确定应纳税金额。"

13. 第 13 条增加一款作为第（6）款，第 13 条全文修正如下：

"**第 13 条**

（1）应付税款到期或纳税期、部分纳税年度、纳税年度结束后 5 年内，税务总干事在下列情形下，可签发欠缴税款评估单：

a. 根据审计结果或其他数据，到期税额未付和/或少付；

b. 纳税单未能按第 3 条第（3）款规定的日期提交，且在发出敦促函后仍未能按该函规定的时间提交；

c. 根据审计结果，不得对货物及服务增值税和奢侈品营业税进行税差补偿，并不得享受零关税之待遇；

d. 第 28 条和第 29 条规定的义务未能履行，因此税收额度无法确定；

e. 纳税人获得纳税人代码或按第 2 条第 (4a) 款规定确认为纳税企业主。

（2）第（1）款 a 项和 e 项所述的纳税评估单中的欠缴税额应以行政处罚金进行补偿，采用每月 2% 的利息补偿形式，补偿时间最长为 24 个月，从税款到期日、纳税期、部分纳税期、纳税年度截止日开始起算至欠缴税额评估单签发之日止。

（3）第（1）款 b 项、c 项和 d 项所述的纳税评估单中的税额应以行政处罚金进行补偿，额度增加如下：

a. 一个年度中欠缴税额或未缴税额的 50%；

b. 未代缴的或少代缴的、未征收的或少征收的、未汇付的或少汇付的、虽已代扣或征收但未汇付或少汇付之所得税的 100%；

c. 未支付的或少支付的货物或服务增值税或奢侈品营业税的 100%。

（4）如按第（1）款规定的 5 年期间纳税申报单未签发，则从税款到期日或纳税期、部分纳税期、纳税年度截止日之后，纳税人在纳税单中申报的所得税金额依税法规定将固定不变。

（5）即使第（1）款所述的 5 年期已过，欠缴评估单仍可签发并附加相当于欠缴或少缴税额 48% 的行政处罚，即便在上述期限后，纳税人因在税收领域的犯罪或其他可能导致国家财政收入损失的犯罪而被判刑的情况亦不例外。

（6）第（5）款所述的欠缴税款评估单之签发程序由财政部部长管控。"

14. 第 13 条和第 14 条之间增加一条，作为第 13A 条，具体如下：

"**第 13A 条**

如纳税人因过失未能提交纳税单或提交的纳税单内容不真实、不完整或随附数据含有不真实内容因而可能导致国家财政收入损失的，若纳税人属于初犯，且付清税款余额以及最高相当于欠缴税额 200% 的行政处罚金，则纳税人可免于刑事处罚。"

15. 第 14 条修正如下：

"**第 14 条**

（1）在下列情况下，税务总干事可签发征税单：

a. 当年所得税未付和/或少付；

b. 根据纳税单审查结果，查出因误写、误算导致的税款缺口；

c. 纳税人需缴纳、罚款和/或利息的行政处罚金；

d. 企业主已确认为应纳税人，但未做出税务发票或未及时做出税务发票；

e. 企业主已确认为应纳税人，但未完整填写 1984 年增值税法第 13 条第（5）款及其修正案所述的税务发票，但下列情况除外：

①1984 年增值税法第 13 条第（5）款 b 项及其修正案所述的买方身份；

②在纳税企业主以零售商的身份实现交割的情况下，1984 年增值税法第 13 条第（5）款 b 项和 g 项及其修正案所述的买方身份以及名称和签名；

f. 企业主申报纳税发票不适合于税务发票的签发期限；或

g. 应纳税企业主获得 1984 年增值税法第 9 条第（6a）款及其修正案所规定的进项税补偿。

（2）第（1）款所述征税单与税收评估单具有同等法律效力。

（3）第（1）款 a 项和 b 项所述征税单中的应付税款余额，加上每月 2% 的最长为 24 个月的行政处罚金，从应纳税款到期日、纳税期满日、部分纳税期、纳税年度截止日开始起算至签发征税单之日止。

（4）第（1）款 d 项、e 项和 f 项所述的企业主或应纳税企业主应分别接受行政制裁，方式为缴纳相当于税基 2% 的罚金。

（5）第（1）款 g 项所述的应纳税企业主应接受行政制裁，方式为缴纳相当于重征税款 2% 的罚金，时间从签发返还超额税款决议之日起至签发税款征收单之日止，不足一个月的以一个月计。

（6）税款征收单签发程序由财政部部长调控。"

16. 第 15 条修正如下：

"第 15 条

（1）在税收到期日、纳税期、部分纳税年度或纳税年度终止后 10 年内，在进行审计后，如因新数据的发现而使得税款额增加，则税务总干事可签发额外的欠缴税款评估单。

（2）第（1）款所述的额外的欠缴税款评估单中的余额另加行政处罚金，金额应在应纳税款余额的基础上追加一倍。

（3）如额外的欠缴税款评估单是根据纳税人自己提供的书面数据而签发的，在税务总干事尚未进行审计的情况下，第（2）款所述的追加额不适用。

（4）如第（1）款所述 5 年期已过，当纳税人在 5 年期后因在税收领域犯罪或其他可能导致国家财政收入损失的犯罪而被判刑的情况下，税务总干事可随时签发额外的欠缴税款评估单，征收相当于欠缴或少缴税额 48% 的利息作为行政处罚金。

（5）第（4）款所述的额外欠缴税款评估单之签发程序由财政部部长调控。"

17. 第 16 条修正如下：

"第 16 条

（1）税务总干事可依职权或应纳税人的要求整改下列文件：税务评估单、征税单、反对决议、减低行政处罚决议、取消行政处罚决议、减低税收评估决议、取消税收评估决议、超额纳税初步返还决议或准许利息补偿协议，上述协议在签发时，包含了误写、误算或在运用税法规定时出现错误。

（2）在接到要求后 6 个月内，税务总干事就第（1）款中纳税人提交的返还申请书签发决议。

（3）如第（2）款规定的时间已过，而税务总干事仍未签发任何决议，则返还申请即视为已获批准。

（4）纳税人申请批准部分第（1）款中所述之文件时，如税务总干事拒绝批准，则须提供基本书面信息说明原因。

18. 第 17 条修正如下：

"第 17 条

（1）审计后，如税收抵免额或已付税额大于应付税额，则税务总干事应签发超额税收评估单。

（2）根据纳税人的申请，税务总干事在验证税款的真实性之后，可根据本法下受财政部部长调控的有关规定签发超额税款评估单。

（3）如果根据审计结果或新的数据，超额税款大于已规定税款的多余量，则仍可签发超额税款评估单。"

19. 第 17A 修正如下：

"第 17A 条

（1）审计后，如税收抵免额或已付税额等同于应付税额、税额尚未到期、不存在税收抵免或税款，则税务总干事可签发无税评估单。

（2）无税评估单的签发程序由财政部部长调控。"

20. 第 17B 条修正如下：

"第 17B 条

（1）在对除第 17C 条和第 17D 条当中所述纳税人提交的税额税款返还申请书进行审计后，税务总干事应在接到完整的申请书之日后 12 个月内签发税收评估单。

（1a）第（1）款之规定不适用于根据财政部部长规定正在接受在税收领域犯罪调查的纳税人。

（2）如第（1）款规定的期限已过，而税务总干事尚未做出任何决议，则超额税收返还申请视为获得批准，相应地，在上述期限过后一个月内，应签发超额税收评估单。

（3）如超额税收评估单的签发迟于第（2）款规定之时间，则纳税人应获每月 2% 的利息补偿，时间从第（2）款规定期限期满日起算至超额税收评估单签发之日止。

（4）如第（1a）款所述的对税收领域犯罪的初始证据的审计调查不再继续或虽继续但不进行犯罪指控或虽继续并进行犯罪指控，但根据法院判决判定无罪或不需承担法定费用，而在纳税人接到超额税收评估单的情况下，则纳税人应获每月 2% 的利息补偿，最长持续 24 个月，从第（1）款所述期限期满日起算至超额税收评估单签发之日止，不足一个月的以一个月计。"

21. 第 17C 条修正如下：

"第 17C 条

（1）税务总干事在对符合某些特定条件的纳税人提交的超额税款返还申请进行审验

后，应签发超额税款初始返还决议，如果是所得税方面的，则在接到申请后 3 个月内签发；如果是增值税方面的，则在接到申请后 1 个月内签发。

（2）上述特定条件包括：

a. 准时提交纳税申报单；

b. 无任何拖欠税款，已获准分期纳税或延迟纳税的除外；

c. 财务报表连续 3 年接受会计师事务所或政府财政监管机关审计；

d. 最近 5 年内无任何税务犯罪记录。

（3）符合第（2）款所述各项条件的纳税人由纳税总干事以决议形式进行确定。

（4）税务总干事可对第（1）款规定的纳税人进行审计，并在实现初始超额税款返还后签发税收评估单。

（5）如根据第（4）款所述审计结果，税务总干事签发了欠缴税收评估单，则应对欠缴税额追加行政处罚金，金额相当于欠缴税额的 100%。

（6）在下列情况下，第（1）款所叙述的纳税人不得享有超额税款初始补偿：

a. 纳税人正在接受纳税犯罪调查；

b. 纳税人连续 2 个纳税期迟交定期纳税单；

c. 纳税人在一年中连续 3 个纳税期迟交定期纳税单；或

d. 纳税人迟交年度纳税单。

（7）确定符合某些条件的纳税人的程序由财政部部长管控。"

22. 在第 17C 条和第 18 条之间加入两条，分别为第 17D 条和第 17E 条，具体如下：

"**第 17D 条**

（1）税务总干事在对满足某些特定条件的纳税人提交的超额税款返还申请进行审验后，应签发超额税款初级返还决议，如果是所得税方面的，则在接到申请后 3 个月内签发；如果是增值税方面的，则在接到申请后 1 个月内签发。

（2）第（1）款所述的享受返还待遇的纳税人应为：

a. 不经营独立企业或不从事独立工作的个人纳税人；

b. 营业额达到或超过一定数量的经营独立企业或从事独立工作的个人纳税人；

c. 营业额达到或超过一定数量的企业纳税人；

d. 提交定期增值税纳税单且缴税额达到一定数量的纳税企业主。

（3）第（2）款所述营业额、交付额及超过额之限定由财政部部长调控。

（4）税务总干事可对第（1）款所述的纳税人进行审计并在完成初级超额税收返还后签发税收评估单。

（5）如根据第（4）款所述审计结果，税务总干事应签发欠缴税收评估单，且应对欠缴税额追加行政处罚金，金额相当于欠缴税额的 100%。"

23. 第 18 条修正如下：

"**第 18 条**

（1）如任何征税单、欠缴评估单、额外欠缴评估单、整改决议、反对决议、上诉决议以及司法审查决议导致上缴税额增加，则其可作为征税的基础。

（2）已废除。"

24. 第 19 条修正如下：
"**第 19 条**

（1）如欠缴评估单、额外欠缴评估单、整改决议、反对决议、上诉决议以及司法审查决议导致上缴税额增加，则到税款应付日时，未付或少付的税额应缴纳每月 2% 的利息作为行政处罚金，贯穿所有纳税期，从期满日起算至支付日或征税单签发之日止，不足一个月的以一个月计。

（2）获准分期纳税或延期纳税的纳税人应每月缴纳相当于未付税额 2% 的利息，不满一个月的以一个月计。

（3）如纳税人获准推迟提交纳税单，且根据暂定计算，第 3 条第（5）款所述的应付税额低于实际的应纳税额，则差额部分应每月交纳 2% 的利息，计算时间从第 3 条第（3）款 b 项或 c 项所述的纳税单提交的最后截止日起至应付税额付讫日止，不足一个月的以一个月计。"

25. 第 20 条修正如下：
"**第 20 条**

（1）按照第 9 条第（3）款或第（3a）款所述的期限，基于征税单、欠缴评估单、额外欠缴评估单、整改决议、反对决议、上诉决议以及司法审查决议中的应付税额导致纳税担保人上缴税额增加的情况，则按照税法规定，应付税额以扣押令形式进行征收。

（2）除第（1）款规定外，在下列情形下，应付税款即时将一次性整笔征收完毕：

a. 纳税担保人将永久或意欲离开印度尼西亚的；

b. 为停止、缩减公司业务或个人的工作，纳税担保人将其拥有的或控制下的商品转让与他人的；

c. 有迹象表明，纳税担保人欲解散其法人团体、将其企业进行兼并、扩大企业规模、将企业进行转让或将公司转为其他形式的；

d. 国家欲解散法人团体；或

e. 纳税担保人的财产被第三方征收或有破产迹象的。

（3）扣押令征税应按照税法规定执行。"

26. 第 21 条修正后全文如下：
"**第 21 条**

（1）国家对属于纳税担保人的财产拥有税收优先权。

（2）第（1）款规定的税收优先权包括正税、以利息、罚款或增税为表现形式的行政处罚金或征税费用。

（3）税收优先权应优于其他优先权，但以下费用除外：

a. 由拍卖动产和/或不动产导致的处罚性的法庭费用；

b. 为抢救上述财物而产生的费用；

c. 拍卖和处置遗产产生的法庭费用。

（3a）如纳税人宣告破产或进行清算，在将纳税人资产用于缴纳税款前，监护人、清算人、被指派处理该案的人员或团体不得与其他股东或债权人分派该纳税人的资产。

（4）在导致税额增加的征税单、欠缴评估单、额外欠缴评估单、整改决议、反对决议、上诉决议以及司法审查决议等文件签发之日起两年后，税收优先权作废。

（5）优先权期限计算如下：

a. 如官方发出支付令，则第（4）款所述的 5 年期从该支付令发出日起算；或

b. 如获准递延纳税或分期纳税，则该 5 年期从递延期限期满日起算。"

27. 第 22 条修正后全文如下：

"**第 22 条**

（1）包括利息、罚款、增税令以及征税费在内的征税权，自征税单、欠缴评估单、额外欠缴评估单、整改决议、反对决议、上诉决议以及司法审查决议签发之日起 5 年后失效。

（2）下列情形下，第（1）款所述征税期满日将递延：

a. 支付令已发出；

b. 承认纳税人无论直接或间接的税债；

c. 第 13 条第（5）款所述的欠缴税款评估单或第 15 条第（4）款所述的额外欠缴税款评估单已签发；

d. 已启动税务领域犯罪调查。"

28. 第 23 条修正如下：

"**第 23 条**

（1）已废除。

（2）纳税人或纳税担保人针对下述提起诉讼：

a. 支付令的执行、没收令或拍卖通知；

b. 征税框架预防决议；

c. 除第 25 条第（1）款和第 26 条规定外的关于执行纳税的决议；

d. 发布的不符合税法规定之程序和机制的纳税评估单或异议决议，只可向税务法院提起诉讼。

（3）已废除。"

29. 第 24 条修正后全文如下：

"**第 24 条**

消除纳税及消除纳税额度的程序由财政部部长根据规定裁决。"

30. 第 25 条修正后全文如下：

"**第 25 条**

（1）如对下述有异议，纳税人只可向税务总干事提请：

a. 欠缴税款评估单；

b. 额外欠缴税款评估单；

c. 超额税款评估单；

d. 无税评估单；

e. 第三方依照税法规定进行的代扣或征缴。

（2）异议应使用印尼语以书面形式提请，其中须提到应付税额、已预提或征收的税额、纳税人根据其计算得出的亏损额，但须提供计算依据。

（3）异议须在送达纳税评估单后或在第（1）款所述的代扣、代征之日后3个月内提请，纳税人能证明由于不可抗力导致上述时限无法满足的情况除外。

（3a）如纳税人对税收评估单提出异议，在提交异议书之前，纳税人应最低限度缴纳其认可的纳税额度。

（4）未满足第（1）款、第（2）款、第（3）款及第（3a）款之条件的异议不视为异议，故不予考虑。

（5）税务总局之官员给出的异议接收证据，用挂号信或财政部部长规定的其他方式寄出异议的证据，应作为异议接收证明。

（6）如纳税人为提出异议之目的而提出要求，则税务总干事应给出书面说明，指出征税、损失计算及代扣的依据。

（7）如纳税人提出异议，则第9条第（3）款或（3a）款所述的在提交异议时尚未支付的税款的结算期限应从发布税收评估书之日起递延一个月。

（8）在提交上述异议书时尚未支付的税款额不包括第11条第（1）款和（1a）款所述的应付税款。

（9）如纳税人的异议被拒绝或只是部分获准，则纳税人需缴纳行政处罚金，相当于基于异议决议税额的50%，扣除提交异议前已支付的税额。

（10）如纳税人提出上诉申请，则不得征收第（9）款所述行政处罚金。"

31. 第26条修正如下：
"**第26条**

（1）在接到异议后12个月内，税务总干事应就提交的异议做出决定。

（2）在决定做出前，纳税人可提交书面补充说明。

（3）税务总干事给出的决议可全部或部分地接受、否定或补充应付税额。

（4）如纳税人对第13条第（1）款b项和d项中规定的税收评估单提出异议，则纳税人应有充分理由证明该评估单的失真性。

（5）如第（1）款规定的期限已过，而税务总干事又未做出决议，则该提交的异议视同接受。"

32. 第26条和第27条之间加入新条款，作为第26A条，具体如下：
"**第26A条**

（1）提交和解决异议的程序由财政部部长管控。

（2）提交和解决第（1）款中所述异议的程序尤其规定了授予纳税人出庭证实或就其异议获得解释的权利。

（3）如纳税人未行使第（2）款所述的权利，则异议的处理仍将持续。

（4）如纳税人在异议处理的过程中公开了账目、档案、数据、信息或其他评论，而上述资料又非纳税人在审计时从第三方获得的，则上述账目、档案、数据、信息或其他评论在异议处理过程中不予以考虑。"

33. 第 27 条修正后全文如下：

"第 27 条

（1）纳税人只可向税务法院就第 26 条第（1）款所述异议决议提起上诉申请。

（2）税务法院的决议为国家行政法院框架内的特别法院决议。

（3）第（1）款所述申请应使用印尼语以书面形式说明原因，申请应在接到异议决议后 3 个月内提交，并随附异议决议复印件。

（4）已废除。

（4a）如纳税人为提交上诉申请之目的而提出请求，则税务总干事应以书面形式提供作为异议决议依据的事项之信息。

（5）已废除。

（5a）如纳税人提起上诉，则第 9 条第（3）款、第（3a）款或第 25 条所述税款结算期应从发布上诉决议之日起顺延一个月。

（5b）在提交第（5）款所述的上诉申请时仍未支付的税额不包括第 11 条第（1）款和第（1a）款所述的应付税款。

（5c）在上诉决议发布前，提交上诉申请时尚未支付的税额不得变为应付税款。

（5d）如上诉申请遭到回绝或仅为部分接受，纳税人须根据上诉决议交纳相当于税款 100% 的行政处罚金，扣除在提交异议时已缴纳的税额。

（6）第（1）款和第 23 条第（2）款所述的税务法院受法律监控。"

34. 第 27A 条修正如下：

"第 27A 条

（1）如异议或上诉申请获得部分或全部接受，而欠缴税款评估单、额外欠缴税款评估单、无税评估单和已付超额税款评估单中所述的税债均已支付，并导致超额纳税，则超额部分应返还，并给予纳税人以每月 2% 的利息为赔偿，最长赔偿时间为 24 个月，具体如下：

a. 如为欠缴税款评估单或额外欠缴税款评估单，则从支付日起算至发布异议决议、上诉决议或司法审查决议之日止；

b. 如为无税评估单或超额税款评估单，则从发布税款评估单之日起算至发布异议决议、上诉决议或司法审查决议之日止。

（1a）因整改决议、减低税收评估单决议获得部分或完全接受而导致的超额纳税亦应给予第（1）款所述的利息赔偿，具体如下：

a. 如为欠缴税款评估单或额外欠缴税款评估单，则从导致超额部分的支付日起算至发布整改决议、减低税收评估决议或废止纳税评估决议之日止；

b. 如为无税评估单或超额税款评估单，则从发布税款评估单之日起算至发布整改决议、减低税收评估决议或废止纳税评估决议之日止；

c. 如为征税单，则从导致超额部分的支付日起算至发布整改决议、减低税收评估决议或废止纳税评估决议之日止。

（2）第（1）款所述利息赔偿亦适用于第 14 条第（4）款所述的行政处罚金，亦适用于因发布异议决议、上诉决议或部分及完全地批准纳税人申请的司法审查决议而导致的减低或废除行政处罚金决议之基础上产生的第 19 条第（1）款所述的利息。

（3）超额税款返还之计算方法及利息补偿之提供方式均受财政部部长管控。"

35. 第 28 条修正如下：

"**第 28 条**

（1）所有在印尼从事独立业务活动或工作的个人纳税人或企业纳税人应进行簿记。

（2）除履行第（1）款所述的簿记义务外，从事独立业务活动或工作的个人纳税人仍应制作记录，按照税法，允许其通过使用净收入计算准则来计算净收入，非从事独立业务活动或工作的个人纳税人亦应做记录。

（3）在做簿记或记录时，应注重商誉，并须反映真实情况或业务活动。

（4）应在印尼当地做簿记或记录，使用拉丁字母、阿拉伯数字，以卢比为货币单位，使用印尼语或财政部部长允许的外国语言。

（5）做簿记应遵循一致性原则，采用权责发生制或现金制。

（6）任何簿记方法或会计年度的变更应首先获得税务总干事的批准。

（7）簿记应至少包括资产、负债、资本、收入和成本，以及购销，以保持应付税款额的可计算性。

（8）在获得财政部部长批准后，纳税人可使用非印尼语和非卢比货币制做簿记。

（9）第（2）款所述的记录应包括以常规方式采集的有关总营业额、收入或总收入的数据，均作为应付税款的计算依据，包括非纳税收入和（或）最后税款收入。

（10）已废除。

（11）作为簿记或记录依据的账本、记录本和文件以及其他类文件应在印尼保留 10 年，即保留于业务所在地、个人纳税人的居住地或企业纳税人的住所。

（12）第（2）款所述的记录之模式和程序由财政部部长管控。"

36. 第 29 条修正后全文如下：

"**第 29 条**

税务总干事有权进行审计借以评估纳税人在履行纳税义务时是否合规，并在执行税法规定的框架下，完成其他目标。

（2）为达审计之目的，审计人员应持有审计员识别卡和审计令，并向被审计纳税人出示。

（3）被审计纳税人应：

a. 出示或出借作为审计所依据的账簿、记录和文件，其他与纳税人在商业活动、独立工作中收入的相关文件或应纳税的标的；

b. 提供地方和协助，确保审计能顺利进行，并提供其他必要信息。

（3a）在提出要求后一个月内，纳税人应提供第（3）款所述的账簿，记录以及数据和其他信息。

（3b）如从事独立业务活动或独立工作的个人纳税人未能满足第（3）款所述之要求，因而应纳税额无法计算，则该应纳税额可依税法规定进行计算。

（4）如要求对账簿、档案或文件与信息进行披露，而纳税人又有对此进行保密的义务，为第（1）款所述之审计，则应取消上述义务。"

37. 第 29 条和第 30 条之间加入第 29A 条，具体如下：

"**第 29A 条**

可对下述企业纳税人进行审计：上市声明已被资本市场监督局宣布有效的；而其提交的纳税单却附有会计师事务所不合格评语的，即

a. 年度纳税单证明了第 17B 条所述的超额纳税；

b. 基于风险分析而被选择进行审计；

c. 通过内勤审计进行的审计。"

38. 第 30 条修正如下：

"**第 30 条**

（1）如纳税人未能履行第 29 条第（3）款 b 项所述义务，则税务官有权查封纳税人某些地点、房间以及某些动产和/或不动产。

（2）第（1）款所述查封行动之步骤由财政部部长管控。"

39. 第 31 条修正后全文如下：

"**第 31 条**

（1）审计程序由财政部部长管控。

（2）第（1）款所述审计程序尤其应规定以下内容：在审计、再审计期间，向纳税人通告审计结果之义务以及纳税人在规定时间内就审计结果进行上诉的权利。

（3）除非纳税人在接受审计时履行了第 29 条第（3）款所述义务，从而应纳所得税之计算得以顺利进行，否则税务官将不向纳税人通告审计结果，亦不给予纳税人在规定时间内就审计结果进行上诉的权利。"

40. 第 32 条修正如下：

"**第 32 条**

（1）纳税人在依税法行使权利和履行义务时，其所出代表如下：

a. 如为团体，则为执行委员会；

b. 如为已宣告破产的团体，则为监管人；

c. 解散过程中的团体，则为负责看守的个人或董事局；

d. 清算中的团体，则为清算人；

e. 如为不可分割之遗产，则为执行遗嘱的继承人或被继承财富的照管人；

f. 如为未成年人或处于监护之下的人，则为代理人或监护人。

（2）第（1）款所述代理人应以个人方式和/或集体方式缴纳应付税款，除非其可以证明并让税务总干事确信他们所处情形无法担负纳税责任。

（3）个人或团体可通过特别授权的方式指定代理人依税法行使权利和履行义务。

（3a）第（3）款所述代理人应满足财政部部长设定或受财政部部长调控的要求。

（4）第（1）款 a 项所述执行委员会的定义应包括那些在公司的运营中拥有参与制定政策或决议之权利的人士。"

41. 第 33 条已废除。

42. 第 34 条修正如下：
"**第 34 条**
（1）任何官员不得向其他方泄露其所掌握的信息，亦不得在其职权范围内接收纳税人的任何信息。

（2）第（1）款所述禁令亦适用于税务总干事指定的协助执行税法规定的专家。

（2a）在下列情况下，上述官员和专家不适用于第（1）款和第（2）款的规定：

a. 担任证人的官员和专家或在法院审理过程中的专家证人；

b. 由财政部部长指定的向被授权在国家金融领域进行审计工作的其他机构的官员、出示证言的官员和专家。

（3）为国家利益，财政部部长有权向指定的其他方签发来自纳税人或与纳税人有关的书面证据。

（4）按刑法典或民法典，应法官之要求，为对刑事犯罪或民事犯罪进行调查，财政部部长可签发许可令，允许第（1）款所述官员和第（2）款所述专家索要有关纳税人的书面证据和信息。

（5）第（4）款中所述法官之要求中应提及嫌疑人或被告的姓名、所需的信息，以及相关罪犯或民事案件与所需信息之间的联系。"

43. 第 35 条修正如下：
"**第 35 条**
（1）如在执行税法规定时需要源自银行、会计师事务所、公证人、税务咨询人员、行政人员和/或其他第三方的与被审计纳税人有关的信息或证据，则当税务总干事提出要求时，上述各方应出让上述的信息或证据。

（2）如第（1）款所述各方有对上述信息或证据保密的义务，然出于审计、征税或对税务领域犯罪进行调查之目的，上述保密义务应取消，然银行的保密义务的取消须向财政部部长递交书面申请。

（3）对第（2）款所述各方索要证据或信息的程序由财政部部长管控。"

44. 在第 35 条和第 36 条之间第 35A 条，具体如下：

"第 35A 条

（1）所有政府部门、机构、协会或其他方应遵守第 35 条第（2）款之规定，向税务总局出让与税收相关的数据和信息。

（2）如上述数据和信息不充分，则为国家税收利益计，税务总干事有权依法搜集所需数据和信息。"

45. 第 36 条修正如下：

"第 36 条

（1）税务总干事可：

a. 如果因为纳税人的无知或无过错行为而被处罚，减低或取消依照税法已到期的行政处罚金，如利息、罚款或增税等；

b. 减低或废除失实的税收评估单；

c. 减低或取消第（14）款所述的失实征税单；

d. 将审计结果或将源于税务审计的纳税评估单作废而无须：

①通报审计结果；

②向纳税人披露审计结果。

（1a）纳税人只可就第（1）款 a 项、b 项和 c 项所述的申请事项最多提出两次。

（1b）纳税人只可就第（1）款 d 项所述事项提出一次申请。

（1c）税务总干事须在接到上述申请后 6 个月内就申请事项做出决定。

（1d）如第（1c）款所述期限已过，而税务总干事仍未做出决议，则该款申请视为已被接受。

（1e）如纳税人提出要求，则税务总干事应就回绝或部分批准纳税人申请事项的原因做出书面说明。

（2）第（1）款、第（1a）款、第（1b）款、第（1c）款、第（1d）款和第（1e）款所规定的技术性指令由财政部部长管控。"

46. 第 36A 条修正如下：

"第 36A 条

（1）税务官员因过失或故意违背税法规定对税款进行计算或规定的，应依法受到惩处。

（2）在执行任务时，如税务官发生越权的，受害人可向财政部内部机构申诉，该机构有权对此展开调查，如证实税务官的确做出上述行为，将依法对其进行惩处。

（3）如发现税务官在执行任务时为一己之私敲诈或威胁纳税人的，则其将承担刑法典第 268 条所规定的刑事责任。

（4）税务官为一己之私滥用职权，强迫纳税人给予好处的，应按 1999 年第 31 号反腐败法及其修正案第 12 条之规定予以惩处。

（5）如税务官依税法规定善意履行职责，则不得对其提起刑事或民事诉讼。"

47. 在第 36A 条和第 37 条之间增加第 36B 条、第 36C 条、第 36D 条，具体如下：

"**第 36B 条**

（1）财政部部长应为税务总局所属人员制定行为准则。

（2）税务总局所属人员应遵守上述行为准则。

（3）如税务总局所属人员因违背行为准则而遭到投诉，在对其进行处理时，应由行为准则委员会依照财政部部长的规定进行监督。

第 36C 条

财政部部长应依法建立税收监督委员会。

第 36D 条

（1）如税务总局达到一定的业绩，可给予奖励。

（2）第（1）款所述的奖励的授予可通过国家收支预算进行规定。

（3）授予和利用第（1）款所述奖励的程序由财政部部长管控。"

48. 在第 37 条和第 38 条之间增加第 37A 条，具体如下：

"**第 37A 条**

（1）在 2007 年之纳税年度前提交年度所得税申报整改单从而导致未付税款增加，且在本法实施后一年内发现的，可扣除或取消针对该纳税人因迟交所缺税额而产生的采用利息形式的行政处罚金。

（2）在本法实施后一年内积极注册并获得纳税人代码的个人纳税人，可免除其在获取纳税代码前之纳税年度内因欠缴或少缴税款而被征收的行政处罚金，亦不对其进行税务审计，除非另有资料或数据证明该纳税人提交的年度纳税单不真实或超额付款。"

49. 第 38 条修正后全文如下：

"**第 38 条**

任何人因过失而：

a. 未能提交纳税单；或

b. 虽提交了纳税单，但其内容不真实、不完整或附加了虚假信息因此给国家税收带来损失，

则其应被处以罚款，金额最低相当于欠缴或少缴金额数，最高相当于欠缴或少缴金额的两倍，并将被处以 3 个月以上一年以下的有期徒刑。"

50. 第 39 条修正后全文如下：

"**第 39 条**

（1）任何人如故意：

a. 不通过登记获得纳税人代码或不申报其业务以期成为有效应纳税企业主；

b. 滥用、非法使用纳税人代码或应纳税企业主身份；

c. 不提交纳税申报单；

d. 提交不正确、不完整的纳税申报单和/或信息；或

e. 拒绝进行第 29 条所述的审计；或

f. 出示虚假的或伪造的账簿、档案或其他看似真实，实则未描述实际情况的文件；或

g. 未做账簿或档案，不出示或出借账目、档案或其他文件；或

h. 未保留可作为记账或存档用的账目、档案或文件，包括第 28 条所述的以电子方式进行管理或在印尼通过网上申请进行记账时处理数据的结果；或

i. 未汇付代扣或代征的税款，

故而对政府税收带来潜在影响的，将被判处最高 6 年的徒刑，并处以最低两倍于欠缴或少缴税款，最高 4 倍于欠缴或少缴税款的罚金。

（2）如第（1）款所述的纳税人在出狱后 1 年内在税收领域再次犯罪，则第（1）款所述刑期加倍。

（3）任何试图通过以下手段进行刑事犯罪的人员将被判处 6 年以上的有期徒刑，并被处以最高两倍于要求返还、赔偿或抵免之金额的罚款：

a. 滥用或非法使用第（1）款 b 项所述的纳税人代码或应纳税企业主身份；或

b. 在申请税额返还、赔偿或抵免时，提交第（1）款 d 项所述的不正确、不完整的申报单或信息。"

51. 在第 39 条和第 40 条之间增加第 39A 条，如下：

"**第 39A 条**

任何人如果故意：

a. 签发或使用未基于实际交易之上的税务发票、征税单、代缴单或税款支付单；或

b. 在未成为有效纳税企业主之前擅自签发税务发票，

将被判处 2 年以上 6 年以下有期徒刑，并被处以罚款，金额最低相当于税务发票、征税单、代缴单或税款支付单中税额的两倍，最高不超过 6 倍。"

52. 第 41 条修正后全文如下：

"**第 41 条**

（1）因玩忽职守而未能对第 34 条所述事项履行保密义务的官员将被判处 1 年以下有期徒刑，并处以最高 25 000 000.00 卢比的罚款。

（2）故意不履行职责的官员或任何使第 34 条所述官员未能履行义务的个人，将被判处 2 年以下有期徒刑，并处以最高 50 000 000.00 卢比的罚款。

（3）只有在接到有关个人就其隐私权遭到侵害而投诉时，方可针对第（1）款和第（2）款所述犯罪行为提起公诉。"

53. 第41A条修正后全文如下：

"**第41A条**

任何人，如故意不提供本法第35条要求的信息和证据或提供不正确的信息和证据，将被判处1年以下有期徒刑，并处以最高25 000 000.00卢比的罚款。"

54. 第41B条修正后全文如下：

"**第41B条**

任何人，如故意妨碍针对税收领域的犯罪调查，将被判处3年以下有期徒刑，并处以最高75 000 000.00卢比的罚款。"

55. 在第41B条和第42条之间加入第41C条，具体如下：

"**第41C条**

（1）任何人，如故意不履行第35A条第（1）款所述之义务，将被判处1年以下有期徒刑，并处以最高1 000 000 000.00卢比的罚款。

（2）任何人，如故意使官员或其他方无法履行第35A条第（1）款所述之义务，将被判处10年以下有期徒刑，并处以最高800 000 000.00卢比的罚款。

（3）任何人，如故意不向税务总干事提供第35 A条第2款所述之数据和信息，将被判处10年以下有期徒刑，并处以最高800 000 000.00卢比的罚款。

（4）任何人，如故意滥用税收数据和信息，致使国家遭受损失，将被判处1年以下有期徒刑，并处以最高500 000 000.00卢比的罚款。"

56. 第43条修正后全文如下：

"**第43条**

（1）如纳税人代表、代理人、雇员或其他方，命令、参与、建议或协助税务领域的犯罪，则第39条和第39A条之规定亦适用。

（2）第41A条和第41B条之规定亦适用于命令、参与、建议或协助税务领域的犯罪的任何一方。"

57. 在第9章第44条之前第43A条，如下：

"**第43A条**

（1）根据信息、数据、报告和投诉，税务总干事有权在启动针对税务领域犯罪调查之前对初始证据进行审验。

（2）如有迹象表明税务总局官员涉嫌税务领域犯罪，则财政部部长可指派财政部内部审计处查验初始证据。

（3）如在初始证据中发现腐败事实，应依照反腐败法规对牵涉的税务总局所属人员进行处理。

（4）第（1）款和第（2）款所述初始证据之审验程序由财政部部长管控。"

58. 第 44 条修正后全文如下：

"第 44 条

（1）只有税务总局的文职官员方可对税收领域的刑事犯罪进行调查，按照现行刑法法典，上述官员拥有特殊权利担任税收领域刑事犯罪的调查员。

（2）第（1）款所述调查员的权限如下：

a. 受理、搜查、采集和审验与税务领域刑事犯罪相关的信息或报告，使其更加完整和清楚；

b. 审验、搜查、采集有关个人和团体的信息，查明税务领域刑事犯罪行为的真相；

c. 从个人、团体处索取与税务领域刑事犯罪相关的信息和证据；

d. 审验与税务领域刑事犯罪相关的账目、档案和其他文件；

e. 搜查住所以获取关于记账、存档或其他文件的证据并将证据没收；

f. 寻求专家的帮助，对税务领域刑事犯罪展开调查；

g. 如审计正在进行，可禁止个人离开房间或地点，并对其身份以及获得的第 e 项所述文件进行查验；

h. 对涉嫌税务领域刑事犯罪之个人进行拍照；

i. 传唤嫌疑人、证人提供证词或进行质询；

j. 停止调查；

k. 根据相关法律，采取其他必要行动确保调查的顺利进行。

（3）按现行刑法典，第（1）款所述调查员应通过印尼警署调查员通知检察官调查启动，并将调查结果向其汇报。

（4）在执行第（1）款所述之调查权时，调查员可寻求其他法律强制手段。"

59. 第 44B 条修正后全文如下：

"第 44B 条

（1）为国家收入计，如财政部部长提出要求，则总检察长可在接到请求后 6 个月内中断对税务领域刑事犯罪的调查。

（2）只有当纳税人结清欠缴税款、少缴税款后或证明纳税人不应得到返还且应被处以相当于欠缴税款、少缴税款额 4 倍的行政处罚金后，方可中止对第（1）款所述税务领域刑事犯罪的调查。"

第 2 条

1. 1983 年第 6 号税法通则之规定已做过数次修正，最新版为 2000 年第 16 号，适用于 2001 年纳税年度至 2007 年纳税年度期间所有未了结的税收权利与义务。

2. 除第 1 点所述规定外，关于纳税期、部分纳税年度或纳税年度 2000 年及此前的所有规定，除第 13 条第（5）款或第 15 条第（4）款所述之规定外，在 2013 纳税年度前失效。

3. 本法自 2008 年 1 月 1 日起生效。为使公众周知，本法将于印度尼西亚共和国法典中予以颁布。

CONSOLIDATION OF LAW OF THE REPUBLIC OF INDONESIA NUMBER 7 OF 1983 CONCERNING INCOME TAX AS LASTLY AMENDED BY LAW NUMBER 36 OF 2008

CHAPTER I   GENERAL PROVISION

Article 1

Income tax shall be imposed on any taxable person in respect of income during a taxable year.

CHAPTER II   TAXABLE PERSON

Article 2

(1) Tax Subject consists of:

a. ① individual;

② undivided inheritance as a unit in lieu of the beneficiaries;

b. entity; and

c. permanent establishment.

(1a) A permanent establishment is a Tax Subject which, for taxation purposes, is treated as a corporate taxpayer.

(2) Tax Subject consists of resident and non-resident taxpayer.

(3) The term "resident taxpayer" means:

a. an individual who resides in Indonesia, an individual who has been presenting in Indonesia for more than 183 (one hundred and eighty-three) days within any 12 (twelve) months period, or an individual who has been residing in Indonesia within a particular taxable year and intends to reside in Indonesia;

b. an entity established or domiciled in Indonesia, except part of government bodies which fulfills these criteria as follows:

① its establishment is pursuant to the laws;

② financed by State Budget or Local Government Budget;

③ its revenues are included in State Budget or Local Government Budget; and

④ its book keeping is audited by the government auditor;

c. any undivided inheritance as a unit in lieu of beneficiaries.

(4) The term "non-resident taxpayer" means:

a. an individual who does not reside in Indonesia, has been presenting in Indonesia for not more than 183 (one hundred and eighty-three) days within any 12 (twelve) months period, and an entity which is not established and is not domiciled in Indonesia conducting business or carrying out activities through a permanent establishment in Indonesia; and

b. any individual who does not reside in Indonesia, has been presenting in Indonesia for not more than 183 (one hundred and eighty-three) days within any 12 (twelve) months period, and any entity which is not established and is not domiciled in Indonesia, which may receive or accrue income from Indonesia other than from conducting business or carrying out activities through permanent establishment.

(5) A permanent establishment is an establishment used by an individual who does not reside in Indonesia, an individual who has been present in Indonesia for not more than 183 (one hundred and eighty-three) days within any period of 12 (twelve) months, and an entity which is established outside Indonesia and is not domiciled in Indonesia conducting business or carrying out activities which may include:

a. a place of management;

b. a branch;

c. a representative office;

d. an office;

e. a factory;

f. a workshop;

g. a warehouse;

h. a space for promotion and selling;

i. a mine and a place of extraction of natural resources;

j. an area of oil and gas mining;

k. a fishery, animal husbandry, agriculture, plantation, or forestry;

l. a construction, installation or assembly project;

m. any kind of services provided by employees or any other persons, provided that the services were done in more than 60 (sixty) days within a period of 12 (twelve) months;

n. an individual or entity acting as a dependent agent;

o. an agent or employee of an insurance company which is established outside Indonesia and is not domiciled in Indonesia, receiving insurance premium or insuring risk in Indonesia; and

p. computers, electronic agents or automatic equipments owned, rented, or used by any electronic transaction provider to conduct business through Internet.

(6) The residence of an individual or the domicile of an entity shall be stipulated by Director General of Taxes in accordance with the real situation.

Article 2A

(1) Tax obligations of an individual referred to in paragraph (3) subparagraph a of Article 2, shall commence at the time the individual is born, is present, or intends to reside in Indonesia and shall cease at the time such person passes away or leaves Indonesia permanently.

(2) Tax obligations of an entity referred to in paragraph (3) subparagraph b of Article 2, shall commence at the time the entity is established or domiciled in Indonesia and shall cease at the time the entity is dissolved or is no longer domiciled in Indonesia.

(3) Tax obligations of an individual or an entity referred to in paragraph (4) subparagraph a of Article 2, shall commence at the time the individual or the entity starts its business or engages in activities referred to in paragraph (5) of Article 2 and shall cease at the time the businesses or activities through a permanent establishment are terminated.

(4) Tax obligations of an individual or an entity referred to in paragraph (4) subparagraph b of Article 2, shall commence at the time the individual or the entity derives income from Indonesia and shall cease at the time the individual or the entity no longer derives such income.

(5) Tax obligations of an undivided inheritance referred to in paragraph (1) subparagraph a point ② of Article 2, shall commence at the time the undivided inheritance starts to exist and shall cease at the time the inheritance is divided.

(6) In case tax obligations of an individual who resides or is present in Indonesia consist only a fraction of a taxable year, such fraction shall be treated as a taxable year.

Article 3

Tax Subject referred to in Article 2 does not include the following:

a. representative office of foreign countries;

b. officials of diplomatic and consular missions, or any other foreign official and any individual who work for and stay with them provided that they are not Indonesian citizens, and in Indonesia they do not receive nor accrue income other than from their position and their official duty in Indonesia, provided that the aforementioned country grants reciprocal treatment;

c. any international organization provided that:

① Indonesia is a member of the aforementioned organization; and

② they do not conduct business or engage in other activities to derive income from Indonesia, except providing the government with loan which the fund comes from the members' contribution;

d. the officials of the representative of international organizations as referred to in subparagraph c, provided that they are not Indonesian citizens and do not conduct any business, engage in activities, nor other employment to derive income from Indonesia.

CHAPTER Ⅲ   TAXABLE OBJECT

Article 4

(1) Taxable object is income, which is defined as any increase in economics capacity received by or accrued by a taxpayer from Indonesia as well as from which may be utilized for consumption or increasing the taxpayer's wealth, in whatever name and form, including:

a. compensation or remuneration received or accrued in respect of employment or service rendered, including salary, wage, allowance, honorarium, commission, bonus, gratuity, pension, or other forms of remuneration, unless otherwise stipulated by this Law;

b. lottery prizes, or gifts in respect of employment or activities, and rewards;

c. business profits;

d. gains from the sale or transfer of property, including:

① gains from a transfer of property to a company, a partnership, and other entity in exchange for shares or capital contributions;

② gains accrued by a company, a partnership or other entities from the transfer of property to its shareholders, partners or members;

③ gains from a liquidation, merger, consolidation, expansion, split-up, acquisition, or reorganization in whatever name and form;

④ gains from transfer of property in the form of grant, aid or donation, unless they are given to relatives within one degree of direct lineage, and to religious body, educational or other social entities including foundation, cooperative, or to any individual who is conducting micro and small business which stipulated by Minister of Finance, provided that aforementioned parties have no business, employment, ownership nor control relationship; and

⑤ gains from the sale or the transfer of part of or all mining rights, participation in financing, or capitalization in a mining company;

e. refund of tax payments which has already deducted as an expense and any additional payments of tax refund;

f. interest including premium, discounts, and compensation for loan repayment guarantees;

g. dividends, in whatever name and form, including dividends from an insurance company to its policyholders, and distribution of net income by a cooperative;

h. royalties or compensation from the use of rights;

i. rents and other income from the use of property;

j. annuities;

k. gains from the discharge of indebtedness up to a certain amount stipulated by the Government Regulations;

l. gains from foreign exchange;

m. gains from revaluation of assets;

n. insurance premium;

o. contribution received by or accrued by an association from its members who are taxpayers engaged in business or independent services;

p. an increase in net wealth from income which has not been taxed;

q. income from sharia business;

r. compensation as stipulated by Laws concerning General Provisions and Tax Procedures; and

s. surplus of Bank of Indonesia.

(2) The following income may be subject to a final income tax:

a. income in the form of interest from deposit and other savings, interest bonds and state bonds, interest paid by a cooperative to its individual members;

b. income in the form of lottery prizes;

c. income from a transaction of shares and other securities, derivative transactions traded in exchange, and sales of share or transfer of capital contribution from its company partner received by a venture-capital company;

d. income from transfer of property such as land and/or buildings, construction services business, real estate business, and renting land and/or buildings; and

e. other incomes which are stipulated by or based on a Government Regulation.

(3) These shall be excluded from taxable object:

a. ① aids or donations, including zakat received by Amil Zakat Board or other amil zakat institutions established or approved by the Government and received by eligible zakat recipients or compulsory religious donation for the followers of religions acknowledged by the Government, received by religious institutions established and approved by the Government and received by eligible donations recipients, which are stipulated by or based on a Government Regulation; and

② gifts received by relatives within one degree of direct lineage, and to religious body, educational or other social entities including foundation, cooperative, or to any individual who conducting micro and small business which stipulated by or based on a Minister of Finance Regulation, provided that aforementioned parties have no business, employment, ownership or control relationship;

b. inheritance;

c. assets including cash received by an entity referred to in Article 2 paragraph (1) subparagraph b, in exchange for shares or capital contribution;

d. consideration or remuneration in the form of benefits in kinds in respect of employment or services received or accrued from a taxpayer or the Government, except given by a non-taxpayer, taxpayer which is imposed by final tax, or taxpayer using deemed profit as referred to in the Article 15;

e. payments by an insurance company to an individual in connection with health, accident, life or education insurance;

f. dividends or distribution of profit received by or accrued by a resident limited corporation, cooperative, state-owned enterprises, or local government-owned enterprises through ownership in enterprise established and domiciled in Indonesia, provided that:

① dividends are paid out from retained earnings; and

② limited corporations and state-owned enterprises and local-owned enterprises receiving the dividends must own at least 25% (twenty-five percent) of the total paid-in capital;

g. contributions received or accrued by a pension fund which its establishment is approved by the Minister of Finance, either paid by an employer or an employee;

h. income from a capital investment of the pension fund as referred to in subparagraph g, in certain sectors as determined by the Minister of Finance Decree;

i. distribution of profit received or accrued by a member of a limited partnership, whose capital does not consists of shares, partnership, association, firma, and kongsi, including a unit holder of collective investment contract ;

j. deleted;

k. income received or accrued by a venture-capital company in the form of profit distribution of a joint-venture company established and conducting business or engage in activities in Indonesia, provided that:

① the investee is a micro, small, medium-sized enterprise, or engaged in activities in business sectors stipulated by or based on the Minister of Finance Regulation; and

② the investee's shares are not traded in the stock exchange in Indonesia;

l. scholarships that fulfill certain requirements which are stipulated by or based on the Minister of Finance Regulations;

m. a surplus received or accrued by an institution or a non-profit organization engaged in education and/or research and development, which has been listed in corresponding institutions, which is reinvested in the forms of infrastructures of education and/or research and development, within no more than 4 (four) years period of time since it is received or accrued, as stipulated by or based on the Minister of Finance Regulations;

n. aid or donation paid by the Social Security Agency to a certain taxpayer, as stipulated by or based on the Minister of Finance Regulations.

Article 5

(1) Taxable object of a permanent establishment consists of:

a. income from its businesses or activities and from its owned or controlled properties;

b. income of the head office from businesses or activities, sales of goods, or furnishing services in Indonesia which are similar to those undertaken by the permanent establishment in Indonesia;

c. income referred to in Article 26 received or accrued by the head office provided that the properties or activities giving rise to the aforementioned income is effectively connected with a permanent establishment.

(2) Expenses related to gross income referred to in paragraph (1) subparagraph b and c may be deducted from the permanent establishment's income.

(3) In calculating the profit of a permanent establishment:

a. administrative expenses incurred by the head office for the purpose of the permanent establishment is deductible subject to limitations regulated by the Director General of Taxes;

b. the following payments to its head office are not deductible:

① royalties or other payments paid in respect of the use of properties, patents, or other rights;

② payments in respect of management services or other services;

③ interest, except in banking business;

c. payments referred to in subparagraph b received or accrued from the head office shall not be included in taxable object, except interest in banking business.

Article 6

(1) Resident taxpayers and permanent establishments are entitled to claim the deductions in the form of expenses to earn, to collect and secure income from their gross income, including:

a. costs which are directly or indirectly related to business, among others:

① costs of materials;

② costs in relation with employment or services including wages, salaries, honoraria, bonuses, gratuities and remuneration in the form of money;

③ interest, rents and royalties;

④ travel expenses;

⑤ waste processing expenses;

⑥ insurance premiums;

⑦ advertisement and selling expenses as stipulated by or based on the Minister of Finance Regulation;

⑧ administrative expenses;

⑨ taxes other than income tax;

b. depreciation of tangible assets and amortization of rights and other expenditures which have effective life of more than 1 (one) year as referred to in Article 11 and Article 11A;

c. contributions to a pension fund which its establishment is approved by the Minister of Finance;

d. losses incurred from the sale or transfer of properties owned and used in business or used for the purpose of earning, collecting and securing income;

e. losses from foreign exchange;

f. costs related to research and development carried out in Indonesia;

g. scholarships, apprenticeships and training expenses;

h. debts which are actually uncollectible, provided that:

① it has been expensed in commercial profit and loss statement;

② the taxpayer shall submit the list of bad debts to the Directorate General of Taxes;

③ the case has been filed to court or government agencies which handle state's receivables, or there is a written agreement on the discharge of indebtedness between the debtor and creditor, or it has been published in the media, or there is creditor's which states certain amount of bad debts have been written off;

④ the requirement stated in point ③ does not apply for small debtors as specified in Article 4 paragraph (1) subparagraph k, and the procedure of which shall be stipulated by or based on the Minister of Finance Regulations;

i. donation for national disaster which is stipulated by a Government Regulation;

j. donation for research and development conducted in Indonesia which is stipulated by a Government Regulation;

k. costs of social infrastructure development which are stipulated by a Government Regulation;

l. donation in the form of education facilities which is stipulated by a Government Regulation;

m. donation for sport enhancement which is stipulated by a Government Regulation.

(2) The loss incurred, after subtracting the deductions referred to in paragraph (1) from gross income, shall be carried forward for a maximum of 5 (five) successive years.

(3) An individual who is a resident taxpayer is entitled to claim personal exemptions as referred to in Article 7.

Article 7

(1) The amount of personal exemptions is as follows:

a. Rp 15,840,000.00 (fifteen million eight hundred and forty thousand rupiah) for an individual taxpayer;

b. additional Rp 1,320,000.00 (one million three hundred and twenty thousand rupiah) for a married taxpayer;

c. additional Rp 15,840,000.00 (fifteen million eight hundred and forty thousand rupiah) for married taxpayers' spouse provided they file a joint tax return as referred to in paragraph (1) of Article 8;

d. additional Rp 1,320,000.00 (one million three hundred and twenty thousand rupiah) for each dependent family member related by blood and by marriage in a direct lineage, and an adopted child with a maximum of three dependents.

(2) The application of paragraph (1) is based on the facts and circumstances at the beginning a taxable year or fraction of a taxable year.

（3） The Minister of Finance, after consultation with the House of Representatives, shall stipulate the adjustment of personal exemptions.

Article 8

（1） Income or losses of a married woman at the beginning of a taxable year or fraction of a taxable year, including loss originating from previous years that have not been offset as referred to in paragraph （2） of Article 6, shall be deemed as income or loss of her husband, except where the income is received or accrued exclusively from one employer and from which tax has been withheld in accordance with Article 21 and the employment is not related to the business or independent personal service of her husband or any other relative.

（2） Income of a married individual shall be taxed separately if:

a. they live separately based on a court decision;

b. it is requested in writing by both the husband and the wife on the basis of an agreement for the separation of property and income;

c. it is requested by the wife who chooses to meet her tax right and obligation separately.

（3） The net income of a married individual referred to in paragraph （2） subparagraph b and c shall be taxed on aggregate net income of the married individual, and the amount of tax to be paid by each of them shall be in proportion to their respective net income.

（4） The income of a minor child shall be added to the income of the parents.

Article 9

（1） In determining the taxable income of a resident taxpayer and a permanent establishment, the following are not deductible:

a. distribution of profit in whatever name or form, such as dividends, including dividends paid by an insurance company to its policyholders, and any distribution of the surplus by a cooperative;

b. expenses charged or incurred for the personal benefit of shareholders, partners or members;

c. formation or accumulation of reserves, except:

① reserve for bad debt of a bank and other business which conduct business as a creditor, financial lease company, consumer finance company and factoring company;

② reserves in an insurance business including reserve for social aid made by the Social Security Agency;

③ guarantee reserve for the Deposit Guarantor Institutions;

④ reserves for cost of reclamation in general mining;

⑤ reserve for cost of reforestation in forestry business;

⑥ reserve for closing and maintaining industrial waste site conducted by industrial waste processing business, and the terms and conditions of which shall stipulated by or based on the Minister of Finance Regulation;

d. insurance premiums for health, accident, life, dual purpose, and education insurance which are paid by an individual taxpayer, except those paid by an employer where premiums is treated as income of the taxpayer;

e. consideration or remuneration related to employment or services given in the form of a benefit in kind, except provision of food and beverages for employees or consideration or remuneration given in the form of a benefit in kind in certain regions and in connection with employment as stipulated by or based on the Minister of Finance Regulation;

f. excessive compensation paid to shareholders or other associated parties as a consideration for work performed;

g. gifts, aid, donations, and inheritances as referred to in Article 4 paragraph (3) subparagraph a and b, except donations as referred to in Article 6 paragraph (1) subparagraph i to m and zakat received by an Amil Zakat Board or other amil zakat institutions established or approved by the Government or compulsory religious donation for the followers of religions acknowledged by the Government, received by religious institutions established and approved by the Government, which are stipulated by or based on a Government Regulation;

h. income tax;

i. cost incurred for the personal benefit of a taxpayer or his dependents;

j. salary paid to a member of an association, firm, or limited partnership, the capital of which does not consist of stocks;

k. administrative penalty in the form of interest, fines, and surcharges, as well as criminal penalty in the form of fines imposed pursuant to the tax laws.

(2) Expenditures for earning, collecting, and securing of income having an effective life of more than 1 (one) year, shall not be charged directly to income but shall be deducted through depreciation or amortization as referred to in Article 11 or Article 11A.

Article 10

(1) Acquisition cost or selling price in an arm's length transaction referred to in paragraph (4) of Article 18 shall be the amount actually paid or actually received; whereas, in a transaction between related taxpayers, is the amount which should have been paid or received.

(2) Acquisition value or selling value in the case of an exchange of assets shall be the amount which should be paid or received on the basis of the market price.

(3) Acquisition value or transfer value of transferred assets in the case of liquidation, merger, split-up, spin-off, split-off, or taking over of a business shall be the amount which should be paid or received in accordance with the market price except the Minister of Finance otherwise determines.

(4) In case of a transfer of assets:

a. that qualifies for paragraph (3) subparagraph a and subparagraph b of Article 4, the basis of the assets in the hands of the transferee shall be the book value in the hands of the transferor or other value determined by the Director General of Taxes;

b. that does not qualify for paragraph (3) subparagraph a of Article 4, then the basis of the assets in the hands of the transferee shall be the market value of the assets.

(5) In case of a transfer of assets referred to in paragraph (3) subparagraph c of Article 4, the basis of the transferred assets in the hands of the transferee shall be the market value of the assets.

(6) Inventories and the use of inventories for the calculation of the cost of goods sold shall be valued at cost under weighted average or first-in first-out method.

Article 11

(1) Depreciation with respect to costs of purchasing, erecting, expanding, improving, or replacing tangible assets, except land that bears ownership right, a right to build, a right to cultivate, and a right to use that is held for earning, collecting, and securing of income that has an effective life of more than 1 (one) year, shall be calculated on a straight line basis over the effective life stipulated for the assets.

(2) Depreciation with respect to tangible assets as referred to in paragraph (1), other than building, may also be calculated under the declining balance method over the effective life of the asset by applying the rate of depreciation to the book value, and at the end of the effective life the remaining of the book value shall be fully depreciated, provided that the method is adopted consistently.

(3) Depreciation shall commence in the month when the expenditures are incurred; except for the asset still in progress, the depreciation shall commence in the month when the process is completed.

(4) Subject to the approval of the Director General of Taxes, a taxpayer may start to claim depreciation at the beginning of the month the asset is used to earn, to collect and to secure income or of the month the asset produces income.

(5) If a taxpayer revalues the assets as referred to in Article 19, then the basis of depreciation for the assets shall be the value resulting from the revaluation.

(6) For the purpose of calculating depreciation, the effective life and the rate of depreciation for tangible assets shall be as follows:

Group of Tangible Assets	Effective Life	Rate of Depreciation under	
		Paragraph (1)	Paragraph (2)
I. Non-building Class:			
Group 1	4 years	25%	50%
Group 2	8 years	12.5%	25%
Group 3	16 years	6.25%	12.5%
Group 4	20 years	5%	10%
II. Building Class:			
Permanent	20 years	5%	
Non-permanent	10 years	10%	

(7) Further regulations related to depreciation of tangible assets owned and used in certain business shall be stipulated by a Minister of Finance Regulation.

(8) If there is a transfer or withdrawal of assets as referred to in paragraph (1) subparagraph d of Article 4 or a withdrawal of assets for other reasons, then the remaining book value of the assets shall be deducted as a loss and the selling price or insurance payment received or accrued shall be treated as income in the year the assets are withdrawn.

(9) If the insurance payment can only be identified at a later date, then subject to the approval of the Director General of Taxes, the amount of the loss as referred to in paragraph (8) shall be deducted at a later date.

(10) If there is a transfer of tangible assets which qualifies for paragraph (3) subparagraph a and subparagraph b of Article 4, then the remaining book value of the assets may not be treated as a loss by the transferor.

(11) Further regulations related to classification of tangible assets according to their effective life as referred to in paragraph (6) shall be stipulated by the Minister of Finance Regulations.

Article 11A

(1) Amortization with respect to cost of acquiring intangible assets and other costs including cost of extending right to build, right to cultivate, right to use, and goodwill that has an effective life of more than 1 (one) year which is used to earn, to collect and to secure income shall be calculated under straight line method or declining balance method by applying the amortization rate to the costs or the book value and at the end of the effective life the remaining of the book value shall be fully amortized, provided that the method is adopted consistently.

(1a) Amortization shall commence in the month when the expenditures are incurred except for certain businesses which shall be stipulated by the Minister of Finance Regulations.

(2) For the purpose of calculating amortization, the effective life and the rate of amortization shall be as follows:

Group of Intangible Assets	Effective Life	Rate of Amortization under	
		Straight Line Method	Declining Balance Method
Group 1	4 years	25%	50%
Group 2	8 years	12.5%	25%
Group 3	16 years	6.25%	12.5%
Group 4	20 years	5%	10%

(3) Expenditures incurred prior to the establishment and the capital expansion of an entity shall be deducted in the year the expenditures are incurred or amortized as stipulated in paragraph (2).

(4) Amortization of expenditures to acquire rights and other expenditures that have an effective life of more than 1 (one) year in oil and gas industries shall be calculated under the

unit of production method.

(5) Amortization of expenditures to acquire mining rights other than referred to in paragraph (4), rights on forestry concession and rights on the exploitation of natural resources and other natural products that have an effective life of more than 1 (one) year, shall be calculated using the unit of production method, up to a maximum of 20% (twenty percent) per year.

(6) Expenditures incurred prior to commercial operations, which have effective life of more than 1 (one) year, shall be capitalized and amortized as stipulated in paragraph (2).

(7) In case of transfer of intangible assets or rights referred to in paragraph (1), (4) and (5), the book value of the assets or the rights shall be deducted as a loss and the payment received shall be treated as income in the year the transfer occurred.

(8) In case of a transfer of intangible assets that complies with the conditions as referred to in paragraph (3) subparagraph a and subparagraph b of Article 4, the book value of such assets shall not be treated as a loss by the transferor.

Article 12

Deleted.

Article 13

Deleted.

Article 14

(1) Deemed profit to determine net income shall be formulated and adjusted from time to time, and issued by the Director General of Taxes.

(2) An individual taxpayer whose gross income of business activities or independent services in one year is less than Rp 4,800,000,000.00 (four billion eight hundred million rupiah), may calculate his net income by applying the deemed profit as referred to in paragraph (1), provided that it is communicated to the Director General of Taxes within the first 3 (three) months of the taxable year concerned.

(3) A taxpayer who calculates net income using the deemed profit as referred to in paragraph (2), shall be obliged to keep records as referred to in the provisions of the Law on General Rules and Procedures of Taxation.

(4) A taxpayer who fails to inform the Director General of Taxes to choose deemed profit as referred to in paragraph (2) is deemed to choose to keep books of account.

(5) A taxpayer who is obliged to keep books of account or records including a taxpayer as referred to in paragraphs (3) and (4), but fails to keep or completely keep records or books of account, or fails to reveal records or books of account or supporting evidence, in such case the net income will be calculated using deemed profit and the gross income will be calculated in other basis as stipulated by or based on the Minister of Finance Regulations.

（6）Deleted.

（7）The amount of gross income as referred to in paragraph（2）may be adjusted by the Minister of Finance Regulations.

Article 15

Specific deemed profit for calculating net income of a certain taxpayer whose income cannot be calculated by the provision of paragraph（1）or（3）of Article 16 shall be determined by the Minister of Finance.

CHAPTER Ⅳ   METHODS OF TAX CALCULATION

Article 16

（1）Taxable income of a resident taxpayer in a taxable year shall be income as referred to in paragraph（1）of Article 4 reduced by allowable deductions as referred to in paragraph（1）and（2）of Article 6, paragraph（1）of Article 7, and paragraph（1）subparagraph c, subparagraph d, subparagraph e and subparagraph g of Article 9.

（2）Taxable income of taxpayer as referred to in Article 14 shall be calculated by applying deemed profit as stipulated in that article, and in case of an individual taxpayer, the amount as calculated by applying the deemed profit is deducted with personal exemptions as referred to in paragraph（1）of Article 7.

（3）Taxable income of a non-resident taxpayer conducting business or engaged in activities through a permanent establishment in Indonesia in a taxable year, shall be income as referred to in paragraph（1）of Article 5 with regard to paragraph（1）of Article 4 reduced by allowable deductions, as referred to in paragraph（2）and（3）of Article 5, paragraph（1）and（2）of Article 6, and paragraph（1）subparagraph c, d, e, and g of Article 9.

（4）In case the tax obligation of an individual resident taxpayer covers only a fraction of a taxable year as referred to in paragraph（6）of Article 2A, his/her taxable income is calculated by multiplying the net income with a fraction which would arrive at a full year net income.

Article 17

（1）The tax rate applicable to each taxable income brackets is as follow:

a. resident individual taxpayer:

Taxable Income Tax Brackets	Tax Rate
Rp 50,000,000.00 (fifty million rupiah) or less	5% (five percent)
Over Rp 50,000,000.00 (fifty million rupiah) – Rp 250,000,000.00 (two hundred fifty million rupiah)	15% (fifteen percent)
Over Rp 250,000,000.00 (two hundred fifty million rupiah) – Rp 500,000,000.00 (five hundred million rupiah)	25% (twenty-five percent)
Over Rp 500,000,000.00 (five hundred million rupiah)	30% (thirty percent)

b. tax rate applicable to entities as a resident taxpayer and permanent establishment is 28% (twenty-eight percent).

(2) The highest tax rate as referred to in paragraph (1) subparagraph a may be lowered but shall not be lower than 25% (twenty-five percent) which is stipulated by the Government Regulations.

(2a) The tax rate as referred to in paragraph (1) subparagraph b becomes 25% (twenty-five percent) which applies starting from the tax year of 2010.

(2b) Entity as a resident taxpayer and public company whose at least 40% (forty percent) of their paid-in capital are traded in the Indonesian stock exchange and meet other certain requirements can obtain a rate of 5% (five percent) lower than the tax rate as referred to in paragraph (1) subparagraph b and paragraph (2a), which is stipulated by or based on the Government Regulations.

(2c) Tax rate applicable to dividends received by an individual resident taxpayer is a maximum of 10% (ten percent) and final in nature.

(2d) Further regulations related to tax rate as referred to in paragraph (2c) shall be stipulated by the Government Regulations.

(3) The amount of taxable income brackets as referred to in paragraph (1) subparagraph a may be adjusted by the Minister of Finance Decree.

(4) For the purpose of the application of tax rates as referred to in paragraph (1), the amount of taxable income shall be rounded down in thousands.

(5) Where an individual resident taxpayer's obligation covers only a fraction of a taxable year referred to in paragraph (4) of Article 16, his/her tax payable is calculated by the fraction of the number of days divided by 360 (three hundred sixty) and multiplied by the amount of the tax payable for one full year.

(6) For the purpose of the calculation of tax payable as referred to in paragraph (5), one month is deemed to be 30 (thirty) days.

(7) A special rate on income as referred to in paragraph (2) of Article 4 may be applied by virtue of the Government Regulations, provided that it does not exceed the highest marginal rate as referred to in paragraph (1).

Article 18

(1) The Minister of Finance is authorized to issue a regulation on debt equity ratio for the purpose of computing tax payable in accordance with this Law.

(2) The Minister of Finance is authorized to determine as when dividends accrued by a resident taxpayer on participation in an offshore company other than public companies, provided that one of the following condition is met:

a. the taxpayer owns at least 50% (fifty percent) of the paid-in capital of the company; or

b. the taxpayer together with other resident taxpayer own at least 50% (fifty percent) of the paid – in capital of the company.

(3) The Director General of Taxes is authorized to reallocate income and deductions between related parties and to characterize debt as equity for the purposes of the computation of taxable income to assure that the transactions are those which would have been made between independent parties using price comparison method between independent parties, resale price method, cos-plus method, or other methods.

(3a) The Director General of Taxes is authorized to conclude an agreement with a taxpayer and with a tax authority from other countries on transfer pricing method between related taxpayers as referred to in paragraph (4) which may cover a certain period and to evaluate it as well as to renegotiate after the agreement is expired.

(3b) A taxpayer who purchases shares or assets of other entities through a special-purpose company can be deemed as the real party who conducts the transaction, provided that such taxpayer is the affiliation of the special-purpose company and the price of the transaction is unfairly settled.

(3c) The sale or transfer of shares of a conduit company or special-purpose company which is established or domiciled in tax haven countries and the conduit company or the special-purpose company is the affiliation of an entity established or domiciled in Indonesia or a permanent establishment in Indonesia, could be deemed as the sale or transfer of shares of an entity that is established or domiciled in Indonesia or permanent establishment in Indonesia.

(3d) The amount of income that individual resident taxpayer has received from an employer which is the affiliation of non-resident entity may be adjusted by the Tax Authority, in case of the employer transfers the payment in forms of expenses or other expenditures which are paid to his affiliation.

(3e) The implementation of regulations as referred to in paragraph (3b), (3c) and (3d) shall be stipulated by or based on the Minister of Finance Regulations.

(4) The term "related taxpayer" as referred to in paragraph (3) to paragraph (3d), paragraph (1) subparagraph f of Article 9, and paragraph (1) of Article 10 means:

a. a taxpayer who owns directly or indirectly at least 25% (twenty five percent) of equity of other taxpayers; a relationship between taxpayer through ownership of at least 25% (twenty five percent) of equity of two or more taxpayer, as well as relationship between two or more taxpayer concerned;

b. a taxpayer who controls other taxpayer, or two or more taxpayers are directly or indirectly under the same control;

c. a family relationship either through blood or through marriage within one degree of direct or indirect lineage.

(5) Deleted.

Article 19

(1) The Minister of Finance is authorized to issue a regulations concerning revaluation of assets and adjustment factors when elements of expenditures and income are inappropriate due to inflation.

(2) By virtue of the Minister of Finance Regulations, a certain tax rate, not more than the rate applied as referred to in paragraph (1) of Article 17, shall be applied to the excess value of revaluation of assets.

CHAPTER V TAX PAYMENT DURING THE CURRENT YEAR

Article 20

(1) The income tax payable in any taxable year shall be paid up by way of withholding by other persons and self payment by the taxpayer.

(2) The tax payment referred to in paragraph (1) shall be carried out on a monthly basis or other period to be prescribed by the Minister of Finance.

(3) The tax payment referred to in paragraph (1) shall be treated as a tax installment which may be credited against income tax payable at the end of taxable year concerned, except for final tax which is applicable to a certain type of income.

Article 21

(1) The following persons are obliged to withhold tax on remuneration in whatever form received or accrued by individual resident taxpayer in respect of employment, services rendered, or any other similar activities:

a. an employer who pays salaries, wages, honoraria, allowances, and other similar remuneration in respect of an employment exercised either by permanent employees or non-permanent employees;

b. a government treasurer who pays salaries, wages, honoraria, allowances, and other similar remuneration in respect of an employment, services, and any other similar activities;

c. pension fund or other entity that pays pension and any other similar remuneration in whatever form in consideration of past employment;

d. an entity that pays honoraria or other similar remuneration in respect of services rendered, including professional services or any other activities of an independent character; and

e. a person who organizes an activity and pays remuneration in respect of services connected therewith.

(2) Notwithstanding the preceding provisions, a diplomatic agent or an international organization as referred to in Article 3 are not obliged to withhold tax as referred to in paragraph (1) subparagraph a.

(3) An income to be withheld monthly derived by a permanent employee or a retired person shall be the amount of gross income after deducted by an official expenditure or pension expenditure determined by the Minister of Finance Regulations, pension contribution, and personal exemption.

(4) An income to be withheld derived by a daily wage earner, weekly wage earner, and other non-permanent employees shall be the amount of gross income after deducted by a portion of income which is exempt from withholding tax as determined by the Minister of Finance Regulations.

(5) A rate applicable to income as referred to in paragraph (1) shall be the rate under paragraph (1) subparagraph a of Article 17, except otherwise determined by the Government Regulations.

(5a) The tax rate applicable as referred to in paragraph (5) for unregistered resident taxpayer is 20% (twenty percent) higher than those registered resident taxpayer.

(6) Deleted.

(7) Deleted.

(8) Regulation concerning guidelines for withholding of tax on income in connection with any employment, services, or activities shall be stipulated by or based on the Minister of Finance Regulations.

Article 22

(1) The Minister of Finance may designate:

a. government treasurers to withhold tax in connection with payment for supply of goods;

b. certain entities to withhold tax from taxpayer who conduct in import activities or other business activities; and

c. certain entities to withhold tax from taxpayer who purchase luxurious goods.

(2) Regulations governing the tax base for withholding purposes, the criterion, characteristics and amount of withholding of taxes as referred to in paragraph (1), shall be stipulated by or based on the Minister of Finance Regulations.

(3) Withholding tax rate as referred to in paragraph (2) for unregistered resident taxpayer is 100% (one hundred percent) higher than those registered resident taxpayer.

Article 23

(1) The following income, in whatever name and form, paid, apportioned to be paid, or on the due date of payment by a government institution, a resident taxable entity, a person who organizes an activity, a permanent establishment or a representative of any other non-resident enterprises to a resident taxpayer or a permanent establishment, shall be subject to withholding tax of:

a. 15% (fifteen percent) of the gross amount of:

① dividends as referred to in paragraph (1) subparagraph g of Article 4;

② interest as referred to in paragraph (1) subparagraph f of Article 4;

③ royalties; and

④ prizes, awards, bonus, and similar payments other than those that have been withheld under paragraph (1) subparagraph e of Article 21;

b. deleted;

c. 2% (two percent) of the gross amount of:

①rent and other income in connection with the use of property, except rent and other income in connection with the use of property that has been withheld under paragraph (2) of Article 4;

②compensation in connection with technology, management, construction, consultation and other services, except those that have been withheld under Article 21.

(1a) Withholding tax rate as referred to in paragraph (1) for unregistered resident taxpayer is 100% (one hundred percent) higher than those registered resident taxpayer.

(2) Further regulations related to other services as referred to in paragraph (1) subparagraph c point ② shall be stipulated by or based on the Minister of Finance Regulations.

(3) An individual resident taxpayer may be appointed by the Director General of Taxes as a withholding agent as referred to in paragraph (1).

(4) Withholding tax as referred to in paragraph (1) shall not apply to:

a. income paid or owed to a bank;

b. lease payment in finance lease agreements;

c. dividends as referred to in paragraph (3) subparagraph f of Article 4 and dividends received by individual taxpayers as referred to in paragraph (2c) of Article 17;

d. deleted;

e. distributed profit as referred to in paragraph (3) subparagraph i of Article 4;

f. profit which is distributed by a cooperative to its members;

g. deleted; and

h. income paid or payable to a financial service entity which serves as a loan intermediary and/or financing stipulated by the Minister of Finance Regulations.

Article 24

(1) Tax paid or tax payable in foreign countries on offshore income by resident taxpayer may be credited in the same taxable year against the tax payable under this Law.

(2) The amount of allowable tax credit as referred to in paragraph (1) shall be equal to the amount of foreign tax, but shall not exceed the tax payable calculated under this Law.

(3) In calculating the limit of allowable tax credit, the source of income shall be determined as follows:

a. the source of income from shares and other securities and capital gain from transfer of share is the country where the issuing company resides;

b. the source of income in the form of interest, royalties, and rent in connection with the use of movable assets is the country where the payer or the party who claims the deductions there from is a resident;

c. the source of income in the form of rent in connection with the use of immovable assets is the country where the assets are located;

d. the source of income in the form of compensation for services, employment and other activities is the country where the payer or the party who claims deductions there from is a resident;

e. the source of income of a permanent establishment is the country where the permanent establishment conducts business or is engaged in activities;

f. the source of income of the transfer of some parts of or all mining rights or the proof of participating in financing or funding in the mining company is the country where the location of the mines is situated;

g. gains derived from transfer of immovable assets is the country where the immovable assets is located; and

h. gains derived from transfer of assets that is part of a permanent establishment is the country where the permanent establishment is situated.

(4) The determination of the source of income other than income as referred to in paragraph (3) shall adopt the same principles contained therein.

(5) If foreign tax on offshore income that has been credited is later either reduced or refunded, the amount of tax payable pursuant to this Law shall be added to the amount for the year in which the reduction or refund is made.

(6) The implementation of tax credits in respect of offshore income shall be stipulated by or based on the Minister of Finance Regulations.

Article 25

(1) Monthly tax installment during the current taxable year that must be paid by taxpayers shall be equal to the tax payable according to the tax return of the preceding year, less the following:

a. income tax withheld as referred to in Article 21 and 23, and income tax withheld as referred to in Article 22; and

b. foreign tax paid or payable that is allowable for tax credit as referred to in Article 24, divided by 12 (twelve) or the number of months of a fraction of the taxable year.

(2) The monthly tax installment for periods prior to the due date of income tax return lodgment is equal to the monthly tax installment of the latest month of the preceding taxable year.

(3) Deleted.

(4) If during a current taxable year an assessment notice of the preceding taxable year is issued, the monthly tax installment shall be recalculated according to the notice and shall commence from the following month after the issuance of the notice.

(5) Deleted.

(6) The Director General of Taxes is authorized to stipulate the calculation of monthly tax installment during the current taxable year in the following circumstances:

a. taxpayer is entitled to loss carry forward;

b. taxpayer receives irregular income;

c. Annual Tax Return for the preceding year is filed after the due date;

d. taxpayer is granted an extension of the due date to file the Annual Tax Return;

e. taxpayer amends the Annual Tax Return on his own initiative that results in monthly tax installment greater than the monthly tax installment before the amendment; and

f. there is a change in taxpayer's business or activities.

(7) The Minister of Finance determines the calculation of the amount of tax installment for:

a. new taxpayer;

b. banks, state-owned enterprises, local state-owned enterprises, listed companies, and other taxpayers according to any prevailing law obliged to make periodic financial statements;

c. individual taxpayer as certain entrepreneur with rate not more than 0.75% (zero comma seventy-five percent) from the gross revenue.

(8) Individual resident taxpayer who does not have a Tax Identification Number, 21 (twenty-one) years old or more, or travel abroad shall pay taxes in accordance with the Government Regulations;

(8a) The provisions as referred to in paragraph (8) applies until 31 December, 2010.

(9) Deleted.

Article 26

(1) The following income, in whatever name and form, paid, apportioned to be paid, or on the due date of payment by a government institution, resident taxable entity, a person who organizes activities, permanent establishment, or a representatives of a non-resident company to a non-resident taxpayer other than a permanent establishment in Indonesia, shall be subject to withholding tax of 20% (twenty percent) of the gross income:

a. dividends;

b. interest including premium, discount, and compensation for loan repayment guarantees;

c. royalties, rent and other income in connection with the use of the property;

d. compensation in connection with services, works, and activities;

e. prizes and awards;

f. pension and other periodic payments;

g. premium of swap and other hedging transactions; and/or

h. gains from the discharge of indebtedness.

(1a) The domicile country of the foreign taxpayer other than those who conducting business or performing business through a permanent establishment in Indonesia referred to in paragraph (1) is the country or where the foreign taxpayer resides where he or she actually receives benefit from that income (beneficial owner).

(2) Gains from the sale or transfer of assets in Indonesia other than that governed by paragraph (2) of Article 4, derived by a non-resident taxpayer other than a permanent establishment in Indonesia, and insurance premiums paid to a foreign insurance company, shall be subject to withholding tax of 20% (twenty percent) on the deemed profit.

(2a) Gains from the sale or transfer of shares as referred to in paragraph (3c) of Article 18 is subject to withholding tax of 20% (twenty percent) of the estimated net income.

(3) The implementation of the regulations as referred to in paragraph (2) and (2a) is stipulated by or based on the Minister of Finance Regulations.

(4) Taxable income after deducted from income tax of a permanent establishment in Indonesia is subject to be taxed of 20% (twenty percent), unless the profit is re-invested in Indonesia, the further regulation is stipulated by or based on the Minister of Finance Regulations.

(5) The withholding tax as referred to in paragraph (1), (2), (2a), and (4) is treated as final tax, unless:

a. the withholding tax on income as referred to in paragraph (1) subparagraph b and c of Article 5; and

b. the withholding tax on income received or accrued by a non-resident individual or non-resident company that has changed its status into a resident taxpayer or a permanent establishment.

Article 27

Deleted.

CHAPTER VI CALCULATION OF TAX AT THE END OF THE YEAR

Article 28

(1) Resident taxpayers and permanent establishments are entitled to claim tax credit against tax payable for the same taxable year:

a. tax withheld on income from employment, personal services and activities referred to in Article 21;

b. tax withheld on income in connection with payment on import activities or other business activities referred to in Article 22;

c. tax withheld on dividends, interest, royalties, rent, gifts and rewards, and compensation for services referred to in Article 23;

d. creditable foreign tax paid or payable on offshore income referred to in Article 24;

e. self tax payments during current taxable year referred to in Article 25;

f. tax withheld on income referred to in paragraph (5) of Article 26.

(2) An administrative penalty in the form of interest, fine and surcharge, or a criminal penalty in the form of a fine in connection with the implementation of the prevailing tax laws, may not be credited against tax payable referred to in paragraph (1).

Article 28A

In case tax payable in a taxable year is less than the allowable tax credit referred to in paragraph (1) of Article 28, then after a tax audit is conducted, the excess tax shall be refunded after being offset against outstanding tax and penalties.

Article 29

In case tax payable in taxable year is greater than the allowable tax credit as referred to in paragraph (1) of Article 28, the outstanding tax shall be paid before the Annual Tax Return is submitted.

Article 30

Deleted.

Article 31

Deleted.

CHAPTER VII   OTHER PROVISIONS

Article 31A

(1) Taxpayer who invests capital in certain sectors and/or certain regions that are high priority in the national scale, may be given tax facilities in the form of:

a. up to 30% (thirty percent) investment allowance;

b. accelerated depreciation and amortization;

c. extended loss carried forward but shall not exceed 10 (ten) years; and

d. the imposition of income tax on dividends as referred to in Article 26 of 10% (ten percent), unless the tax rate under the relevant tax treaty is lower.

(2) Further regulations concerning certain sectors and/or certain regions that are high priority in the national scale as well as the tax facilities as referred to in paragraph (1) shall be stipulated by the Government Regulations.

Article 31B

Deleted.

Article 31C

(1) Tax revenue collected from individual resident taxpayers and Income Tax of Article 21 withheld by the employer, shall be shared with the share of 80% (eighty percent) for the central Government and 20% (twenty percent) for the Local Government where the taxpayer is registered.

(2) Deleted.

Article 31D

The provisions on taxation for businesses in the sectors of oil and gas, geothermal, general mining including coal mining, and sharia-based business shall be stipulated by or based on the Government Regulations.

Article 31E

(1) Resident entity taxpayer with gross income of Rp 50,000,000,000.00 (fifty billion rupiah) receives facilities in the form of reduction of the rate by 50% (fifty percent) of the rate as referred to in paragraph (1) subparagraph b and (2a) of Article 17 imposed on taxable income from the part of the gross revenue of Rp 4,800,000,000.00 (four billion eight hundred million rupiah).

(2) The amount of the gross revenue as referred to in paragraph (1) can be increased with the Minister of Finance Regulations.

Article 32

The procedure in relation to the imposition of tax and its penalties under this Law shall be governed by Law Number 6 Year 1983 on the General Provisions and Tax Procedures as lastly amended by Law Number 28 of 2007 on the Third Amendment of the Law No. 6 Year 1983 on the General Provisions and Tax Procedures.

Article 32A

The government is authorized to conclude an agreement with the government of foreign countries for the avoidance of double taxation and the prevention of tax evasion.

Article 32B

The provisions on the imposition of taxes on interest or discounts on the State Bond traded in other countries based on reciprocal treatment agreements with other countries is stipulated by the Government Regulations.

CHAPTER VIII   INTERIM PROVISIONS

Article 33

(1) A taxpayer whose accounting year is ended on the 30th of June, 1984, and those ended between the 30th of June, 1984 and the 31st of December, 1984 may elect Corporate Income Tax Ordinance of 1925 or Individual Income Tax Ordinance of 1944 or this Law in calculating its tax.

(2) Tax incentives that have been granted on or before December 31, 1983:

a. where the incentives extend to a certain period of time, the taxpayers can continue to enjoy such incentives until the time expired;

b. where the incentives do not have any time limit, they can be enjoyed up to taxable year before 1984 taxable year.

(3) Taxable income received or accrued from the oil or natural gas sector or other mining sectors in the form of a Contract of Work or a Production Sharing Contract that remains in force at the time this Law takes effect, shall be governed by Corporate Income Tax Ordinance of 1925 and the Tax Law on Interest, Dividends and Royalties of 1970 and their implementing regulations.

Article 33A

(1) Taxpayers whose accounting year ends after the 30th June, 1995 shall be obliged to calculate their taxes based on the provisions of Law Number 7 of 1983, as lastly amended by this Law.

(2) Taxpayers who have been granted tax incentives and have obtained a notification of the commencement of commercial production before the 1st January, 1995 may continue to enjoy the incentives in accordance with the time period stipulated therein.

(3) Except as provided in paragraph (2), any existing tax incentives previously granted shall cease to exist as of the 31st December, 1994.

(4) Income tax payable of taxpayers who conduct businesses in the oil, natural gas, and general mining sectors and other mining sectors under a Production Sharing Contract, Contract of Work, or other cooperation agreement that remains valid at the time this Law takes effect, shall be computed on the basis of the provisions contained in the Production Sharing Contract, Contract of Work, or cooperation agreement until the termination of the contract or agreement.

Article 34

As this Law takes effect, all implementing regulations related to income tax, shall remain valid provided that they are not contrary to the provisions of this Law.

CHAPTER IX   CLOSING PROVISIONS

Article 35

Matters that are not dealt with in this Law is further stipulated by the Government Regulations.

印度尼西亚共和国 1983 年第 7 号所得税法 2008 年第 36 号修正案

第一章　总则

第 1 条

在税收年度的收入方面，任何应纳税人员均应征税。

第二章　应纳税者

第 2 条

（1）纳税主体包括：

a. ①个人；

②任何作为整体而未分割给受益人的遗产；

b. 实体；

c. 常设机构。

（1a）常设机构系指为纳税目的被视为公司型纳税人的纳税主体。

（2）纳税主体由居民纳税人和非居民纳税人组成。

（3）"居民纳税人"指：

a. 在印尼居住的个人；任意 12 个月期间内，在印尼居留时间超过 183 天的个人；在特定课税年度居留在印尼并拟在印尼居住者；

b. 在印尼建立且住所位于印尼境内的实体，满足以下标准的部分政府机构除外：

①依照法律建立；

②资金来自国家预算或地方政府预算；

③其收益进入国家预算或地方政府预算；并且，

④账簿由政府审计人员进行审计。

c. 任何作为整体而未分割给受益人的遗产。

（4）"非居民纳税人"指：

a. 不在印尼居住，在任意 12 个月期间，在印尼居留时间不超过 183 天的个人；设立及场所均不在印尼，但经印尼常设机构开展业务或从事活动的实体。

b. 不在印尼居住，在任意 12 个月期间，在印尼居留时间不超过 183 天的个人，以及设立及场所均不在印尼的实体，即使不通过印尼常设机构开展业务或从事活动但从印尼获得收益者。

（5）常设机构是指不在印尼居住的，或在任意 12 个月期间，在印尼居留时间不超过 183 天的个人所使用的设施；或在印尼境外设立，（经营）场所不在印尼，但在印尼开展业务或从事活动的实体所使用的设施，可包括：

    a. 经营场所；

    b. 分部；

    c. 代表处；

    d. 办公室；

    e. 工厂；

    f. 车间；

    g. 库房；

    h. 促销和销售场所；

    i. 矿区和自然资源开采场所；

    j. 油气开采区；

    k. 渔场、牧场、农场、种植园或林场；

    l. 建设、安装或装配项目；

    m. 所有由雇员或其他任何人提供的在 12 个月期间超过 60 天的服务；

    n. 充当非独立代理人的个人或实体；

    o. 设立及经营场所均在印尼境外的保险公司的代理或雇员，但在印尼收取保险费或投保；

    p. 电子交易服务商所有、租赁或使用的通过互联网开展业务的电脑、电子媒介或自动化设备。

（6）个人住所或实体的正式地址应由税务局长根据实际情况加以规定。

第 2A 条

（1）第 2 条第（3）款 a 项所述的个人纳税义务的时间从个人出生、个人存在或个人有意在印尼居住始，至该个人去世或永久离开印尼止。

（2）第 2 条第（3）款 b 项所述的实体纳税义务的时间从实体设立或驻在印尼始，至该实体解散或撤离印尼止。

（3）第 2 条第（4）款 a 项所述的个人或实体，其纳税义务的时间从该个人或实体开始营业或开展业务（见第 2 条第 5 款）始，至通过常设机构开展的经营活动结束止。

（4）第 2 条第（4）款 b 项所述的个人或实体，其纳税义务的时间从该个人或实体从印尼获得收入始，至个人或实体不再取得该项收入止。

（5）第 2 条第（1）款 a 项第 2 点所述的未分割遗产，其纳税时间从该未分割遗产产生始，至该遗产被分割止。

（6）在印尼居住或居留的个人，如其纳税义务不足一个纳税年度的，以一个纳税年度计算。

第 3 条

第 2 条所述主体不包含以下各项：

a. 外国的办事处；

b. 使领馆官员或任何其他为使领馆工作的官员，前提是其非印尼公民，且其不接受工作职责以外的任何收入，且该待遇仅限于互惠的国家；

c. 国际组织，前提是：

①印尼为其成员之一；

②这些组织未开展业务或从事其他活动进而从印尼获取收益（为政府提供贷款除外，贷款的资金来自成员国的分摊额）；

d. c 项所述国际组织的官员和代表，前提是其非印尼公民并且未在印尼开展业务、从事活动进而从印尼获取收益。

第三章　征税对象

第 4 条

（1）征税对象为收益，该收益是指纳税人从印尼或海外获得的财力的增收，这些收益或用于消费，或增加了纳税人的财富（无论以何种名义和形式），其包括：

a. 由于雇佣关系或提供服务而获得的补偿或薪酬，包括工资、补贴、谢礼、佣金、奖金、小费、退休金或其他形式的薪酬，本法另有规定的除外；

b. 由于雇佣关系或其他活动而获得的诸如彩票奖金、礼品、奖励等；

c. 经营利润；

d. 出售或转让财产获得的收益，包括：

①通过向公司、合伙企业或其他实体出让财产以换取股票或资本认购而获取的收益；

②公司、合伙企业或其他实体通过向其股东、合伙人或成员出让财产而获取的收益；

③通过任何形式的清算、兼并、合并、扩张、分立、收购或重组而获取的收益；

④以授予、援助或捐赠形式转让财产而获得的收入，除非上述财产的受让方为直系亲属、宗教团体、教育或其他社会机构（包括基金会、合作社等），或经营微小企业的个人（经财政部部长许可），前提是上述各方不经营企业，也不存在雇佣关系、所有权或控制关系；

⑤通过出售或转让（部分或全部）开采权，参加矿业公司的融资或出资而获得的收益；

e. 退税或退税增加额；

f. 各种收益包括保险费、贴现、还贷保证补偿金；

g. 各种名义和形式的红利，包括保险公司付给保单持有人的红利和合作社派发的净收入；

h. 使用权的提成或补偿；

i. 产权使用获得的租金和其他收入；

j. 年金；

k. 从政府制定份额的债务免除中所获得的收益；

l. 外汇收益；

m. 财产升值收益；

n. 保险费；

o. 协会组织从其会员处获得的捐助，其会员为从事生意或独立服务的纳税人；

p. 来自未纳税收入的净财富的增长；

q. 来自伊斯兰教生意的收入；

r. 税法通则规定的补偿金；以及

s. 印度尼西亚银行盈余。

（2）以下收入应缴纳最终所得税：

a. 来自存款、其他储蓄、升息债券或国债的收入，或合作社向其个体成员支付的利息；

b. 彩票中奖收益；

c. 来自股票和其他证券交易的收入、外汇中的衍生交易收入、合作伙伴向风险投资公司出售股票或转让出资额而获取的收入；

d. 来自财产转让的收益，例如土地和/或建筑物、建筑服务企业、房地产业，或租赁土地和/或建筑物等获取的收益；以及

e. 政府法规规定的或基于政府法规的其他收入。

（3）非征税对象：

a. ①援助款或捐赠，包括阿米尔天课局或其他阿米尔天课机构（由政府建立或批准）接受的天课和其他适任的天课接受者所接受的天课，或向政府承认的宗教信徒、向政府设立或批准的宗教机构以及向政府规定的适任捐款接受人的义务捐赠；以及

②直系亲属接受的赠品，或宗教团体、教育及其他社会机构（包括基金会、合作社等）、经营微小企业的个人（经财政部部长规定许可的）所接受的赠品，前提是上述各方不经营企业，也没有雇佣关系、所有权或控制关系；

b. 遗产；

c. 实体因出售股票或资本认购而得到的包括现金在内的资产［见第2条第（1）款 b 项］；

d. 由于雇佣关系或提供服务而从纳税人或政府处获得的实物形式的对价或酬劳，从非纳税人、最终纳税人或使用核定利润的纳税人（见第15条）处获得的除外；

e. 保险公司向个人支付的有关健康、事故、人寿或教育保险的款项；

f. 在印尼设立和驻扎，因拥有所有权而获得红利或利润分配的企业，包括常驻有限公司、合作社、国有企业或地方政府所属企业，前提是：

①红利由存留收益支出；以及

②获得红利的有限公司，国有企业或地方企业至少拥有实缴资本的25%；

g. 雇主或雇员缴纳的注入退休基金的资金，该退休基金须由财政部部长批准；

h. 用 g 项所述的退休基金在财政部部长令规定的领域进行投资所得的收益；

i. 有限合伙制成员（包括集体投资协议的单位持有者）获得的利润分配，其资本不包含分摊、合伙、联合、商号及公司所得；

j. 已删除；

k. 风险投资公司以从合资企业（在印尼设立、开展业务并从事经营活动）利润分配的形式获取的收益，前提是：

①被注资企业为微、小、中型企业，或开展活动的行业在或基于财政部部长规章规定的领域内；以及

②被注资企业的股票不在印尼的股票交易所进行交易；

l. 满足财政部部长规定的某些要求的奖学金；

m. 已列入名单的相应的教育、科研和/或发展机构或非营利组织所接受或获得的盈余，按财政部部长规章规定，该盈余从接收起 4 年内须用来对教育、科研和/或发展等基础设施进行再投资；

n. 社会安全局向财政部部长规章规定的某一纳税人支付的资助或捐款。

第 5 条

（1）对常设机构的征税对象包括：

a. 其业务、经营活动或其拥有、掌控的财产所带来的收入；

b. 总部从与印尼常设机构从事的相似的业务、活动、销售或服务中获取的收益；

c. 总部获得的第 26 条所述的收益，前提是产生上述收益的财产或活动与常设机构密切相关。

（2）与第（1）款 b 项和 c 项所述的与总收入相关的费用可从常设机构的收益中扣除。

（3）在计算常设机构的利润上：

a. 总部为了常设机构而导致的管理费可按照税收总干事规定的限额扣除；

b. 下列支付给总部的款项不可扣除：

①由于使用财产、专利或其他权利而支付的提成或其他款项；

②管理服务或其他服务的支付款项；

③银行业务以外的利息；

c. 从总部获得的 b 项所述的款项不包括在征税对象中，银行业务中的利息除外。

第 6 条

（1）居民纳税人或常设机构有权以费用的名义索取扣税额以从其总收益中获取和保证收入，其包括：

a. 与业务直接或间接相关的费用，其包括：

①原材料费用；

②雇用或服务成本，包括各种货币形式的工资、谢礼、奖金、小费及薪酬；

③利息、租金和提成；

④差旅费；

⑤垃圾处理费；

⑥保险费；

⑦基于财政部部长规章规定的广告及销售费用；

⑧管理费；

⑨税费和其他所得税；

b. 有形资产的折旧、权利的分期偿还和其他第 11 条及第 11A 条所述的有效使用期为 1 年以上的其他支出；

c. 对经财政部部长批准设立的养老基金的资助；

d. 由销售或财产转让导致的损失，上述财产在业务中拥有和使用或用来获取和保障收益之用；

e. 外汇交易损失；

f. 与在印尼实施的研究与发展（项目）相关的费用；

g. 奖学金、学徒费和培训费用；

h. 不可回收债务，前提是：

①债务已在商业利润和亏损报表中勾销；

②纳税人应向税务总干事提交坏账清单；

③该案已起诉至法院或负责国家应收账款的政府部门，或债务人和债权人已签署书面协议同意解除债务，或已在媒体中公示，或债权人声明部分坏账已经注销；

④第 3 点所述的要求不适用于第 4 条第（1）款 k 项中规定的小型债务人，其办理程序应由财政部部长规章进行规定；

i. 由政府规章规定的国难捐款；

j. 由政府规章规定的对在印尼进行的研发捐款；

k. 由政府规章规定的社会基础设施建设费用；

l. 由政府规章规定的教育设施形式的捐款；

m. 由政府规章规定的用于体育改进的捐款。

（2）在从总收益中减去第（1）款所述的扣除额后，招致的亏损应最多不超过连续 5 年。

（3）作为居民纳税人的个人有权索求个人免税（见第 7 条）。

第 7 条

（1）个人免税额如下：

a. 个人纳税者为 15 840 000.00 卢比；

b. 已婚纳税人追加 1 320 000.00 卢比；

c. 如夫妇二人联合报税［见第 8 条第（1）款］，则已婚纳税人的配偶可追加 15 840 000.00 卢比；

d. 对于直系血缘或姻亲，每位家属可追加 1 320 000.00 卢比；收养一个儿童，最多可带三位家属。

（2）第（1）款的应用基于纳税年度起始或纳税年度之中的现实情况。

（3）在与众议院协商后，财政部部长应对个人免税的调整情况进行规定。

第 8 条

（1）已婚妇女在纳税年度起始或纳税年度之中的收入或亏损，包括来自上一年度未抵消的亏损［见第 6 条第（2）款］，应被视为其丈夫的收入或亏损，除非该项收入均从唯一的雇主处获取，并已按第 21 条从其处预提所得税，且此雇佣关系与其丈夫或亲属的生意或独立的个人服务无关；

（2）下列情况下，已婚个人的收入应单独纳税：

a. 根据法院判决，二人分开居住；

b. 夫妇二人在协定的基础上书面申请分离财产和收入；

c. 妻子选择独自行使纳税权利和义务。

（3）在对已婚个人［见第（2）款 b 项和 c 项］的净收入征税时，应对夫妻二人净收入总和进行征税，二人的纳税额按其各自净收入之比例缴纳。

（4）未成年人的收入应计入父母的收入中。

第 9 条

（1）在确定居民纳税人和常设机构的应纳税收入时，下列各项不可扣除：

a. 任何名义或形式的利润分配，例如股息（包括保险公司付给投保人的红利）、合作社的盈余分配等；

b. 为股东、合伙人或会员的个人利益而收取或产生的费用；

c. 储备金的形成和累积，除非：

①银行或其他机构的坏账储备金，其他机构包括债权人、金融租赁公司、小额贷款公司和代收公司等；

②保险企业的储备金，包括社会保障局用于社会援助的储备金；

③存款担保机构的保障储备金；

④矿业开发费用储备金；

⑤林业企业重新造林费用储备金；

⑥工业垃圾处理企业用于维护和关闭工业垃圾处理站的储备金，其条款和情况应为或基于财政部长规定；

d. 个人纳税人支付的针对健康、事故、人寿或双重目的的保险费以及教育保险等，除非上述费用由雇主支付（此种情况下，上述费用视为纳税人的收入）；

e. 实物形式的对价或薪酬，其中雇员的食物和饮料供应或与财政部部长规章规定的雇佣关系相关的某些行业的实物薪酬除外；

f. 作为工作回报的付给股东或其他相关方的超量的补偿；

g. 礼品、资助、捐赠和遗产，见第 4 条第（3）款 a 项和 b 项，但不包括第 6 条第（1）款 i 项到 m 项下的捐赠，以及阿米尔天课，局或其他阿米尔天课机构（由政府建立或批准）接受的天课，或捐给政府承认的宗教之信徒的强制性宗教捐款（由政府设立或批准的宗教机构接收）；

h. 所得税；

i. 因纳税人或其亲属个人利益产生的费用；

j. 付给协会、商号或资本金中不包含股票的有限合伙制企业的成员的工资；

k. 利息、罚款或附加费等形式的行政处罚以及依照税法对刑事处罚实施的罚款。

（2）为获取和保障有效年限在一年以上的收入而导致的支出不可征税，但应通过折旧或分期支付的方式扣除（见第 11 条和第 11A 条）。

第 10 条

（1）公平交易中的购置成本或售价［见第 18 条第（4）款］应为实付或实收金额；反之，如果是相关纳税人之间进行交易，则采用实际应付或应收的金额。

（2）资产交换中的购置价值或售价的金额应为基于市场价的实收或实付金额。

（3）在企业清算、兼并、分拆、分立或收购中的被转移资产的购置价值或转移价值的金额应为基于市场价格的实收或实付金额，财政部部长另有规定的除外。

（4）如果资产的转让：

a. 满足第 4 条第（3）款 a 项和 b 项，则受让人手中的资产以出让人手中的账面价值或税务总干事确定的价值为基础；

b. 未满足第 4 条第（3）款 a 项，则受让人手中的资产以该资产的市场价为基础。

（5）若出现第 4 条第（3）款 c 项所述的资产转让，则受让人手中的被转让资产以该资产的市场价为基础。

（6）以计算已售货物的成本为目的的库存或库存的使用，使用加权平均成本或先进先出法对其进行计价。

第 11 条

（1）在购买、安装、扩展、改进或代替有形资产费用方面的折扣应在资产规定的有效使用期内采用直线折旧法，但不包括有所有权、建筑权、耕作权及使用权的土地，这些土地是用来获得和保障有效年限在一年以上的收益。

（2）除了建筑物外，有关第（1）款所述的有形资产的折旧也可针对资产有效使用期采用余额递减折旧法，方法是把折旧率应用在账面价值上，在有效使用期快结束时，账面价值的剩余部分应全部折旧，前提是坚持使用该办法。

（3）折旧从开始出现支出的月份算起，如资产仍处于使用中，则其折旧从使用结束的月份开始计算。

（4）在税务总干事许可的情况下，纳税人可在资产被用于获取和保障收入的月份之初要求折旧，或资产开始产生收益月份之初进行折旧。

（5）如纳税人对资产重新估价（见第 19 条），则资产折旧以重新估价后得出的价值为基础。

（6）为计算折旧计，有形资产的有效年限和折旧率如下：

有形资产组	有效年限	折旧率	
		第 1 款	第 2 款
1. 非建筑物类			
第 1 组	4 年	25%	50%
第 2 组	8 年	12.5%	25%
第 3 组	16 年	6.25%	12.5%
第 4 组	20 年	5%	10%
2. 建筑物类			
永久型	20 年	5%	
非永久型	10 年	10%	

（7）对在某些领域拥有和使用的有形资产折旧的进一步管控，由财政部部长规章加以规定。

（8）如资产发生转移或如第 4 条第（1）款 d 项所述的撤出，或因其他原因撤出，则资产的剩余账面价值应作为亏损进行扣除，所收取的售价或保险费应视为资产撤离年度的收益。

（9）如保险费只能在稍后日期确定，则经税务总干事的批准，亏损金额［见第（8）款］应在稍后日期扣除。

（10）如有形资产的转让合乎第 4 条第（3）款 a 项和 b 项，则资产的剩余账面价值可不视为出让方的亏损。

（11）对与有形资产分类（按有效年限）相关的进一步管控，由财政部部长规章加以规定。

第 11A 条

（1）与获得无形资产的费用相关的摊销，或与有效年限在一年以上并用于获取和保障收益的其他费用，诸如扩建权、耕作权、使用权以及商誉等相关的摊销，应通过将摊销率运用于成本或账面价值以直线法或余额递减法进行计算。在有效使用年限届满时，剩余账面价值应足额摊销，前提是坚持使用上述办法。

（1a）摊销应从产生支出的月份算起，财政部部长规章加以规定的某些业务除外。

（2）为对摊销进行计算，有效使用期和摊销率如下：

无形资产组	有效年限	摊销率	
		直线法	余额递减法
第 1 组	4 年	25%	50%
第 2 组	8 年	12.5%	25%
第 3 组	16 年	6.25%	12.5%
第 4 组	20 年	5%	10%

（3）在实体成立或资本扩张前产生的支出应在支出产生的当年扣除或摊销［见第（2）款］。

（4）为获取权利的费用或在油气工业上有效年限超过一年的其他费用在摊销时应采用工作量法进行计算。

（5）对为获取第（4）款下以外的开采权、林地特许权以及自然资源和其他天然产物的开发权（有效年限在一年以上）而导致的支出的摊销应采用工作量法进行计算，每年最多20%。

（6）商业运营之前产生的费用，且有效年限超过一年的，应资本化并按第（2）款进行摊销。

（7）如转让无形资产或第（1）、（4）、（5）款下的权利，则此资产或权利的账面价值应作为亏损扣除，收到的款项应视为资产转移年度的收入。

（8）如符合第4条第（3）款a项和b项的无形资产发生转移，则此资产的账面价值应视为出让人的亏损。

第12条

已删除。

第13条

已删除。

第14条

（1）决定净收入的核定利润应不时进行规划和调整，由税务总干事发布。

（2）从事经营活动或提供个人服务获取的年度总收入少于4 800 000 000.00卢比的个体纳税人，可运用上述核定利润计算其净收入，前提是在相关纳税年度的前3个月和税务总干事进行沟通。

（3）使用核定利润计算其净收入［见第（2）款］的纳税人应做好税法通则所要求的记录。

（4）未能通知税务总干事采用核定利润［见第（2）款］的纳税人将被视为选择了记账（方式）。

（5）必须作账或做记录的纳税人，包括第（3）款和第（4）款所述的纳税人，如果未能作账或做记录，或未能完整地作账或做记录，或未能披露账目、记录或支持性证据，在此种情况下，净收入将采用核定利润计算，总收入将按财政部部长规章规定的依据进行计算。

（6）已删除。

（7）第（2）款所述的总收入的金额可由财政部部长规章加以调整。

第15条

如纳税人的收入不能采用第16条第（1）款或第（3）款的规定进行计算，则由财政部部长确定特种核定利润对其净收入进行计算。

第四章　计税方法

第 16 条

（1）纳税人在纳税年度的应纳税收入应为第 4 条第（1）款所述的收入减去免税的部分［见第 6 条第（1）款和第（2）款，第 7 条第（1）款及第 9 条第（1）款 c、d、e、g 项］。

（2）第 14 条所述的纳税人的应纳税收入应采用该条规定的核定利润进行计算，如为个体纳税人，则采用核定利润计算的金额要扣除个人免税额［见第 7 条第（1）款］。

（3）通过在印尼的常设机构从事经营或开展活动的非居民纳税人在纳税年度的应纳税金额应为第 5 条第（1）款所述的关于第 4 条第（1）款的收入减去免税部分［见第 5 条第（2）款和第（3）款，第 6 条第（1）款和第（2）款，以及第 9 条第（1）款 c、d、e、g 项］。

（4）如个体居民纳税人的纳税义务仅涵盖纳税年度的一部分［见第 2A 条第（6）款］，则其应纳税收入计算方式为：（实际）净收入 ×（实际）时间长度 = 全年净收入。

第 17 条

（1）适用于各种应纳税收入级次的税率如下：

a. 个体居民纳税人：

应纳税收入级次	税率
50 000 000.00 卢比及以下	5%
50 000 000.00 卢比以上至 250 000 000.00 卢比	15%
250 000 000.00 卢比以上至 500 000 000.00 卢比	25%
500 000 000.00 卢比及以上	30%

b. 适用于作为居民纳税人的实体和常设机构的税率为 28%。

（2）最高税率［见第（1）款 a 项］可减降，但按政府规定不得低于 25%。

（2a）第（1）款 b 项所述的税率从纳税年度 2010 年开始变为 25%。

（2b）作为居民纳税人的实体和上市公司（至少 40% 的实缴资本在印尼股票交易所进行交易并满足其他要求）可按政府规定享受比第（1）款 b 项和第（2a）款所述的税率低 5% 的税率。

（2c）适用于个体居民纳税人所得股息的税率最高为 10% 并视为最终税率。

（2d）有关第（2c）款所述税率的进一步监管由政府法规加以规定。

（3）应纳税收入税级的金额［见第（1）款 a 项］可由财政部部长令进行调整。

（4）为实施第（1）款所述税率，应纳税收入的金额以千为单位进行四舍五入。

（5）如个体居民纳税人的纳税义务仅涵盖纳税年度的一部分［见第 16 条第（4）款］，则其应缴税款＝实际天数÷360×全年的应缴税款额。

（6）就应纳税款［见第（5）款］的计算而言，一个月被视为 30 天。

（7）在不超过最高边际税率［见第（1）款］的前提下，根据政府规定可对第 4 条第（2）款所述收入实行特殊税率。

第 18 条

（1）为依照本法计算应缴税款，财政部部长有权发布针对负债与产权比率的规定。

（2）财政部部长有权决定居民纳税人在投资海外公司（非上市公司）时获取红利的具体时间，前提是满足下列条件之一：

a. 纳税人拥有该公司至少 50% 的实缴资本；或，

b. 纳税人和其他居民纳税人共同拥有该公司至少 50% 的实缴资本。

（3）税务总干事有权重新分派相关方的收入和扣除额，并为了计算应纳税收入，把债务描述成权益，目的是通过运用价格比较法、转售价格法、成本加成法和其他方法确保交易在独立各方之间达成。

（3a）税务总干事有权就相关纳税人［见第（4）款］之间的转让定价法与纳税人和外国税务机关签订协议，该方法可持续一段时间，当协议期满后，有权对其进行评估以及重新进行协商。

（3b）通过特殊目的公司购买其他实体的股票或资产的纳税人可视为从事该项交易的真正方，前提是该纳税人是该特殊目的公司的关联方，且交易定价不合理。

（3c）在避税港国家设立或驻在的中介公司或特殊目的公司之股份的出售或转让，如该中介公司或特殊目的公司附属于某个在印尼设立或驻在的实体或位于印尼的常设机构，应被视为在印尼设立或驻在的实体或位于印尼的常设机构的股份之出售或转让。

（3d）个体居民纳税人从雇主（非居民实体的关联方）处获得的收入总额可由税务机关进行核算，以防雇主以费用或支出的形式向其关联方转移款项。

（3e）第（3b）款、第（3c）款和第（3d）款之规定的执行由财政部长规章加以规范。

（4）"相关纳税人"［见第（3）款至第（3d）款、第 9 条第（1）款 f 项以及第 10 条第（1）款］是指：

a. 直接或间接拥有其他纳税人至少 25% 股权的纳税人，纳税人拥有两个或两个以上纳税人至少 25% 股权以及两个或两个以上相关纳税人之间的关系；

b. 控制其他纳税人的纳税人，或两个（或两个以上）的纳税人间接或直接地处于同样的控制之下；

c. 一代以内的直系或非直系的由血缘或姻亲建立的家庭关系。

（5）已删除。

第 19 条

（1）当支出和收入的要素因通货膨胀而变得不适宜时，财政部部长有权就资产的重新评估和调整系数问题发布规定。

（2）根据财政部部长规章，在不超过第 17 条第（1）款所述的税率的情况下，应针对资产法定升值后的超额价值运用某种税率。

第五章　本年度税款

第 20 条

（1）任何纳税年度的应缴所得税款应通过纳税人自己或经别人预提付讫。

（2）第（1）款所述的税款应按月支付或按财政部部长规定的时限支付。

（3）第（1）款所述的税款应视为分期缴税，可抵免相关纳税年度年终时的所得税款，某些适用最终税款的收入除外。

第 21 条

（1）下列各方有义务就个体居民纳税人因雇佣关系、提供服务或从事任何其他活动所接受的或获取的任何形式的薪酬预提税款：

a. 向终身员工或者临时员工因雇佣关系而支付工资、谢礼、津贴或其他类似的薪酬的雇主；

b. 因雇佣关系、提供服务或从事任何其他活动而支付工资、谢礼、津贴或其他类似的薪酬的政府财务主管；

c. 鉴于以前的雇佣关系以不同形式支付养老金或其他类似薪酬的退休基金或其他实体；以及

d. 就所接受的服务（包括专业服务或其他独立性的活动）支付谢礼或其他类似薪酬的实体；

e. 组织活动并就与之相关的服务支付薪酬的个人。

（2）尽管存在上述规定，外交机构或国际组织（见第 3 条）无须预提税款〔见第（1）款 a 项〕。

（3）终身员工或退休人员获得的税后收入额应为总收入扣除正式支出或退休金支出，以上支出由财政部部长规章、退休金缴纳额和个人免税额所决定。

（4）日薪者、周薪者或其他临时员工获得的税后收入额应为总收入扣除免预提税的收入（由财政部部长规章确定）。

（5）适用于第（1）款所述的收入的税率应为第 17 条第（1）款 a 项下的税率，除非政府另有规定。

（5a）对未经注册的居民纳税人来说，第（5）款所适用的税率要比注册的居民纳税人高 20%。

（6）已删除。

（7）已删除。

（8）关于税款预提（针对因雇佣关系、服务或活动而导致的收入而言）的指导方针应由财政部部长规章加以规定。

第 22 条

（1）财政部部长可指派：

a. 政府财务主管就物资提供的支付款征收预提税；以及

b. 某些实体向从事进口业务或其他业务活动的纳税人征收预提税；

c. 某些实体向购买奢侈品的纳税人征收预提税。

（2）有关预提税税基、标准、特点以及金额［见第（1）款］的规定应由财政部部长规章加以确定。

（3）对未经注册的居民纳税人来说，第（2）款所述的预提税率要比注册的居民纳税人高 100%。

第 23 条

（1）由政府机关、居民型纳税实体、活动组织者、常设机构或任何其他非居民实体的代表向居民纳税人或常设机构支付、分摊支付的，或已到支付期的无论何种名义或形式的收入均应按下列比例缴纳所得税：

a. 以下各项总金额的 15%：

①红利［见第 4 条第（1）款 g 项］；

②利息［见第 4 条第（1）款 f 项］；

③版税；以及

④奖励、奖品、奖金和类似款项［第 21 条第（1）款 e 项下已预提税款的除外］；

b. 已删除；

c. 以下各项总金额的 2%：

①租金和与财物使用有关的其他收入［不包括第 4 条第（2）款下的与使用财物有关的租金和其他收入，这些收入已进行税款预提］；

②与技术、管理、施工、咨询和其他服务有关的补偿金，按第 21 条规定已进行税款预提的除外。

（1a）对未经注册的居民纳税人来说，第（1）款所述的预提税率要比注册的居民纳税人高 100%。

（2）第（1）款 c 项第②点所述的其他服务，由财政部部长规章进行进一步规定。

（3）税务总干事可指定个人居民纳税人作为扣缴义务人［见第（1）款］。

（4）第（1）款所述的预提税率不适合下列情况：

a. 已付的或拖欠银行的所得；

b. 金融租赁协议中的租金；

c. 红利收入［见第 4 条第（3）款 f 项］和个体纳税人获得的红利［见第 17 条第（2c）款］；

d. 已删除；

e. 分派利润［见第 4 条第（3）款 i 项］；

f. 合作社分配给成员的利润；

g. 已删除；以及

h. 已付或应付给金融中介机构的收益，该机构受财政部部长规章指定从事贷款中介和/或融资业务。

第 24 条

（1）居民纳税人针对海外收入已在外国缴纳的或应缴的税款可在同一纳税年度抵免其按本法的应缴税款。

（2）第（1）款中所述的免税额应与外国税金额相等，但不得超过按本法计算的应缴税款。

（3）在计算纳税抵免限额时，按以下规定确定收入来源：

a. 来自股票和其他债券的收入及股权交易的资本收益，其来源为发行公司所在的国家；

b. 因使用动产而获得的利息、提成或租金形式的收入，其来源为纳税人或从中索要扣除额一方所在之国家；以及

c. 与使用不动产相关的租金收入，其来源为该不动产所在国；

d. 因服务、雇用和其他活动而获得的补偿金形式的收入，其来源为纳税人或从中索要扣除额一方所在之国家；

e. 常设机构的收入来源为常设机构开展业务或从事经营活动的国家；

f. 因转让部分或全部采矿权或因参与矿业公司融资和投资而获得的收入，其来源为矿区所在地；

g. 因转让不动产而获取的收益，其来源为该不动产所在国家；以及

h. 因转让属于常设机构一部分的资产而获取的收益，其来源为常设机构所在国。

（4）除第（3）款规定以外的其他收益，应采用相同的原则确定其来源。

（5）针对海外收入进行抵免的外国税收，如在后期产生减降或退税，则按本法，其应缴税额须补入上述产生减降或退税年度之税额中；

（6）在海外收入方面的税额抵免，其具体执行应由财政部部长规章进行规定。

第 25 条

（1）在当前纳税年度期间纳税人须按月缴纳的税额应与按上一年度的纳税单的应缴税额相等，并扣除下列各项：

a. 根据第 21 条和第 23 条规定扣除的所得税，根据第 22 条规定征收的所得税；以及

b. 按照第 24 条规定可作为抵免的已付或应付的外国纳税，除以纳税年度的 12 个月或实际月数。

（2）在规定的纳税申报提交日期之前的按月分期纳税额应与上一纳税年度最后月份的纳税额相等。

（3）已删除。

（4）如在当前纳税年度期间发出了上一年度的评税通知书，则按月分期纳税额应根据该通知书重新核算，并从发出通知的下一个月开始计算。

（5）已删除。

（6）税收总干事有权就下列情况规定本年度按月纳税的计算方式：

a. 纳税人有权结转亏损；

b. 纳税人获得的是不定期收入；

c. 上一年度的纳税单逾期申报；

d. 准许纳税人延期申报年度纳税；

e. 因纳税人主动修改纳税申报单而导致按月纳税额多于修改前的按月纳税额；以及

f. 纳税人业务或活动发生变化。

（7）财政部部长确定以下分期纳税额的计算：

a. 新纳税人；

b. 银行、国有企业、地方企业、上市公司和按照现行法律规定须定期制作财务报表的其他纳税人；

c. 作为雇主的个体纳税人，其税率不超过总收入的 0.75%。

（8）21 岁或以上的没有纳税身份编号或旅居国外的个体居民纳税人应按政府之规定纳税。

（8a）第 8 款之规定至 2010 年 12 月 31 日前有效。

（9）已删除。

第 26 条

（1）由政府机关、居民型纳税实体、活动组织者、常设机构或任何非居民型公司的代表向除常设机构以外的非居民纳税人支付的、分摊支付的或已到支付期的无论何种名义或形式的收入均应缴纳占总收入 20% 的预提税，包括以下

a. 股息；

b. 包括保险费的利息、折扣、偿还贷款保证金；

c. 提成费、租金或其他与财产使用有关的收入；

d. 与服务、工作或活动相关的补偿金；

e. 奖品与奖项；

f. 退休金及其他定期付款；

g. 公平保费和其他套头交易；和/或

h. 来自解除债务的收益。

（1a）除通过在印尼的常设机构开展业务的外国纳税人以外的外国纳税人之居住国指纳税人的所在国家或居住地，在此地该纳税人从该收入中获得利益（实益拥有人）。

（2）除印尼常设机构外的非居民纳税人所获得的除第 4 条第（2）款规定外的来自资产出售或转让的收益，或向外国保险公司支付的保险费，应收取核定利润的 20% 作为预提税。

（2a）第 18 条第（3c）款所述的出售或转让股份所获得的收益应收取预计净收入的 20% 作为预提税。

（3）第（2）款和第（2a）款之规定的执行由财政部部长规章加以规定。

（4）印尼的常设机构的应纳税收入，在扣除所得税后，应缴纳 20% 的税款，除非该利润重新投资于印尼，具体事宜由财政部部长规章进一步加以规定。

（5）除以下情况外，第（1）款、第（2）款、第（2a）款及第（4）款所述的预提税视为最终纳税：

a. 第 5 条第（1）款 b 项和 c 项下所述收入的预提税；以及

b. 针对已经转变为居民纳税人或常设机构的非居民个人或非居民公司所收到或获取的收入所征收的预提税。

第 27 条

已删除。

第六章　年终税收之计算

第 28 条

（1）居民纳税人和常设机构有权针对同一纳税年度的应缴税额请求抵免：

a. 按第 21 条规定的针对出自雇用、个人服务或活动的收入征收的预提税；

b. 按第 22 条规定的针对源自进口活动或其他业务付款而得到的收入征收的预提税；

c. 对第 23 条所述的红利、利息、版税、租金、礼物、奖励和服务补偿金征收的预提税；

d. 第 24 条所述的可用于抵免的针对海外收入的已付或应付的纳税额；

e. 第 25 条所述的在当前纳税年度期间的自付税款；

f. 第 26 条第（5）款所述的收入征收的预提税。

（2）以权益、罚款或追加罚款形式进行的行政处罚或按现行法规采用罚款形式的刑事处罚不可抵免应缴税款［见第（1）款］。

第 28A 条

如纳税年度的应缴税款低于第 28 条第（1）款所述的税收抵免额，则在进行税收审计后，超出的部分在冲销未付的税款和处罚后（如有），应返给纳税人。

第 29 条

如纳税年度的应缴税款高于第 28 条第（1）款所述的税收抵免额，则所欠税款应在提交年度纳税单之前即行支付。

第 30 条

已删除。

第 31 条

已删除。

第七章　其他规定

第 31A 条

（1）投资于国家重点行业和/或地区的纳税人可享受如下税收优惠：

a. 最高 30% 的投资补贴；

b. 加速折旧和摊销；

c. 可延长亏损年限，但不得超过 10 年；以及

d. 对第 26 条所述的红利征收 10% 的所得税，但根据相关税收协定，税率更低的除外。

（2）对第（1）款所述的国家重点行业和/或地区以及税收优惠政策由政府法规作进一步规定。

第 31B 条

已删除。

第 31C 条

（1）来自个体居民纳税人的税赋和第 21 条中雇主代为扣缴的所得税，其中 80% 收归中央政府，20% 收归纳税人注册地所在的地方政府。

（2）已删除。

第 31D 条

对于油气、地热，包括采煤在内的采矿类企业以及基于伊斯兰教规的企业，其税收条款由政府法规进行规定。

第 31E 条

（1）总收入达 50 000 000 000.00 卢比的常驻实体纳税人可享受第 17 条第（1）款 b 项和第（2a）款所规定的对总收入中的 4 800 000 000.00 卢比所征收的应税收入额的 50% 的减税优惠。

（2）第（1）款所述的总收入的金额可根据财政部部长规章加以提高。

第 32 条

本法下的征税及处罚规定，其程序遵从 1983 年颁布的关于税收总则和税收程序的第 6 号法令，该法令前次经由 2007 年第 28 号法令进行修改，合并成为第三次修正案。

第 32A 条

政府有权和外国政府签订协议，以避免双重征税和防止逃税。

第 32B 条

针对基于国家间的互惠协议而在其他国家进行交易的国家债券之利息和贴现的征税条

款由政府法规进行规定。

第八章　过渡条款

第 33 条

（1）会计年度截止日期在 1984 年 6 月 30 日或在 1984 年 6 月 30 日和 1984 年 12 月 31 日之间的纳税人，在计算税款时，可选择遵从 1925 年企业所得税条例，或 1944 年个人所得税条例，或者本法。

（2）1983 年 12 月 31 日当天或之前允准的税收激励政策：

a. 激励政策延长至某一时间段的，则纳税人可继续享受该政策，直至届满；

b. 激励政策无时间限制的，则在 1984 年纳税年度前，纳税人可一直享受该政策。

（3）石油天然气行业或其他开采性行业以作业合同或产量分成合同形式接受的或获取的应纳税收入，如在本法开始生效时，上述合同仍然处于有效期，则其应纳税收入应遵从 1925 年颁布的企业所得税条例和 1970 年颁布的利息、红利和特许权使用费税法及相关的执行规定。

第 33A 条

（1）会计年度在 1995 年 6 月 30 日后截止的纳税人，应按照经本法修正的 1983 年第 7 号令之规定计算所得税。

（2）获准税收优惠的纳税人，如在 1995 年 1 月 1 日前获得可以启动商业生产的通知，可按当时规定的时限继续享受税收优惠。

（3）第（2）款规定以外的任何先前允准的税收优惠均截至 1994 年 12 月 31 日。

（4）如纳税人按照产量分成合同、作业合同或其他合作协议从事石油天然气业务、采矿业务或其他开采性行业，如在本法开始生效时，上述合同或协议仍然处于有效期，则其应付所得税应根据上述合同或协议中的规定进行计算，直至该合同或协议终止。

第 34 条

当本法生效时，所有与所得税相关的执行规定仍然有效，与本法之规定相矛盾的除外。

第九章　最终条款

第 35 条

本法未尽事宜由政府法规进一步加以规定。

CONSOLIDATION OF LAW OF INDONESIA NUMBER 8 YEAR 1983 CONCERNING VALUE ADDED TAX AS LASTLY AMENDED BY LAW NUMBER 18 YEAR 2000

CHAPTER I   GENERAL PROVISION

Article 1

In this Law the meaning of:

1. Customs Area is the territory of the Republic of Indonesia, which covers land, sea, and air as well as specific areas within the Exclusive Economic Zone and the Continental Shelf within which Law Number 10, Year 1995 on Customs apply.

2. Goods are tangible Goods, which according to their nature and legal status are movable or immovable Goods, and intangible assets.

3. Taxable Goods are Goods referred to in point 2, which are subject to tax according to this Law.

4. Supply of Taxable Goods is any business activity of supplying Taxable Goods referred to in point 3.

5. Services are any service activities under a contractual agreement or legal arrangement which makes available for using Goods, facilities or rights, including Services provided on order or request, for which the material is provided by the customer.

6. Taxable Services are a service referred to in point 5, which are subject to tax according to this Law.

7. Rendering of Taxable Service is any activity to provide a Taxable Service referred to in point 6.

8. Utilization of Taxable Service from outside the Customs Area is any activity of Utilization of Taxable Service obtained from outside the Customs Area within the Customs Area.

9. Import is entry of Goods into the Customs Area.

10. Utilization of intangible Taxable Goods from outside the Customs Area is any activity of utilization of intangible Taxable Goods obtained from outside the Customs Area by an arrangement within the Customs Area.

11. Export is exit of Goods outside the Customs Area.

12. Trade is any business activity to buy and sell, including barter of Goods without changing their form or nature.

13. Entity is a group of individual and/or capital as a union, whether conducts business activities or not, covering a limited company, partnership, other partnership, a state-owned enterprise or company owned by a regional government in whatever name and form, "firma", "kongsi", "cooperative", permanent establishment, foundation or such kind of organizations, institutes and other business forms.

14. Firm is an individual or an Entity referred to in point 13, which in the course of business or work, produces Goods, imports Goods, exports Goods, engages in trading activities, utilizes intangible Goods obtained from outside the Customs Area, provides business Services or utilities Services obtained from outside the Customs Area.

15. Taxable Person for VAT (Value Added Tax) Purposes is a Firm referred to in point 14 which supplies Taxable Goods and or renders Taxable Services which are subject to tax according to this Law, excluding small Firms with a turnover not exceeding a limit determined by the Minister of Finance Decree, but including small Firms which choose to be confirmed as Taxable Person for VAT Purposes.

16. Manufacture is an activity which changes the form or nature of Goods to become new Goods, or to obtain new uses from the Goods, or an activity to process natural resources, including having another individual or Entity carried out the Manufacture.

17. Tax Base is the Sales Price or Consideration, or Import Value or Export Value, or such other value as may be determined by the Minister of Finance Decree, to be used as the basis for calculating tax payable.

18. Sales Price is the value in money, including all costs charged or which should be charged by a seller, on Supply of Taxable Goods, excluding tax withheld in accordance with this Law and any rebate which is written in the Tax Invoice.

19. Consideration is the value in money, including all costs charged or which should be charged by a Firm rendering a service, arising from the Rendering of a Taxable Service, excluding tax withheld in accordance with this Law and any rebate which is written in the Tax Invoice.

20. Import Value is the value in money, which forms the basis for calculating import duties plus other levies incurred under the Customs Regulations on the Import of Taxable Goods, excluding tax withheld in accordance with this Law.

21. Buyer is an individual, or an Entity, or government institution which receives or should receive a Supply of Taxable Goods and which pays or should pay the Taxable Goods.

22. Recipient of Services is an individual, or an Entity, or government institution which receives or should receive a Rendering of Taxable Services and which pays or should pay for the Taxable Services.

23. Tax Invoice is proof of tax withheld by a Taxable Person for VAT Purposes on Supply of

Taxable Goods, or Rendering of Taxable Services, or by the Directorate General of Customs and Excise on the importation of Taxable Goods.

24. Input Tax is Value Added Tax which should have been paid by a Taxable Person for VAT Purposes who obtains Taxable Goods, and/or Taxable Services, and/or the Utilization of intangible Taxable Goods obtained from outside the Customs Area, and/or the Utilization of Taxable Services obtained from outside the Customs Area, and/or the importation of Taxable Goods.

25. Output Tax is Value Added Tax payable withheld by a Taxable Person for VAT Purposes on a Supply of Taxable Goods, or Rendering of Taxable Services, or the exportation of Taxable Goods.

26. Export Value is the value in money, including all costs charged or should be charged by an exporter.

27. Withholding Agent of Value Added Tax is government treasurer, an Entity or government institution appointed by the Minister of Finance to withhold, deposit and report on the tax payable from a Taxable Person for VAT purposes arising from a Supply of Taxable Goods, and/or Rendering of Taxable Services to the Government Treasurer, Entity or government institution concerned.

Elucidation of Article 1

Sufficiently clear.

Article 1A

(1) The meaning of Supply of Taxable Goods shall include of the following:

a. transfer of title over Taxable Goods under the terms of an agreement;

b. Supply of Taxable Goods under a hire-purchase agreement or a leasing agreement;

c. Supply of Taxable Goods to an intermediate trader or to an auctioneer;

d. Taxable Goods for personal use and/or Taxable Goods provided free of charged;

e. Taxable Goods and assets originally acquired not for sale, which remain available at the time of dissolution of the company, provided Value Added Tax on the acquisition of such assets may be credited in accordance with the rule;

f. Supply of Taxable Goods from a head office to a branch or vice versa and Supply of Taxable Goods between branches;

g. Supply of Taxable Goods by consignment.

(2) The meaning of Supply of Taxable Goods shall exclude of the following:

a. Supply of Taxable Goods to a broker referred to in the Commercial Law;

b. Supply of Taxable Goods as collateral for loans;

c. Supply of Taxable Goods referred to in paragraph (1) subparagraph f where a Taxable Person for VAT Purposes has obtained permission to centralize payment of tax payable.

Elucidation of Article 1A

Paragraph (1)

Subparagraph a

According to this provision, agreements cover sales transaction, barter, purchase by installments, or other agreements which result in the transfer of rights over Goods.

Subparagraph b

A Supply of Taxable Goods may occur under a hire purchase or finance leasing agreement. A finance leasing agreement means a supply caused by a finance leasing agreement by a right of opts. Although a transfer of rights over Taxable Goods has not taken place and the payment of the Taxable Goods price is carried out in stages, because authority over the Taxable Goods has already moved from the seller to the Buyer or from the lesser to the lessee, this Law stipulates that a Supply of Taxable Goods is considered to occur at the time of signing the agreement, unless the time of de facto change authority over the Taxable Goods occurred prior to the signing of the agreement.

Subparagraph c

An intermediate trader is an individual or an Entity, which in the course of business activities or professional work in its own name, concludes an agreement or contract on behalf of another Firm and thereby obtains wages or compensation for Services, such as a commission. An auctioneer is a Government Auctioneer or one appointed by the Government.

Subparagraph d

Personal use means the use for the interest of one's own Firm, management or employees, whether self products or oneself products. Provision free of charge means without payment in return, whether self products or non-self products, including, among others, the provision of samples for promotional purposes to a contact or a Buyer.

Subparagraph e

Inventory of stock and assets, which according to their original purposes, are not intended to be traded, and which remain on the dissolution of a Firm are considered as being the sambas those for personal use, and are therefore considered as falling within a Supply of Taxable Goods.

Assets which, according to their original purposes are not for sale, are only subject to Value Added Tax if they fulfill a specific condition, namely that the Value Added Tax paid at the time the Goods are obtained may be credited.

Subparagraph f

In case a Firm has more than one place where tax is payable, namely the places where a Supply of Taxable Goods is made to another party, whether as a head office or as a branch office, this Law construes the movement of Taxable Goods between the places as constituting a Supply of Taxable Goods. A branch in this regulation is a business location, representative office, marketing unit and others of the same type.

225

Subparagraph g

Where a supply occurs as a consignment, the Value Added Tax paid at the time the Taxable Goods are handed over may be credited against Output Tax for the taxable period in which the Taxable Goods are consigned. If, however, the consigned Taxable Goods are not sold but are returned to their owner, the Firm which receives the consignment may use the provisions on return of Taxable Goods as contained in Article 4A of this Law.

Paragraph (2)

Subparagraph a

A broker in this Law means a broker in the Commercial Law, who is an intermediate trader appointed by the President or the government official authorized by the President. They run their company by conducting a business activity and thereby obtain wages or certain commission as payment, on mandate and behalf of other people which have no business relationship with the broker.

Subparagraph b

Sufficiently clear.

Subparagraph c

If a Taxable Person for VAT Purposes has more than one place of business, either has a head office or branches, and the Taxable Person for VAT Purposes has permission from the Director General of Taxes to centralize tax payable, the Supply of Taxable Goods from one place of business to another (from a branch to a head office and vice versa, or between branches) is not considered as a Supply of Taxable Goods, except where the Supply of Taxable Goods is between places where tax is payable.

CHAPTER II   TAXABLE PERSON

Article 2

(1) If the Sales Price or Consideration is influenced by special relationship, the Sales Price or Consideration shall be calculated on the basis of a fair market price at the time of a Supply of Taxable Goods or the Rendering of Taxable Services.

(2) A special relationship is deemed to exist:

a. where a Firm owns direct or indirect participation of 25% (twenty-five percent) or more in another Firm; likewise, between 2 (two) or more Firms where there is direct or indirect participation of 25% (twenty-five percent) in each of those Firms by another Firm; or

b. a Firm has control over another Firm, or two or more Firms are under the same control, whether directly or indirectly; or

c. there exists a family relationship either through blood-line or through marriage within one degree of direct or indirect lineage.

Elucidation of Article 2

Paragraph (1)

The influence of a special relationship as meant in this Law shall be the possibility of the price which is set below the market price. In such cases, the Director General of Taxes has the authority to adjust the Sales Price or Consideration which forms the Tax Base to a fair market price applying in a free market.

Paragraph (2)

A special relationship between a Taxable Person for VAT Purposes and a party receiving Supply of Taxable Goods and/or Rendering of Taxable Services may occur due to the dependency of one on the other because of:

—ownership or participation factors;

—the existence of influence through management or technology.

Apart from the above, a special relationship between individual persons may result from a relationship through blood or marriage.

Subparagraph a

A special relationship is considered to exist if there is an ownership relationship in the form of capital participation of 25% (twenty-five percent) or more, either directly or indirectly. Example: If PT A owns 50% (fifty percent) of the shares of PT B, the share ownership of PT A constitutes direct participation. At the same time, if PT B owns 50% (fifty percent) of the shares in PT C, then PT A as a shareholder in PT B has an indirect participation in PT C for 25% (twenty-five percent). Because of this, a special relationship is considered to exist between PT A, PT B and PT C. If PT A also has a 25% (twenty-five percent) shareholding in PT D, a special relationship is also considered to exist between PT B, PT C and PT D. Such ownership relationships may also occur between individuals and entities.

Subparagraph b

A relationship as described in subparagraph a may also occur because of control through management or the use of technology, without regard to the existing of ownership relationship. A special relationship is considered to exist if one or more companies are under control of the same Firm. It also applies to the relationship between the several companies which are under the authority in those mentioned similar Firm.

Subparagraph c

The meaning of blood relationships in direct lineage of one degree are father, mother and child, while blood relationships in indirect lineage of one degree are brothers and sisters. The meaning of relationship through marriage in direct lineage of one degree are parents-in-law and step-children, while relationships in marriage in indirect lineage of one degree are brothers-in-law and sisters-in-law. If, between husband and wife, there is an agreement for the separation of assets and income, a special relationship is construed to exist between the husband and wife under this Law.

CHAPTER II CONFIRMATION OF TAXABLE PERSON FOR VAT PURPOSES

Article 3

Deleted.

Elucidation of Article 3

Deleted.

CHAPTER IIA THE OBLIGATION ON A TAXABLE PERSON TO REPORT HIS BUSINESS ACTIVITIES AND THE DUTY TO WITHHOLD, DEPOSIT, AND REPORT TAX PAYABLE

Article 3A

(1) A Firm making a supply referred to in subparagraph a, c, or f of Article 4 shall be obliged to report its business activities to be registered as a Taxable Person for VAT Purposes and to withhold, deposit and report Value Added Tax and Sales Tax on Luxury Goods which is payable.

(2) A small Firm which chooses to be confirmed as a Taxable Person for VAT Purposes shall be required to carry out the obligation referred to in paragraph (1).

(3) An individual or Entity utilizing intangible Taxable Goods obtained from outside the Customs Area referred to in subparagraph d of Article 4 and or utilizing Taxable Services obtained from outside the Customs Area referred to in subparagraph e of Article 4, shall be obliged to withhold, deposit and report Value Added Tax payable, and the method and procedures shall be determined by the Minister of Finance Decree.

Elucidation of Article 3A

Paragraph (1)

A Firm which supplies Taxable Goods, and/or renders Taxable Services within the Customs Area, and/or exports Taxable Goods is obliged to:

a. report its business activities to be confirmed as a Taxable Person for VAT Purposes;

b. withhold tax payable;

c. deposit Value Added Tax must be paid where Output Tax is greater than creditable Input Tax, and deposit Sales Tax on Luxury Goods payable;

d. report the tax calculation.

Paragraph (2)

A small Firm is allowed to be confirmed as a Taxable Person for VAT Purposes. By doing so, this Law fully applies to that Firm.

Paragraph (3)

Value Added Tax payable on the Utilization of Intangible Taxable Goods or Taxable Services from outside the Customs Area must be withheld by the individual or Entity, which utilizes the intangible Taxable Goods or Taxable Services.

CHAPTER III   TAXABLE OBJECTS

Article 4

Value Added Tax shall be imposed on:

a. a Supply of Taxable Goods carried out in the Customs Area by a Firm;

b. importation of Taxable Goods;

c. Rendering of Taxable Services in the Customs Area by a Firm;

d. Utilization of Intangible Taxable Goods obtained from outside the Customs Area within the Customs Area;

e. Utilization of Taxable Services obtained from outside the Customs Area within the Customs Area; and

f. the Export of Taxable Goods by a Taxable Person for VAT Purposes.

Elucidation of Article 4

Subparagraph a

A Firm conducting a Supply of Taxable Goods covers both a Firm which has been registered as a Taxable Person for VAT Purposes referred to in paragraph (1) of Article 3A and a Firm which should have been confirmed as a Taxable Person for VAT Purposes.

A supply of Goods is subject to tax under the following circumstances:

a. the tangible Goods supplied are Taxable Goods;

b. the intangible Goods supplied are intangible Taxable Goods;

c. the supply is carried out within the Customs Area;

d. the supply is conducted in the course of business or work of the Firm concerned.

Subparagraph b

Tax is also withheld at the time of importation of Taxable Goods. Withholding is carried out through the Director General of Customs and Excise. Other than Supply of Taxable Goods under subparagraph a, whomsoever imports Taxable Goods into the Customs Area, regardless whether the importation is conducted in the course of business or work or not, is subject to tax.

Subparagraph c

A Firm, which conducts a Rendering of Taxable Services, covers both a Firm which has been confirmed as a Taxable Person for VAT Purposes referred to in paragraph (1) of Article 3A and a Firm which should have been confirmed as a Taxable Person for VAT Purposes.

Service rendering is subject to tax under the following circumstances:

a. the Services rendered are Taxable Services;

b. the rendering is carried out in the Customs Area; and

c. the rendering is conducted in the course of business or work of the Firm concerned.

Included in the definition of Rendering of Taxable Services is Taxable Services rendered for personal use and/or Taxable Services rendered for free of charge.

Subparagraph d

In order to give the similar tax treatment as for Imported Taxable Goods, intangible Taxable Goods Imported from outside the Customs Area which is utilized in the Customs Area is also subject to Value Added Tax.

Example: Firm A is domiciled in Jakarta and obtains the right to utilize a trademark owned by Firm B domiciled in Hong Kong. Utilization of the trademark by Firm A within the Customs Area is subject to Value Added Tax.

Subparagraph e

Services originated from outside the Customs Area and utilized within the Customs Area are subject to tax under the provisions of this Law. For example, Taxable Person for VAT Purposes C in Surabaya utilizes a Taxable Service from Firm B located in Singapore. Utilization of the Taxable Service aforesaid is subject to Value Added Tax.

Subparagraph f

Different from the Firm referred to in subparagraph a and/or subparagraph c, a Firm which exports Taxable Goods is only a Firm which has been confirmed as a Taxable Person for VAT Purposes referred to in Article 3A paragraph (1).

Article 4A

(1) The types of Goods referred to in point 2 of Article 1 and the types of Services referred to in point 5 of Article 1, which are not taxable under this Law, shall be determined by the Government Regulations.

(2) The determination of types of Goods which are not subject to Value Added Tax referred to in paragraph (1) shall be based on the following categories:

a. products of mining and drilling, taken directly from the sources;

b. daily necessities needed by public;

c. food and beverages served in hotels, restaurants, and such other places;

d. money, gold, and valuable documents.

(3) The determination of types of Services which are not subject to Value Added Tax

referred to in paragraph (1) shall be based on the following fields of activity:

a. healthcare;

b. social welfare;

c. postal delivery;

d. banking, insurance and financial leasing;

e. religion;

f. education;

g. culture and entertainment which has been imposed by entertainment tax;

h. broadcasting, not include advertising;

i. shipping and inland public transportation;

j. manpower;

k. hotels;

l. Rendering of Services by the Government in efforts to run the Government in general.

Elucidation of Article 4A

Paragraph (1)
Sufficiently clear.
Paragraph (2)
Subparagraph a
The meaning of products of mining and drilling taken directly from the sources are products such as crude oil, natural gas, sand and gravel, iron ore, bauxite, and gold ore.

Subparagraph b
The meaning of daily necessities by this paragraph are rice and seeds, corn, sago, soybean, and salt whether iodized or not.

Subparagraph c
To avoid double taxation, because it has been subject to Regional Tax.

Subparagraph d
Sufficiently clear.
Paragraph (3)
Sufficiently clear.

Article 5

(1) In addition to the imposition of tax referred to in Article 4, Sales Tax on Luxury Goods shall be imposed on:

a. a Supply of Taxable Goods categorized as luxuries by a Firm which produces the Goods within the Customs Area in the course of business or work;

b. the importation of Taxable Goods categorized as luxuries.

(2) Sales Tax on Luxury Goods shall be imposed only once, either at the time of Supply of the Taxable Goods categorized as luxuries by the Firm producing them, or at the time of Import.

Elucidation of Article 5

Paragraph (1)

Considering that:

a. appropriate apportionment of the tax burden between consumers with low incomes and those with high incomes shall be notified;

b. consumption patterns for Taxable Goods categorized as luxuries shall be controlled;

c. small and traditional producers shall be protected;

d. state revenue shall be saved.

A Supply of Taxable Goods categorized as luxuries by a producer or the Import of such Goods is not only subject to Value Added Tax but also Sales Tax on Luxury Goods.

The meaning of Taxable Goods categorized as luxuries by this paragraph are:

① the Goods that are not daily necessities Goods; or

② the Goods are only consumed by certain people; or

③ the Goods are usually consumed by high income people; or

④ the Goods are consumed to show the status; or

⑤ if the Goods is consumed, it could be harmful for health or social morality, and distort social order, such as alcoholic drinks.

The imposition of Sales Tax on Luxury Goods on importation of Taxable Goods categorized as luxuries shall be done irrespective of who imports the Goods and irrespective of whether importation is ongoing or simply a one-off transactions. Moreover, the imposition of Sales Tax on Luxury Goods on a transfer of taxable luxury items is irrespective of whether or not part of the Taxable Goods has been subject to Sales Tax on Luxury Goods in previous transaction.

The term Producing in this paragraph shall include the following activities:

a. assembling: joining separate components of a product to become a semi-processed or finished product, as in car assembly, electronic products, household furniture and others;

b. cooking: the processing of Goods by heating, where heating includes boiling, grilling, smoking, roasting and frying, and whether mixed with other ingredients or not;

c. mixing: combining two or more elements to produce one or more other Goods;

d. packaging: placing a product in material to protect it from damage and/or to increase its marketability;

e. bottling: putting beverages or liquid into a bottle which is closed in a specific way, and other activities which are similar, or have another individual or Entity to carry out the activities.

Subparagraph a

Sufficiently clear.

Subparagraph b

Sufficiently clear.

Paragraph (2)

Input Tax, as generally meant in this Law, applies only to Value Added Tax and not to Sales Tax on Luxury Goods; consequently, Sales Tax on Luxury Goods that has been paid cannot be credited against Sales Tax on Luxury Goods that may be payable.

In effect, withholding of Sales Tax on Luxury Goods is carried out only once, either:

a. at the time of supply by the factory or producer of the Taxable Goods categorized as luxuries; or

b. at the time of importation of Taxable Goods categorized as luxuries.

A supply at subsequent stages is not subject to Sales Tax on Luxury Goods.

Article 6

Deleted.

Elucidation of Article 6

Deleted.

CHAPTER IV   TAX RATE AND METHOD OF CALCULATION

Article 7

(1) The Value Added Tax rate is 10% (ten percent).

(2) The Value Added Tax rate on the Export of Taxable Goods is 0% (zero percent).

(3) The tax rate referred to in paragraph (1) may be adjusted by the Government Regulations to a minimum of 5% (five percent) and a maximum of 15% (fifteen percent).

Elucidation of Article 7

Paragraph (1)

Sufficiently clear.

Paragraph (2)

Value Added Tax is imposed on the consumption of Taxable Goods in the Customs Area. Consequently, Taxable Goods which are exported or consumed outside the Customs Area are subject to 0% (zero percent) Value Added Tax. The 0% (zero percent) rate does not mean exempted from Value Added Tax. Thus, Input Tax paid on exported Goods may still be credited.

Paragraph (3)

Considering the enhancement of economic development and/or a increasing need of fund development, the Government is authorized to adjust the Value Added Tax rate to the minimum rate of 5% (five percent) and the maximum rate of 15% (fifteen percent) while maintaining the principle of a single rate. Any changes proposed in tax rate under this paragraph must be presented to the House of Representatives by the Government in the context of discussion and drafting of a bill on the State Budget.

Article 8

（1）The Sales Tax rate on Luxury Goods shall be a minimum of 10% （ten percent） and a maximum of 75% （seventy-five percent）.

（2）On the Export of Taxable Goods categorized as luxuries shall be imposed by 0% （zero percent） tax rate.

（3）The group of Taxable Goods categorized as luxuries and subject to Sales Tax rate on Luxury Goods referred to in paragraph （1） shall be determined by the Government Regulations.

（4）The types of Goods subject to Sales Tax on Luxury Goods referred to in paragraph （3） shall be determined by the Minister of Finance Decree.

Elucidation of Article 8

Paragraph （1）

The Sales Tax rate on Luxury Goods may be set at different levels, with the minimum rate of 10% （ten percent） and the maximum rate of 75% （seventy-five percent）. The difference between the rate classification is based on the grouping of Taxable Goods classified as luxuries and on which Sales Tax on Luxury Goods is imposed as referred to in paragraph （1） of Article 5.

Paragraph （2）

Sales Tax on Luxury Goods is imposed on the consumption of Taxable Goods classified as luxuries within the Customs Area. Consequently, luxuries which are exported or consumed outside the Customs Area are subject to 0% （zero percent） Sales Tax on Luxury Goods. Sales Tax on Luxury Goods which is paid on the purchase of luxuries and which are exported may be refunded.

Paragraph （3）

In accordance with the Considerations set out in the elucidation of paragraph （1） of Article 5, the grouping of Taxable Goods classified as luxuries are based primarily on the economic capability of that part of society using the Goods, as well as on the value of their usefulness to society in general.

Thus, a high rate of tax is imposed on Goods that are only consumed by the high income segment of society and the consumption of which needs to be constrained, while for Goods which are most needed and consumed in larger quantities by society, the Sales Tax rate on Luxury Goods applied is low.

Paragraph （4）

Sufficiently clear.

Article 9

（1）Value Added Tax payable shall be calculated by multiplying the tax rate referred to in Article 7 by the Tax Base.

(2) Input Tax in one Taxable Period is credited against Output Tax for the same Taxable Period.

(2a) In case Output Tax has not been available in one Taxable Period, Input Tax may still be credited.

(3) In case within a specific Taxable Period, Output Tax is greater than Input Tax, the difference is Value Added Tax, which shall be paid by a Taxable Person for VAT Purposes.

(4) In case within a specific Taxable Period, creditable Input Tax exceeds Output Tax, the difference is surplus tax, which may be refunded or credited in the next Taxable Period.

(5) In case within a specific Taxable Period, a Taxable Person for VAT Purposes conducts both taxable and non-taxable supply, insofar as the part of taxable supply can be identified from the bookkeeping exactly, then the amount of creditable Input Tax shall be the Input Tax related to the taxable supply.

(6) In case within a specific Taxable Period, a Taxable Person for VAT Purposes conducts both taxable and non-taxable supply and insofar as the amount of Input Tax related to the taxable supply cannot be identified from the bookkeeping exactly, the amount of Input Tax which may be credited against taxable supply shall be calculated by using guidelines for crediting Input Tax determined by the Minister of Finance Decree.

(7) The amount of Input Tax which may be credited by a Taxable Person for VAT purposes who pays Income Tax by using deemed profit governed by Law Number 7 of 1983 on Income Tax as amended by Law Number 17 of 2000, may be calculated by using guidelines for crediting Input Tax determined by the Minister of Finance.

(8) Input Tax may not be credited under the procedure referred to in paragraph (2) for costs incurred for :

a. the acquisition of Taxable Goods or Taxable Services before a Firm is registered as a Taxable Person for VAT Purposes;

b. the acquisition of Taxable Goods or Taxable Services which do not have direct connection with a Firm's activities;

c. the acquisition and maintenance of motor vehicles, cars, jeeps, station wagons, vans, and "combi" vehicles, except the vehicles used as merchandised or hired Goods;

d. the Utilization of Intangible Taxable Goods or Taxable Services from outside the Customs Area prior to confirmation as a Taxable Person for VAT Purposes;

e. the acquisition of Taxable Goods or Taxable Services of which proof of tax withholding is in form of a simple Tax Invoice;

f. the acquisition of Taxable Goods or Taxable Services of which Tax Invoice fails to meet the provisions referred to in paragraph (5) of Article 13;

g. the Utilization of Intangible Taxable Goods or Taxable Services from outside the Customs Area for which Tax Invoice fails to meet the provisions referred to in paragraph (6) of Article 13;

h. the acquisition of Taxable Goods or Taxable Services of which Input Tax is collected under the issuance of a tax assessment;

i. the acquisition of Taxable Goods or Taxable Services of which Input Tax is not reported in the Value Added Tax Return, which is found when the return is audited.

(9) Creditable Input Tax that has not been credited against Output Tax for the same Taxable Period, may be credited in subsequent Taxable Period, not later than the third month following the end of the Taxable Period concerned, provided it has not been charged as a cost and has not been audited.

(10) Deleted.

(11) Deleted.

(12) Deleted.

(13) The calculation and procedure of refund of Input Tax overpayment referred to in paragraph (4) shall be determined by the Director General of Taxes Decree.

(14) Deleted.

Elucidation of Article 9

Paragraph (1)

Value Added Tax payable is calculated by multiplying the Sales Price, Consideration, Import Value, Export Value or other value stipulated by the Minister of Finance Decree by the tax rate stipulated in paragraph (1) of Article 7. This tax payable is Output Tax, which is withheld by a Taxable Person for VAT purposes.

The Tax Base may be determined by the Minister of Finance Decree to guarantee a sense of fairness, in the following circumstances:

a. Sales Price, Consideration, Import Value, and Export Value which are difficult to determine; and/or

b. Transfer of Taxable Goods needed by people at large quantities, such as drinking water, electricity, and such other Goods.

Example:

(a) Taxable Person for VAT Purposes A sells Taxable Goods for cash in amount of Rp 25,000,000.00. Value Added Tax payable = 10% × Rp 25,000,000.00 = Rp 2,500,000.00. The Value Added Tax of Rp 2,500,000.00 is the Output Tax which is withheld by A.

(b) Taxable Person for VAT Purposes B renders Taxable Services for Rp 20,000,000.00. Value Added Tax payable = 10% × Rp 20,000,000.00 = Rp 2,000,000.00. The Value Added Tax of Rp 2,000,000.00 is the Output Tax collected by B.

(c) A person imports Taxable Goods from outside the Customs Area with an Import Value of Rp 15,000,000.00. Value Added Tax collected through the Directorate General of Customs and Excise = 10% × Rp 15,000,000.00 = Rp 1,500,000.00.

Paragraph (2)

A Buyer of Taxable Goods, a Recipient of Taxable Services, an importer of Taxable Goods, a party who utilizes intangible Taxable Goods obtained from outside the Customs Area, or a party who utilizes Taxable Services from outside the Customs Area, shall be obliged to pay Value Added Tax and has the right to receive a proof of tax withholding. The Value Added Tax which should have been paid is Input Tax for a Buyer of Taxable Goods, or a Recipient of certain Taxable Services, or an importer of Taxable Goods, or the party which utilizes intangible Taxable Goods from outside the Customs Area, or the party which utilizes Taxable Services from outside the Customs Area, which has been confirmed as a Taxable Person for VAT Purposes.

The Input Tax which should be paid by a Taxable Person for VAT Purposes may be credited against Output Tax withheld for the same Taxable Period.

Paragraph (2a)

In case a Taxable Person for VAT Purposes has not yet produced or supplied Taxable Goods or rendered Taxable Services, or exported Taxable Goods so that the Output Tax has not been available (NIL), Input Tax paid by the Taxable Person for VAT Purposes on the acquisition of Taxable Goods, or receipt of Taxable Services, or Utilization of Taxable Services from outside the Customs Area within the Customs Area, or Utilization of Intangible Taxable Goods, or Import of Taxable Goods, may still be credited in accordance with Article 9 paragraph (2), except Input Tax referred to in Article 9 paragraph (8) .

Paragraph (3)

The difference referred to in this paragraph must be deposited at the State Treasury according to the provisions in the Law on General Provisions and Tax Procedures.

Paragraph (4)

Input Tax referred to in this paragraph is Input Tax, which may be credited. During a Taxable Period, Input Tax, which is creditable may exceed Output Tax. The surplus is refundable or may be credited in the next Taxable Period.

Example:

Taxable Period: May, 2001

Output Tax	= Rp 2,000,000. 00
Input Tax which can be credited	= Rp 4,500,000. 00
	--------- -/-
Surplus Tax paid	= Rp 2,500,000. 00

The overpaid may be refunded or credited in the next Taxable Period in June, 2001.

Taxable Period: June, 2001

Output Tax	= Rp 3,000,000. 00
Input to be credited	= Rp 2,000,000. 00
	--------- -/-
Tax Underpayment	= Rp 1,000,000. 00
Surplus Tax from May, 2001 Taxable Period credited in June	= Rp 2,500,000. 00

--------- -/-

Surplus Tax paid as in June, 2001   = Rp 1,500,000. 00.

Paragraph (5)

In this paragraph, a taxable supply means a supply of Goods or rendering of Services which is subject to Value Added Tax in accordance with the provisions of this Law.

The meaning of non-taxable supply in which Input Tax is not able to be credited is a supply of Goods and rendering of Services which are not imposed to Value Added tax referred to in Article 4A and which are exempt from Value Added Tax referred to in Article 16 Subparagraph b.

A Taxable Person for VAT Purposes which conducts a taxable and non-taxable supply in a specific Taxable Period, may only credit Input Tax in respect of the supply which is subject to tax. A taxable supply must be clearly identified from the bookkeeping of the Taxable Person for VAT Purposes.

Example:

A Taxable Person for VAT Purposes conducts several kinds of supply, which are:

a. taxable supply = Rp 25,000,000. 00, Output Tax = Rp 2,500,000. 00;

b. supply which is not subject to Value Added Tax = Rp 5,000,000. 00;

c. supply exempted from Value Added Tax = Rp 5,000,000. 00, Output Tax = NIL.

Input Tax paid on the acquisition of:

a. Taxable Goods and Services related to taxable supply = Rp 1,500,000. 00;

b. Taxable Goods and Services related to a supply which is not subject to Value Added Tax = Rp 300,000. 00;

c. Taxable Goods and Services related to a supply which is exempted from Value Added Tax = Rp 500,000. 00;

Under this provision, Input Tax which may be credited against Output Tax of Rp 2,500,000. 00 is only Rp 1,500,000. 00.

Paragraph (6)

If Input Tax related to a taxable supply can not be correctly identified, the method of crediting Input Tax shall be based on guidelines determined by the Minister of Finance Decree for the purpose of facilitating and providing certainty to the Taxable Person for VAT Purposes.

Example:

A taxable Person for VAT Purposes makes two supplies as follows:

a. taxable supply = Rp 35,000,000. 00, Output Tax = Rp 3,500,000. 00;

b. non-taxable supply = Rp 15,000,000. 00, Output Tax = NIL.

While Input Tax on the acquisition of Taxable Goods and Services related to the entire supply is Rp 2,500,000. 00, Input Tax related to the taxable supply is not correctly identifiable. According to this provision, not all Input Tax of Rp 2,500,000. 00 may be credited against Output Tax of Rp 3,500,000. 00. The amount of Input Tax which may be credited is calculated by the guidelines determined by the Minister of Finance Decree.

Paragraph (7)

A Firm who is allowed to calculate net income using deemed profit is obliged only to make record which includes gross turnover and gross revenue. Because the creditable Input Tax can not be determined precisely due to lack of record of purchasing, the Minister of Finance is authorized to determine the amount of creditable Input Tax.

Paragraph (8)

In principle, Input Tax may be credited against Output Tax; however, for expenses referred to in this paragraph, Input Tax is not creditable.

Subparagraph a

This paragraph gives legal certainty that Input Tax acquired before a Firm reports its business to be confirmed as a Taxable Person for VAT Purposes cannot be credited.

Example:

Firm A reports its business activities to be registered as a Taxable Person for VAT Purposes on January 3,2001. The confirmation as a Taxable Person for VAT Purposes is given on January 5, 2001 and has been valid since January 3,2001. Input Tax acquired before January 3,2001 cannot be credited based on this paragraph.

Subparagraph b

Expenses directly related to business means expenses for production, distribution, marketing and management activities. This provision applies to all fields of business.

Subparagraph c

Sufficiently clear.

Subparagraph d

This paragraph gives a legal certainty that Input Tax acquired before a Firm is confirmed as a Taxable Person for VAT Purposes cannot be credited.

Example:

A reports its business activities to be confirmed as a Taxable Person for VAT Purposes on January 3,2001. The confirmation as a Taxable Person for VAT Purposes is given on January 5, 2001 and has been valid since January 3, 2001. Input Tax on Utilization of Intangible Taxable Goods or Taxable Services obtained from outside the Customs Area before January 3, 2001 cannot be credited based on this paragraph.

Subparagraph e

A simple Tax Invoice is a Tax Invoice referred to in paragraph (7) of Article 13. Because a simple Tax Invoice does not fully include matters covered in paragraph (5) of Article 13, it can only be used as proof of withholding of Value Added Tax and cannot be used as a basis for crediting Input Tax.

Subparagraph f

Sufficiently clear.

Subparagraph g

Sufficiently clear.

Subparagraph h

A Taxable Person for VAT Purposes may be required to pay Value Added Tax payable on the acquisition or Utilization of Taxable Goods or Taxable Services after the issuance of a tax assessment. The Value Added Tax paid under this provision is not Input Tax that can be credited.

Subparagraph i

In accordance with the system of self-assessment, a Taxable Person for VAT Purposes is obliged to report all its business activities in the Periodic Value Added Tax Return. In addition, a Taxable Person for VAT Purposes is given an opportunity to correct the Periodic Value Added Tax Return. Therefore, it is proper that any Input Tax which is not reported in the Return shall not be allowed to be credited.

Example:

A Periodic Value Added Tax Return reports:

Output Tax	Rp 10,000,000.00
Input Tax	Rp 8,000,000.00

An audit reveals:

Output Tax	Rp 15,000,000.00
Input Tax	Rp 11,000,000.00

In this instance, Input Tax which may be credited is not Rp 11,000,000.00, but only Rp 8,000,000.00 in accordance with the amount reported in the Return. Therefore, the computation based on the audit is:

Output Tax	= Rp 15,000,000.00
Input Tax	= Rp 8,000,000.00
	--------- -/-
Underpayment based on the audit	= Rp 7,000,000.00
Underpayment based on the Return	= Rp 2,000,000.00
	--------- -/-
	= Rp 5,000,000.00

Paragraph (9)

This provision allows a Taxable Person for VAT Purposes to credit Input Tax against Output Tax in a different Taxable Period because of the reasons among other is the late receipt of a Tax Invoice. The crediting of Input Tax in such different Taxable Period concerned is only permitted if it is done no later than three months from the end of the Taxable Period concerned. If such a period has elapsed, the Input Tax may still be credited by correcting the Periodic Value Added Tax Return. The foregoing two methods of crediting can only be implemented if the Input Tax concerned has not been charged as a cost or depreciated in the price paid to obtain the Taxable Goods or Taxable Services concerned, and if the Taxable Person for VAT Purposes has not been audited.

Example:

Input Tax on the acquisition of Taxable Goods which the Tax Invoice dated July 7, 2001 may be credited against Output Tax in the Taxable Period of July, 2001 or in subsequent Taxable Period, not later than Taxable Period of October, 2001.

Paragraph (10)

Deleted.

Paragraph (11)

Deleted.

Paragraph (12)

Deleted.

Paragraph (13)

Sufficiently clear.

Paragraph (14)

Deleted.

Article 10

(1) Sales Tax on Luxury Goods payable shall be calculated by multiplying the tax rate referred to in Article 8 by the Tax Base.

(2) Sales Tax on Luxury Goods which is paid on the acquisition or Import of Taxable Goods categorized as luxuries, may be credited against either Value Added Tax or Sales Tax on Luxury Goods withheld according to this Law.

(3) A Taxable Person for VAT Purposes who exports Taxable Goods categorized as luxuries may request refund on the Sales Tax on Luxury Goods paid on the acquisition of the exported Taxable Goods concerned.

Elucidation of Article 10

Paragraph (1)

Sales Tax on Luxury Goods payable is calculated by multiplying the Sales Price, Import Value, Export Value, or such other values as determined by the Minister of Finance Decree by the tax rate as stipulated in Article 8.

Paragraph (2)

In contrast to Value Added Tax which is withheld at every stage of supply, Sales Tax on Luxury Goods is only withheld at the time of supply by the Taxable Person for VAT Purposes which produces Taxable Goods categorized as luxuries or on the importation of Taxable Goods categorized as luxuries. Hence, Sales Tax on Luxury Goods is not Input Tax, as consequence it cannot be credited. Therefore, Sales Tax on Luxury Goods may be added to the price of the Taxable Goods concerned or charged as a cost in accordance with the provisions of the Law on Income Tax.

Example:

Taxable Person for VAT Purposes A imports Taxable Goods with an Import Value of

Rp 5,000,000.00. In addition to Value Added Tax, the Taxable Goods are subject to Sales Tax on Luxury Goods at, for example, a rate of 20%. The calculation of Value Added Tax and Sales Tax on Luxury Goods payable on the Import of the Taxable Goods is as follows:

Tax Base: Rp 5,000,000.00

Value Added Tax:

10% × Rp 5,000,000.00 = Rp 500,000.00

Sales Tax on Luxury Goods:

20% × Rp 5,000,000.00 = Rp 1,000,000.00

Later, Taxable Person for VAT Purposes A uses the Taxable Goods concerned as a component of other Taxable Goods, which, on supply, are subject to 10% of Value Added Tax and 35% of Sales Tax on Luxury Goods. Due to lack of ability to credit Sales Tax on Luxury Goods paid, the Sales Tax on Luxury Goods of Rp 1,000,000.00 may either be added to the price of the Taxable Goods produced by A, or charged as a cost.

Then, a Taxable Person for VAT Purposes A sells the Taxable Goods produced to Taxable Person for VAT Purposes B for Rp 50,000,000.00. Therefore, the calculation of Value Added Tax and Sales Tax on Luxury Goods payable is as follows:

Tax Base: Rp 50,000,000.00

Value Added Tax:

10% × Rp 50,000,000.00 = Rp 5,000,000.00

Sales Tax on Luxury Goods:

35% × Rp 50,000,000.00 = Rp 17,500,000.00

In this example, a Taxable Person for VAT Purposes A may credit the mentioned Value Added Tax of Rp 500,000.00 against Value Added Tax of Rp 5,000,000.00. The Sales Tax on Luxury Goods of Rp 1,000,000.00, however, cannot be credited against either the Value Added Tax of Rp 5,000,000.00 or the Sales Tax on Luxury Goods of Rp 17,500,000.00.

Paragraph (3)

A Taxable Person for VAT Purposes which has paid Sales Tax on Luxury Goods on the acquisition of Taxable Goods categorized as luxuries, as long as the Sales Tax on Luxury Goods has not been charged as a cost, may refund the Sales Tax on Luxury Goods paid, if the Taxable Person for VAT Purposes concerned has exported the Goods concerned.

Example:

Taxable Person for VAT purposes A buys a car from a sole agent of trademark holder for Rp 100,000,000.00. Value Added Tax and Sales Tax on Luxury Goods paid is Rp 10,000,000.00 and Rp 35,000,000.00. If the car is then exported, A may request for refund of Value Added Tax amounting Rp 10,000,000.00 and Sales Tax on Luxury Goods amounting Rp 35,000,000.00, which have been paid on the acquisition of the car concerned.

CHAPTER V   THE TIME AND THE PLACE IN WHICH TAX IS PAYABLE AND THE REPORT OF TAX CALCULATION

Article 11

(1) Tax shall be payable at the time of:

a. Supply of Taxable Goods;

b. Import of Taxable Goods;

c. Rendering of Taxable Services;

d. Utilization of Intangible Taxable Goods obtained from outside the Customs Area referred to in subparagraph d of Article 4;

e. Utilization of Taxable Services obtained from outside the Customs Area referred to in subparagraph e of Article 4; or

f. Export of Taxable Goods.

(2) If payment is received before Supply of Taxable Goods or Rendering of Taxable Services, or if payment is conducted before the Utilization of Intangible Taxable Goods referred to in subparagraph d of Article 4 or the Utilization of Taxable Services obtained from outside the Customs Area referred to in subparagraph e of Article 4, tax shall be payable at the time of payment.

(3) Deleted.

(4) The Director General of Taxes may determine certain time as the time of tax payable, if the time is difficult to determine or there is a change of rules that may result in unfairness.

(5) Deleted.

Elucidation of Article 11

Paragraph (1)

Value Added Tax withholding basically adheres to the accrual principle, meaning the tax due at the time the Taxable Goods or Taxable Services are supplied or rendered, or at the time the Taxable Goods are imported; although at the time of supply they may not have been, or may not have completely, paid for. The time when tax is payable for transactions conducted by "electronic commerce" follows this provision.

Subparagraph a

Sufficiently clear.

Subparagraph b

Sufficiently clear.

Subparagraph c

Sufficiently clear.

Subparagraph d

If an individual or an Entity uses an intangible Taxable Good from outside the Customs Area within the Customs Area, or utilizes Taxable Services from outside the Customs Area within the Customs Area, the tax due is at the time an individual or an Entity begins utilizing the intangible Taxable Good or Taxable Service within the Customs Area.

This condition relates to the fact that the party which supplies the intangible Taxable Goods or Taxable Services is located outside the Customs Area, and thus he cannot be confirmed as a Taxable Person for VAT Purposes. Consequently, the timing of tax due is not related to the time of supply, but to the time of utilization of the Goods or Services.

Subparagraph e

Sufficiently clear.

Subsection f

Sufficiently clear.

Paragraph (2)

In case the payment is received prior to the Supply of Taxable Goods referred to in subparagraph a of Article 4, before the Rendering of Taxable Services referred to in subparagraph c of Article 4, or before the Utilization of Intangible Taxable Goods from outside the Customs Area referred to in subparagraph d of Article 4 begins, or before the Utilization of Taxable Services from outside the Customs Area referred to in subparagraph e of Article 4 begins, tax shall be payable at the time of payment.

Paragraph (3)

Deleted.

Paragraph (4)

Sufficiently clear.

Paragraph (5)

Deleted.

Article 12

(1) For a Taxable Person for VAT Purposes which conducts supply referred to in subparagraph a, c, and f of Article 4, tax is payable at its places of residence, domicile or business activities or such other places as may be determined by the Director General of Taxes Decree.

(2) On a written request by a Taxable Person for VAT Purposes, the Director General of Taxes may determine one place or more as the place or places where tax shall be payable.

(3) In the case of Imports, tax shall be payable at the point of entry of the Taxable Goods and shall be withheld through the Directorate General of Customs and Excise.

(4) For an individual or an Entity who uses intangible Taxable Goods and or Taxable Services within the Customs Area which are obtained from outside the Customs Area referred to in subparagraph d and e of Article 4, tax shall be payable at the place of residence, domicile or business activities of the individual or the Entity.

Elucidation of Article 12

Paragraph (1)

Individual who has been confirmed as a Taxable Person for VAT Purposes is subject to tax at the place of residence and/or place of business activities, while Entity which has been confirmed as a Taxable Person for VAT Purposes is subject to tax at the place of domicile or business activities.

If a Taxable Person for VAT Purposes has one or more places of business activities outside its residence or place of domicile, each place should be reported as place of tax payable, and the Taxable Person for VAT Purposes is obliged to report his business activities to be confirmed as a Taxable Person for VAT Purposes.

In case a Taxable Person for VAT Purposes has more than one place of tax payable under an office of the Directorate General of Taxes, therefore the Taxable Person for VAT Purposes may choose one place of tax payable which takes responsibility for all the places of his business activities for all those places.

Example 1 :

An individual A, resides in Bogor, has a place of business in Cibinong. If there is no transfer of Taxable Goods and/or Taxable Services at the place of his residence, A shall be obliged to report his business to be confirmed as a Taxable Person for VAT Purposes in Cibinong District Tax Office, because Cibinong is the place in which tax is payable for A. On the contrary, if the Supply of Taxable Goods and Rendering of Taxable Services occurs at the place of his residence, the individual A shall be obliged to register in Bogor District Tax Office. However, if individual A supplies Taxable Goods or Taxable Services both at his place of residence and business activities, A shall be obliged to register both in the Bogor District Tax Office and Cibinong District Tax Office because his taxes are payable at both places.

Different from an individual, an Entity which has been confirmed as a Taxable Person for VAT Purposes shall be obliged to register both at the place of domicile and business activities because an Entity confirmed as a Taxable Person for VAT Purposes is considered to make a Supply of Taxable Goods and/or Rendering of Taxable Services at both places.

Example 2 :

Taxable Person for VAT Purposes A has three places of business activities which are Bengkulu, Curup and Manna, and all of which are under one District Tax Office, namely Bengkulu District Tax Office. Each of the three places of business activities, makes a Supply of Taxable Goods and/or Rendering of Taxable Services, and makes sales and financial administration, hence Taxable Person for VAT Purposes A is subject to tax at the three places or cities. In this instance, Taxable Person for VAT Purposes A shall be obliged to choose one place of business activities, for example the one in Bengkulu, to report its business activities to be registered as a Taxable Person for VAT Purposes in Bengkulu District Tax Office. The Taxable Person for VAT Purposes A in Bengkulu will be responsible to report all the business activities of the three branches.

Paragraph (2)

In case a Taxable Person for VAT Purposes has tax payable in more than one place, hence in fulfilling his tax obligation, he may request in writing to the Director General of Taxes to choose one or more of the places of its activities as the place or places in which tax is payable. The Director General of Taxes, prior to the decision is made, shall conduct an audit to ensure the following:

a. Supply of Taxable Goods or Rendering of Taxable Services for all places of business done only in one or more places of business;

b. the sales and financial administration is centralized on one or more places of business.

Paragraph (3)

Sufficiently clear.

Paragraph (4)

An individual or an Entity either as a Taxable or non-Taxable Person for VAT Purposes who utilizes intangible Taxable Goods from outside the Customs Area within the Customs Area and/or utilizes Taxable Services from outside the Customs Area within the Customs Area, shall be subject to tax in place of residence, domicile or business activities of the individual or an Entity concerned.

Article 13

(1) A Taxable Person for VAT Purposes shall be obliged to issue a Tax Invoice for each Supply of Taxable Goods referred in subparagraph a or f of Article 4, and for each Rendering of Taxable Services referred to in subparagraph c of Article 4.

(2) Notwithstanding the provision of paragraph (1), a Taxable Person for VAT Purposes may issue a single Tax Invoice consisting of all supplies to the same Buyer of Taxable Goods or Recipient of Taxable Services during one calendar month.

(3) If payment is received before the Supply of Taxable Goods or the Rendering of Taxable Services, the Tax Invoice shall be issued at the time of payment.

(4) The time of issuance, format, size, availability, and procedures for submission and correction of a Tax Invoice shall be determined by the Director General of Taxes.

(5) A Tax Invoice shall include information concerning the Supply of Taxable Goods or the Rendering of Taxable Services, which at least consists of the following:

a. the name, address, and Taxpayer Identification Number of the Taxable Person for VAT

Purposes supplying the Taxable Goods or rendering the Taxable Services;

b. the name, address, and Taxpayer Identification Number of the Buyer of the Taxable Goods or Recipient of the Taxable Services;

c. the type of Taxable Goods or Services, total Sales Price or Consideration, and amount of discount;

d. the Value Added Tax withheld;

e. the Sales Tax on Luxury Goods withheld;

f. the code, serial number and date of issuance of the Tax Invoice; and

g. the name, position, and signature of person authorized to sign the Tax Invoice.

(6) The Director General of Taxes may determine certain documents to represent a Tax Invoice.

(7) A Taxable Person for VAT Purposes may issue a simple Tax Invoice of which the conditions shall be determined by the Director General of Taxes Decree.

Elucidation of Article 13

Paragraph (1)

In case there is a Supply of Taxable Goods and/or Rendering of Taxable Services, hence a Taxable Person for VAT Purposes who supplies Taxable Goods or renders Taxable Services shall be obliged to withhold Value Added Tax payable and give a Tax Invoice as a proof of tax withholding. A Tax Invoice is not necessarily made special or different from the Sales Invoice. A Tax Invoice may be a standard Tax Invoice, a simple Tax Invoice, and certain documents determined as a Tax Invoice by the Director General of Taxes.

Paragraph (2)

Not withstanding with the provisions of paragraph (1), in order to simplify administrative burden, a Taxable Person for VAT Purposes is allowed to make a single Tax Invoice, called a Joint Tax Invoice, for the Supply of Taxable Goods or Rendering of Taxable Services which occurs within the same calendar month to the same Buyer or the same Recipient of Services.

Paragraph (3)

Sufficiently clear.

Paragraph (4)

Considering that a Sales Invoice may be made after Supply of Taxable Goods or Rendering of Taxable Services, hence the Director General of Taxes is given the authority to determine the timing of issuance of Tax Invoice.

Likewise, the Director General of Taxes is given the authority to determine uniformity in the form, size, availability, procedures of delivery and the procedures of correcting a Tax Invoice. In this paragraph, the meaning of regulation of availability of Tax Invoice is a regulation of who is responsible to make the Tax Invoice forms, and the requirement to be complied. For instance, the provision of a Tax Invoice form may be issued or printed by the Firm itself, while the form, size and other administrative matters are determined by the Director General of Taxes.

Paragraph (5)

A Tax Invoice is a proof of tax withholding and may be used as a media to credit Input Tax. Consequently, a Tax Invoice must be valid formally and materially. A Tax Invoice must be filled out completely, clearly and faithfully and signed by the person authorized by the Taxable Person for VAT Purposes. However, the filling of information on Sales Tax on Luxury Goods only conducted in case the Supply of Taxable Goods is subject to Sales Tax on Luxury Goods. Incomplete Tax Invoice in accordance with the provision of this paragraph may negate the ability to credit such invoice referred to in paragraph (8) subparagraph f of Article 9. A Tax Invoice which contains information and is completed in accordance with the regulation in this paragraph is called a Standard Tax Invoice.

Paragraph (6)

Not withstanding with the provisions of paragraph (5), the Director General of Taxes may determine a common documentation in ordinary course of business as a Standard Tax Invoice.

This regulation is admitted into the Law because:

a. a Sales Invoice used by a Taxable Person for VAT Purposes is recognized by the public and qualify the administrative standard as Tax Invoice, for example, a telephone bill or an airline ticket;

b. to constitute evidence of tax withholding, there must be a Tax Invoice while the party who is supposed to make the Tax Invoice, such as the party which supplies the Taxable Goods or Services, which located outside the Customs Area.

For the purpose of Utilization of Taxable Services from outside the Customs Area, hence Tax Remittance Slip may be determined as a Tax Invoice.

Paragraph (7)

A simple Tax Invoice is also a proof of tax withholding by a Taxable Person for VAT Purposes to record a direct Supply of Taxable Goods or Rendering of Taxable Services to the last consumer. The Directorate General of Taxes may determine a proof of evidence on a submission or payment as a simple Tax Invoice. A simple Tax Invoice, at least, consists of the following:

a. the name, address, Taxpayers Registration Number of the Taxable Person for VAT purposes who supplies Taxable Goods or renders Taxable Services;

b. the type and quantity of the Taxable Goods or Services;

c. the amount of Sales Price or compensation including tax, or separately, the amount of tax;

e. the date of issuance the simple Tax Invoice is made.

Article 14

(1) An individual or an Entity not registered as a Taxable Person for VAT Purposes is prohibited from issuing a Tax Invoice.

(2) If a Tax Invoice has been issued, the individual or Entity referred to in paragraph (1)

shall deposit the tax amount written in the Tax Invoice to the State Treasury.

Elucidation of Article 14

Paragraph (1)

A Tax Invoice may only be made by a Taxable Person for VAT Purposes. The prohibition on the issuance of Tax Invoice by non-Taxable Person for VAT Purposes is intended to protect the Buyer from improper tax withholding.

Paragraph (2)

Sufficiently clear.

Article 15

Deleted.

Elucidation of Article 15

Deleted.

CHAPTER VA   SPECIAL PROVISIONS

Article 16A

(1) Tax payable on a Supply of Taxable Goods and/or a Rendering of Taxable Services to a Withholding Agent of Value Added Tax shall be withheld, deposited and reported by the Value Added Tax Withholding Agent.

(2) The procedures of withholding, depositing and reporting of tax by the Value Added Tax Withholding Agent referred to in paragraph (1) shall be determined by the Minister of Finance Decree.

Elucidation of Article 16A

Paragraph (1)

In case a Taxable Person for VAT Purposes supplies Taxable Goods or renders Taxable Services to a Value Added Tax agent, the Value Added Tax Withholding Agent is obliged to withhold, deposit and report the tax withheld.

However, the Taxable Person for VAT Purposes still has an obligation to report the tax withheld by the Value Added Tax Withholding Agent.

Paragraph (2)

Sufficiently clear.

Article 16B

(1) It may be determined by the Government Regulations that tax payable shall not be withheld in part or in full, either temporarily or permanently, in respect of:

a. activities in specified zones or specified places within the Customs Area;

b. the supply of specified Taxable Goods or rendering of specified Taxable Services;

c. Imports of specified Taxable Goods;

d. the utilization within the Customs Area of specified intangible Taxable Goods obtained from outside the Customs Area;

e. the utilization within the Customs Area of specified Taxable Services obtained from outside the Customs Area.

(2) Input Tax paid on the acquisition of Taxable Goods and/or Taxable Services on which the supply is not withheld to Value Added Tax, may still be credited.

(3) Input Tax paid on the acquisition of Taxable Goods and/or Taxable Services on which the supply is exempt from the imposition of Value Added Tax, may not be credited.

Elucidation of Article 16B

Paragraph (1)

One of the principles which must be firmly held to in the tax laws is the application of the similar treatment to all taxpayers or to the cases in the field of taxation which, in fact, is the same as holding to the provisions of the valid law.

To this end, each and every tax facility, where truly necessary, must hold to the foregoing principles and steps be taken to ensure that its application does not depart from the purpose and aim for which the facility is granted.

The meaning and purpose of facilities granted are mainly for achieving success in economic sectors of high national priority, encouraging the improvement of business world and enhancing the competition ability, supporting national defense, and also accelerating national development.

Tax facilities under this Article are limited to:

a. encouraging Exports of national priority in Bonded Zones and Export Production Entry Port Zones (EPTE), or other areas within the Customs Area which have been specially designed for such purpose;

b. covering possible agreements between the State and other countries in the fields of trade and investments;

c. encouraging health improvement of the society through the provision of vaccines for the national immunization program;

d. guarantee the availability of tools for Indonesian National Army/Police of the Republic of Indonesia (TNI/POLRI) to protect the Republic of Indonesia either from external or internal threat;

e. guarantee the availability of data base and air photograph of the Republic of Indonesia by Indonesian National Army (TNI) to support national defense;

f. improving the people education and intelligence by helping the provision of text books on general subjects, holy books and religious text books in a quite reachable price;

g. encouraging the building of houses of work ship;

h. guarantee the provision of housing which is attainable by the lower classes such as simple houses, very simple houses, and simple graded houses;

i. encouraging the improvement of national transportation means on inland, at sea, and on air;

j. encouraging national development by helping the provision of strategic Goods, after consulted to the House of Representative.

Paragraph (2)

Special treatment in the form of non-withheld of Value Added Tax due means that Input Tax connected with a Supply of Taxable Goods and/or Rendering of Taxable Services which have been granted the special treatment can still be credited.

In other words, Value Added Tax remains payable but is not withheld.

Example:

Taxable Person for VAT Purposes A produces Taxable Goods which has been granted facilities by the State, in such case, the Value Added Tax payable on the transfer of the Taxable Goods has never been withheld (and not simply postponed).

To produce these Taxable Goods, Taxable Person for VAT Purposes A uses other Taxable Goods and/or other Taxable Services as raw materials, auxiliary materials, capital goods or other cost components.

At the time of purchase of the other Taxable Goods and/or Taxable Services, Taxable Person for VAT Purposes A pays Value Added Tax to the Taxable Person for VAT Purposes who sells or supplies the Taxable Goods or renders Taxable Services.

If Value Added Tax paid by Taxable Person for VAT Purposes A to the supplying Taxable Person for VAT Purposes constitutes Input Tax which may be credited against Output Tax, then the Input Tax can still be credited even though Output Tax is zero because of the non-withheld of Value Added Tax by the State in accordance with the provisions of facilities under paragraph (1).

Paragraph (3)

In contrast to the provisions in paragraph (2), special treatments may be granted in the form of exemption from Value Added Tax, which results in there being no Output Tax; In this instance, Input Tax connected with the Supply of Taxable Goods and/or Rendering of Taxable Services which have been granted tax exemption cannot be credited.

Example:

Taxable Person for VAT Purposes B produces Taxable Goods, which have been granted tax facilities such as any exemption from VAT on their supply by the State. To produce the Taxable Goods, B uses other Taxable Goods and/or Taxable Services as raw materials, auxiliary materials, capital Goods or other cost components. At the time of purchase of the other Taxable Goods and/or Taxable Services, B pays Value Added Tax to the Taxable Person for VAT Purposes selling or supplying the Taxable Goods or rendering the Taxable Services. Although Value Added Tax paid by B to the other Taxable Person for VAT Purposes is Input Tax, which, may be credited, since in fact there is no Output Tax because of the exemption granted under paragraph (1), the Input Tax cannot be credited.

Article 16C

Value Added Tax shall be imposed on self-construction activities conducted outside the course of business or work by an individual or an Entity where the results are for personal use or for other party use whereby such limitations and procedures shall be determined by the Minister of Finance Decree.

Elucidation of Article 16C

Self-construction activities undertaken outside the course of business or work are subject to Value Added Tax considered to prevent avoidance of the imposition of Value Added Tax.

To protect the low income classes from imposition of Value Added Tax on a self-construction activity, the definition of self-construction are stipulated by the Minister of Finance Decree.

Article 16D

Value Added Tax shall be imposed on the transfer of assets originally acquired not for sale by a taxable person, provided the Value Added Tax paid at the time of acquisition is creditable.

Elucidation of Article 16D

A supply of machinery, buildings, tools, furniture or other assets, which originally not for sale by a Taxable Person for VAT Purposes, is subject to tax as long as it falls under the requirement, that Value Added Tax paid at the time of acquisition may be credited in accordance with this Law.

Accordingly, a supply of such assets is not subject to tax if the Value Added Tax paid at the time of acquisition cannot be credited based on the regulations in this Law, except otherwise the rejection of credibility of Value Added Tax due to unqualified evidence according to administrative requirement, such as a Tax Invoice which has not been completed in accordance with the provisions of Article 13 paragraph (5).

CHAPTER VI   OTHER PROVISIONS

Article 17

Matters related to the definition and procedures for tax withholding in relation to the application of this Law and which are not specifically regulated by this Law, shall be subject to the provisions of the Law on General Provisions and Tax Procedures as well as other Laws.

Elucidation of Article 17

Sufficiently clear.

CHAPTER VII INTERIM PROVISIONS

Article 18

(1) With coming into effect of this Law :

a. all Supplies of Taxable Goods or Rendering of Taxable Services and Imports of Taxable Goods, which is conducted before this Law comes into effect, is still taxable under the Law on Sales Tax of 1951 ;

b. in the course when the regulations for implementation of this Law have not been stipulated, the existing regulations which are not against this Law are still applicable.

(2) The implementation regulations referred to in paragraph (1) shall be stipulated further by the Minister of Finance.

Elucidation of Article 18

Paragraph (1)

Subparagraph a

Sufficiently clear.

Subparagraph b

All the existing implementation regulations which have been issued in accordance with the Law on Sales Tax of 1951 which are not against the content and purpose of this Law remain in force as long as it is not abolished yet or replaced by the regulations issued based on this Law.

Paragraph (2)

The provisions of paragraph (2) are intended to overcome the problem arisen within the interim period as consequences of Law on Value Added Tax and Sales Tax on Luxury Goods coming into effect, and Law on Sales Tax of 1951 not coming into effect any more, on the same object for tax imposition such as :

—long-term contract or contract which involves period between those two Laws ;

—the rest of Sales Price or Consideration which is not paid yet ;

—inventory of Goods which the Input Tax is not available yet.

In this respect, the Minister of Finance is given authority to determine other implementation regulations, which are different from paragraph (1) to reduce unfairness in burdening tax and smooth the implementation of this Law.

CHAPTER VIII   CLOSING PROVISIONS

Article 19

Matters that have not been regulated yet by this Law shall be stipulated further by the Government Regulations.

Elucidation of Article 19

Sufficiently clear.

Annotations:

With coming into effect this Law:

a. the postponement of the payment of Value Added Tax and Sales Tax on Luxury Goods, which has been granted before this Law comes into effect, shall be ended in accordance with the period of the postponement granted, but not later than 31st December of 1999.

b. the imposition of Value Added Tax and Sales Tax on Luxury Goods on business in mining of oil and gas, general mining, and other mining under Production Sharing Contract, Contract of Work, or Agreement of Work on Mining Business, which is still applicable at the time this Law comes into effect, shall be calculated in accordance with Production Sharing Contract, Contract of Work, or Agreement of Work on Mining Business concerned until such Production Sharing Contract, Contract of Work, or Agreement of Work on Mining Business terminates.

印度尼西亚共和国 1983 年第 8 号增值税法 2000 年第 18 号修正案

第一章　总则

第 1 条

本法中定义如下：

1. 关税区系指印度尼西亚共和国领土，包括陆地、领海、领空以及专属经济区及大陆架内特定区域。以上区域适用于 1995 年第 10 号海关法。

2. 商品包括有形资产和无形资产，有形资产按其属性和法律地位可分为动产和不动产。

3. 应纳税商品系指第 2 点所述商品，按本法须缴纳税款。

4. 提供应纳税商品指第 3 点所述的提供应纳税商品的一切商业活动。

5. 服务是指由于约定或法定原因而可以有效使用商品、设施或权利的一切服务性活动，也包括在客户提供物资的情况下，应客户的订购或要求而提供的服务。

6. 应纳税服务是指第 5 点所述的服务，按本法应缴纳税款。

7. 提供应纳税服务是指提供第 6 点所述可课税服务的一切活动。

8. 使用关税区外的应纳税服务是指在关税区内使用从关税区外获得的应纳税服务的一切活动。

9. 进口指商品进入关税区。

10. 使用关税区外的无形应纳税商品是指通过约定在关税区内使用从关税区外获得的无形应纳税商品的一切活动。

11. 出口指商品从关税区出境。

12. 贸易是指在不改变形式和性质的前提下进行货物买卖，包括实物交换在内的一切商业活动。

13. 实体是指无论是否从事业务活动的个人或资本组合，它包括有限公司、合伙制、其他合伙制、国有企业或地方政府所辖企业，无论上述企业采用何种名义和形式，例如"商号""公司"或"合作社"等，同时也包括常设机构、基金会或类似的组织、机构或其他商业组织形式。

14. 商号指第 13 点所述的个人或实体，其在业务或工作的过程中，生产商品、进口货物、出口货物、从事贸易活动、使用关税区以外获得的无形商品、提供商业服务或使用关税区以外获得的服务。

15. 增值税的纳税人指第 14 条所述的商号，它所提供的商品或服务应按本法要求纳税，但不包括营业额在财政部部长令规定的限额以下的小型企业，自愿作为增值税纳税人的小型企业除外。

16. 制造是一种活动，它通过改变产品的形态或性质从而使其成为新商品，或获得新用途，它也是一种加工自然资源的活动，包括通过其他个人或实体进行代加工。

17. 税基是指销售价格或对价、进口值或出口值，或由财政部部长令规定的作为计算应缴税款基础之用的其他价值。

18. 销售价格是指以金钱表示的价值，包括卖方因提供应纳税商品而收取的或应收取的费用，但不包括按本法预提的税款或在税务发票中写明的折扣。

19. 对价是指以金钱表示的价值，包括某商号因提供应纳税服务而收取的或应收取的费用，但不包括按本法预提的税款或在税务发票中写明的折扣。

20. 进口值是指以金钱表示的价值，它是计算进口税或海关对进口应纳税货物而制定的其他税收的基础，但不包括按本法预提的税款。

21. 买主是指收到或应收到应纳税商品，并为此支付或应支付货款的个人、实体或政府部门。

22. 服务接受者是指接受或应接受应纳税服务，并为此支付或应支付货款的个人、实体或政府部门。

23. 纳税单据是应纳税人在提供应纳税货物或应纳税服务时所预提增值税的完税凭证，或由海关总局对进口应纳税商品征收的增值税的完税凭证。

24. 进项税是应纳税人在获得应纳税商品或服务，或在关税区以外使用应纳税无形商品或服务，或在进口纳税商品时即应支付的增值税。

25. 销项税是应纳税人在提供应征纳商品或服务时，或在出口应纳税商品时预提的增值税。

26. 出口值是指以金钱表示的价值，包括出口商收取的或应收取的所有费用。

27. 增值税扣缴义务人为政府财务部门、实体或财政部部长指定的政府机构，它们在应纳税人向相关政府财务部门、实体或政府机构提供应纳税商品或服务时，就应纳税人的增值税进行预提、储存和做出报告。

第 1 条司法解释

足够清楚。

第 1A 条

（1）提供应纳税商品之含义包括：

a. 按照约定，应纳税商品之所有权发生转移；

b. 按照分期付款协议或租赁协议，提供应纳税商品；

c. 向中间商或拍卖商提供应纳税商品；

d. 供个人使用的应纳税商品或免费提供的应纳税商品；

e. 原获得的应纳税商品和资产非为出售之目的，在公司解体时仍然存在，前提是获得该资产的增值税按规定可以进行抵免；

f. 总部向分公司提供的应纳税商品，反之亦然，或分公司之间应纳税商品的供应；

g. 托销（寄售）的应纳税商品。

（2）提供应纳税商品不包括：

a. 向商法中所述的经纪人提供应纳税商品；

b. 作为贷款抵押品而提供的应纳税商品；

c. 第（1）款 f 项下提供的应纳税商品，若应纳税人为增值税目的已获得集中支付税款许可的。

第 1A 条司法解释

第（1）款

a 项

按照本规定，协议包括售货事务、易货贸易、分期付款或其他使商品所有权发生转移的协议。

b 项

应纳税商品的提供可因分期付款协议、租购协议或金融租赁协议产生。金融租赁协议是指通过选择权由金融租赁协议导致的供给。虽然对应纳税商品的权利之转移尚未发生且对应纳税商品的价格支付仍在分期进行中，由于对应纳税商品的支配权已经从卖方转向买方，或从出租人转移到承租人，故本法规定协议的签订时间即为提供应纳税商品的时间，除非应纳税商品的实际所有权已在签署协议前发生变化。

c 项

中间商指个人或实体，其在以自己名义从事商业活动或专业服务的过程中，代表其他商号订立合同或协议，并由此获得工资或服务补偿金，例如佣金。拍卖商指政府拍卖人或由政府指定的人选。

d 项

自用是指无论自产产品抑或非自产产品，均用于企业自身、管理层或员工的利益。免费提供是指无论产品自产与否，均无须回报，其中包括用于促销目的对联系人或买主提供的样品。

e 项

按其原来用途非用于交易目的，并且在商号解体时仍然存在的库存和资产，视为与自用相同，并因此视为提供应纳税商品之范畴。

非用于出售目的的资产仅缴纳增值税，但必须满足特定条件，即在获得商品时支付的增值税可以抵免。

f 项

如商号在一个以上地点纳税，即向其他方提供应纳税商品之所在地，无论是总部还是分部，本法均将应纳税商品在其间的移动解释为构成提供应纳税商品。在本规定中，分部指企业场所、代表处、销售单位或其他相同类型的场所。

g 项

如是寄售形式的商品，在应纳税商品移交时缴纳的增值税可抵免应纳税商品寄售期间的销项税。但如果寄售的纳税商品未卖出并退回原主，则接受寄售的商号可使用本法第 5

条第 A 项中规定的关于退回应纳税商品的条款。

第（2）款

a 项

本法中的经纪人即指商法中的经纪人，它是总统指定的或经总统授权的政府官员指定的中间商，经与其无业务关系的他人授权并代表他人开展业务活动，以此经营公司，并由此获得酬金或佣金作为回报。

b 项

足够清楚。

c 项

如增值税纳税人拥有一个以上的营业场所，无论总部还是分部，并且该纳税人得到税务总干事允准可以集中支付税款，则应纳税商品从某营业地向另一营业地的供应（从分部到总部，反之亦然，或各分部间）不被视为提供应纳税商品，除非应纳税商品的供应所在地有纳税要求。

第二章　　纳税义务人

第 2 条

（1）如销售价格或对价受特殊关系影响，则销售价格或对价应以提供纳税商品和服务时的市场价为基础进行计算。

（2）下列情况下视为存在特殊关系：

a. 一个企业在另一个企业直接或间接参股 25% 以上；同样地，两个或两个以上企业之间直接或间接互相持股 25% 以上；或

b. 某企业对另一企业控股，或两个及两个以上企业均直接或间接地受制于该企业；或

c. 存在一代以内的血缘或姻亲关系。

第 2 条司法解释

第（1）款

本法中所谓特殊关系之影响是指定价低于市场价的可能性。在此情况下，税务总干事有权调整销售价格或对价，使之形成公平的市场价，并作为自由市场中的税基。

第（2）款

增值税应纳税人和应纳税商品及服务的接受方之间会因以下情况导致的彼此从属关系而出现特殊关系：

——所有权或参股；

——通过管理或技术而存在的影响。

除此之外，血缘或姻亲关系也可导致个人之间存在特殊关系。

a 项

如存在直接或间接参股25%或更多的所有权关系，则视为存在特殊关系。例如：如果A 有限公司持有 B 有限公司50%的股份，则 A 有限公司对 B 有限公司构成了直接参股。与此同时，如果 B 有限公司持有 C 有限公司50%的股份，则作为 B 有限公司的股东，A 有限公司间接持有 C 有限公司25%的股份。据此，有限公司 A、B 和 C 之间即视为存在特殊关系。若 A 有限公司也持有 D 有限公司25%的股份，则有限公司 B、C 和 D 之间亦视为存在特殊关系。此种所有权关系在个人和实体之间也可能出现。

b 项

第 a 项中描述的关系也可能通过管理或使用技术产生的控制而出现，而无须考虑所有权的问题。如一个或一个以上公司均处于同一企业的控制之下，则视为存在特殊关系，上述几个公司之间也同样适用于此种关系。

c 项

一代以内的直系血缘关系指的是父母和孩子，而一代以内的非直系血缘关系指的是兄弟姐妹。一代以内的直系姻亲关系指的是岳父母和继子女，而一代以内的非直系姻亲关系指的是姐夫或弟妹等关系。如夫妻间订有财产和收入分离协议，按本法即解释为该夫妻间存在特殊关系。

第二章　确认增值税纳税人

第 3 条

已删除。

第 3 条司法解释

已删除。

第二 A 章　纳税人申报业务活动之义务及代扣、储存和报税之责任

第 3A 条

（1）按第4条 a、c 或 f 项所述提供商品的企业有义务申报其业务活动从而登记成为增值税应纳税人，并有代扣、储存和申报增值税及奢侈品营业税之责任。

（2）自愿作为增值税纳税人的小型企业须履行第（1）款所规定的义务。

（3）使用从第4条 d 项所述的从关税区外获得的应纳税无形商品，或使用第4条 e 项所述的从关税区外获得的应纳税服务的个人或实体有义务代扣、储存和申报应纳增值税，

具体方法和程序由财政部部长令进行规定。

第 3A 条司法解释

第（1）款

在关税区内提供应纳税商品和服务，或出口应纳税商品的企业应：

a. 申报其业务活动以确认成为增值税纳税人；

b. 代扣应缴税金；

c. 销项税大于可抵免的进项税时，存储应付增值税，并存储奢侈品营业税；

d. 申报税款的计算。

第（2）款

小型企业可以被确认为增值税义务人。若如此，则本法完全适用于该企业。

第（3）款

因使用从关税区外获得的应纳税无形商品或应纳税服务而应缴纳的增值税，必须由作为使用者的个人或实体进行代扣。

第三章　　纳税对象

第 4 条

下列情况应征收增值税：

a. 企业在关税区内提供应纳税商品；

b. 进口纳税商品；

c. 企业在关税区内提供应纳税服务；

d. 在关税区内使用从关税区外获得的无形应纳税商品；

e. 在关税区内使用从关税区外获得的应纳税服务；以及

f. 增值税纳税义务人出口应纳税商品。

第 4 条司法解释

a 项

从事纳税商品供应的企业包括已按照第 3A 条第（1）款所述登记成为增值税纳税人的企业和应该被确认为增值税纳税人的企业。

在下列情况下，应缴纳商品应纳税：

a. 提供的有形商品为应纳税商品；

b. 提供的无形商品为无形应纳税商品；

c. 供应行为在关税区内；

d. 供应行为在企业的业务或劳务过程中实现。

b 项

在进口应纳税商品时亦代扣税金，由海关总局进行代扣。除第 a 项下应纳税商品的供应外，其他任何人向关税区进口应纳税商品，无论该进口是否是在其业务或劳务的过程中进行，均须纳税。

c 项

提供应纳税服务的企业包括已按照第 3A 条第（1）款所述确认为增值税纳税人的企业和应该被确认为增值税纳税人的企业。

所提供的服务在下列情况下应纳税：

a. 提供的服务为应纳税服务；

b. 供应行为在关税区内进行；以及

c. 供应行为在企业的业务或劳务过程中实现。

为个人目的而提供的应纳税服务或免费提供的应纳税服务，均包括在提供应纳税服务的定义当中。

d 项

为实现与进口应纳税商品相似的课征方式，从关税区外进口的但在关税区内使用的无形应纳税商品亦应缴纳增值税。

例如：A 企业驻在雅加达并获得驻在香港的 B 企业名下商标的使用权，则 A 企业在关税区内使用该商标即应缴纳增值税。

e 项

按照本法规定，源自关税区外但在关税区内使用的服务应缴纳税款。例如，位于泗水的增值税纳税义务人 C 使用了位于新加坡的 B 企业提供的应纳税服务。上述应纳税服务的使用即应缴纳增值税。

f 项

与第 a 项和/或第 c 项中所述的企业不同的是，出口应纳税商品的企业仅指第 3A 条第（1）款所述的已经确认为增值税纳税人的企业。

第 4A 条

（1）按本法不予征税的第 1 条第 2 点所述的商品类型以及第 1 条第 5 点所述的服务类型应由政府法规进行确定。

（2）第（1）款所述的无须缴纳增值税的商品类型之确定应基于下列各类：

a. 从来源地直接开采和钻取的产品；

b. 公众需要的生活必需品；

c. 宾馆、饭店及其他类似场所供应的食物和饮料；

d. 货币、黄金及有价证券。

（3）第（1）款所述的无须缴纳增值税的服务类型之确定应基于以下活动领域：

a. 保健；

b. 社会福利；

c. 邮递；

d. 银行业、保险及融资租赁；

e. 宗教；

f. 教育；

g. 已经征收娱乐税的文化及娱乐活动；

h. 广播，但不包括广告；

i. 海运和内陆公共运输；

j. 劳动力；

k. 宾馆；

l. 政府为正常运营而提供的服务。

第 4A 条司法解释

第（1）款

足够清楚。

第（2）款

a 项

从来源地直接开采和钻取的产品是指诸如原油、天然气、沙子和碎石、铁矿石、铝土矿以及金矿石等产品。

b 项

本项下的生活必需品是指大米、油籽、玉米、西米、大豆、加碘或不加碘食盐。

c 项

为避免双重征税，因其已缴纳地方税。

d 项

足够清楚。

第（3）款

足够清楚。

第 5 条

（1）除了第 4 条所述的征税外，在下列情况下征收针对奢侈品的营业税：

a. 在从事业务或劳务的过程中在关税区内生产商品的企业提供归类为奢侈品的应纳税商品；

b. 进口已归类为奢侈品的应纳税商品；

（2）奢侈品营业税只能征收一次，其征收时间在生产奢侈品的企业供应归类为奢侈品的应纳税商品时，或在进口时。

第 5 条司法解释

第（1）款

鉴于：

a. 将税负在高收入人群和低收入人群中间进行适当分摊；

b. 对归类为奢侈品的应纳税商品的消费模式应加以控制；

c. 小型和传统型的生产商应受到保护；

d. 节省财政收入；

生产商提供归类为奢侈品的应纳税商品或同类产品的进口不仅要缴纳增值税，还要缴纳奢侈品营业税。

本款归类为奢侈品的应纳税商品指：

①非为生活必需品的商品；

②特定人群消费的商品；

③通常为高收入人群消费的商品；

④消费商品的目的为炫耀其社会地位；

⑤商品的消费可能导致对健康或社会道德的危害，并扭曲社会秩序，例如饮酒等。

不论何人进口奢侈品类应纳税商品，亦不论该进口为不间断性交易还是一次性交易，进口奢侈品类应纳税商品一律征收奢侈品营业税。而且，不论在先前的交易中部分纳税商品是否已缴纳奢侈品营业税，在奢侈品发生流转时，仍要征收奢侈品营业税。

本款内的"生产"应包括以下活动：

a. 组装：在车辆组装、电子产品、家居和其他方面，连接配件使之成为半成品或成品；

b. 烹饪：以加热方式加工商品，加热方式包括煮沸、烧烤、熏制、烘焙和煎炸，无论是否和其他配料混合使用；

c. 混合：把两种或两种以上成分合并在一起，生产出一种或多种其他产品；

d. 包装：把产品放置于某种材料中，以防损坏和/或提高可销性；

e. 瓶装：将饮料或液体装入用特殊方法封闭的瓶子中，或其他类似活动，或委托其他个人或实体代工。

a 项

足够清楚。

b 项

足够清楚。

第（2）款

本法中所指的进项税只适用于增值税，不适用于奢侈品营业税。因此，已缴纳的奢侈品营业税不可抵免可能需要缴纳的奢侈品营业税。

事实上，奢侈品营业税的预提只在下列两种情况下进行一次：

a. 在工厂或生产商提供奢侈品类应纳税商品时；或

b. 在进口奢侈品类应纳税商品时。

后来阶段的供应无须缴纳奢侈品营业税。

第 6 条

已删除。

第 6 条司法解释

足够清楚。

第四章 税率及计算方法

第 7 条

（1）增值税税率为 10%。

（2）出口纳税商品的增值税税率为 0。

（3）第（1）款所述税率可由政府法规进行调节，最低至 5%，最高至 15%。

第 7 条司法解释

第（1）款

足够清楚

第（2）款

增值税是对在关税区内消费应纳税货物而征收的。因此，供出口的或在关税区外消费的纳税货物的增值税税率为 0。然而 0 并不意味着免除增值税。因此，在出口货物上支付的进项税仍可抵免。

第（3）款

为促进经济发展和/或鉴于资金需求的不断增长，政府有权在保持单一税率的情况下，对增值税税率进行调整，最低可至 5%，最高可至 15%。对本款下税率提出的任何更改必须由政府提交众议院进行讨论并起草国家预算法案。

第 8 条

（1）奢侈品的营业税税率最低为 10%，最高为 75%。

（2）奢侈品类应纳税商品的出口征收 0 的税率。

（3）归类为奢侈品并须缴纳营业税的应纳税商品的分类由政府法规确定。

（4）第（3）款所述的须缴纳奢侈品营业税的商品类型由财政部部长令进行确定。

第 8 条司法解释

第（1）款

奢侈品增值税可按不同级别设置，最低为 10%，最高为 75%。税率的差异基于奢侈品类应纳税商品的分类情况以及第 5 条第（1）款所述的征收奢侈品营业税的情况。

第（2）款

奢侈品营业税是对在关税区内消费奢侈品类应纳税商品而征收的。因此，供出口的或在关税区外消费的奢侈品的营业税税率为 0。因购买奢侈品并出口而支付的营业税可退税。

第（3）款

根据对第 5 条第（1）款的司法解释规定的对价，奢侈品类应纳税商品的分类主要基于使用该商品的社会人群的经济能力，以及该商品对社会的总体有效价值。

因此，对仅为社会高收入人群所消费的奢侈品要按高税率课税，同时对此种消费行为要加以限制；而对于在社会中大批量需求和消费的商品，则适用的奢侈品营业税税率较低。

第（4）款

足够清楚。

第 9 条

（1）增值税的计算方式是用税基乘以第 7 条所述的税率。

（2）纳税期的进项税与同一时期的销项税相抵免。

（2a）若在纳税期没有销项税，进项税仍可抵免。

（3）如在某一特定纳税期内，销项税大于进项税，则差额即为增值税，并由增值税纳税人缴纳。

（4）如在某一特定纳税期内，可抵免的进项税超过销项税，则差额即为税收盈余，可办理退税或在下个纳税期进行抵免。

（5）如在某一特定纳税期内，增值税纳税义务人从事了应纳税和非纳税的供应，只要应纳税供应部分能够从账簿中确切识别，则可抵免的进项税金额应为与应纳税供应相关的进项税。

（6）如在某一特定纳税期内，增值税纳税义务人同时从事了应纳税和非纳税的供应，如果与应纳税供应相关的进项税的金额不能从账簿中得到确切识别，则可进行抵免的进项税之金额须采用财政部部长令规定的进项税抵免指南进行计算。

（7）如增值税纳税人通过使用 1983 年第 7 号所得税法 2000 年第 17 号修正案规定的核定利润缴纳所得税，则可被增值税纳税义务人进行抵免的进项税之金额可采用财政部部长规定的进项税抵免指南进行计算。

（8）按第（2）款所述的步骤，下列情况下产生的费用，进项税可不抵免：

a. 在企业注册成为增值税纳税人之前对应纳税商品和服务的获取；

b. 对与企业活动无直接关联的应纳税商品和服务的获取；

c. 对机动车辆、小汽车、吉普车、旅行车、货车和两用车等的获取和维修，商品化的或租用的车辆除外；

d. 在被确定为增值税纳税人之前使用关税区以外的应纳税商品或服务；

e. 对以采用简易税务发票形式作为代扣税款证据的应纳税商品或服务的获取；

f. 对其税务发票未能满足第 13 条第（5）款规定的应纳税商品或服务的获取；

g. 对开出的税务发票未能满足第 13 条第（6）款规定的来自关税区以外的无形应纳税商品或服务的使用；

h. 对按照纳税评估书征收进项税的应纳税商品或服务的获取；

i. 对在审计增值税纳税单时发现没有申报进项税的应纳税商品或服务的获取。

（9）如可抵免的进项税未对同一纳税期的进项税进行抵免，则可在其后的纳税期进行抵免，但不得迟于相关纳税期结束后的第 3 个月，前提是其尚未被记账作为成本，亦未被审计。

（10）

已删除。

（11）

已删除。

（12）

已删除。

（13）

第（4）款所述的进项税超额税款之退税的计算方法和程序由税收总干事令加以确定。

（14）

已删除。

第 9 条司法解释

第（1）款

应纳增值税的计算方法是：售价、对价、进口值、出口值或财政部部长令规定的其他价值乘以第 7 条第（1）款规定的税率。此应纳税款为销项税，由增值税纳税人代扣。

在下列情况下，为保证公平，税基由财政部部长令加以确定：

a. 难以确定的售价、对价、进口值或出口值；

b. 公众大量需求的应纳税商品的转移，例如饮用水、电力和其他类似商品；

例如：

（a）增值税纳税义务人 A 出售应纳税商品，获得现金金额 25 000 000.00 卢比。应付增值税 = 10% × 25 000 000.00 卢比 = 2 500 000.00 卢比。则 25 000 000.00 卢比的增值税为 A 代扣的销项税。

（b）增值税纳税义务人 B 提供价值为 20 000 000.00 卢比的应纳税服务。应付增值税 = 10% × 20 000 000.00 卢比 = 2 000 000.00 卢比。则增值税 2 000 000.00 卢比即为 B 代征的销项税。

（c）某人从关税区外进口应纳税商品金额为 15 000 000.00 卢比。经海关总局征收的增值税为 10% × 15 000 000.00 卢比 = 1 500 000.00 卢比。

第（2）款

纳税商品的买主、纳税服务的接受者、纳税商品的进口商、使用从关税区以外获得的无形应纳税商品的一方，或者使用从关税区以外获得的应纳税服务的一方，均应缴纳增值税并有权获得税款代缴证明。对下列已被确认为增值税纳税人的各方来说，应缴纳的增值税为进项税：应纳税商品的买主、某些应纳税服务的接受者、纳税商品的进口商、使用从关税区以外获得的无形应纳税商品的一方、使用从关税区以外获得的应纳税服务的一方。

增值税纳税人应缴纳的进项税可被同一纳税期代扣的销项税抵免。

第（2a）款

如增值税纳税人尚未生产或提供应纳税商品或应纳税服务，或尚未出口应纳税商品以至于不存在销项税（或为零），则由增值税纳税人在下列情况下缴纳的进项税仍可按第 9 条第（2）款进行抵免，第 9 条第（8）款规定的进项税除外：获取应纳税商品、接受应纳税服务、在关税区内使用来自关税区外的应纳税服务、使用无形应纳税商品、进口应纳税商品。

第（3）款

按税法通则的规定，本款所述的差额须存入国库。

第（4）款

本款所述的进项税是可以抵免的进项税。在纳税期内，可抵免的进项税可能会超过销项税。超出部分可退税或在下一个纳税期进行抵免。

例如：

2001 年 5 月纳税期

销项税	＝2 000 000.00 卢比
可抵免的进项税	＝4 500 000.00 卢比
	--------- -/-
纳税盈余	＝2 500 000.00 卢比

超额部分可办理退税或在下一个纳税期，即 2001 年 6 月份进行抵免。

2001 年 6 月纳税期

销项税	＝3 000 000.00 卢比
进行抵免的进项税	＝2 000 000.00 卢比
	--------- -/-
欠缴部分	＝1 000 000.00 卢比
2001 年 5 月纳税期用于抵免的纳税盈余	＝2 500 000.00 卢比
	--------- -/-
2001 年 6 月的纳税盈余	＝1 500 000.00 卢比

第（5）款

在本款中，应纳税供应指提供按照本法规定应交纳增值税的商品或服务。

进项税不能进行抵免的非纳税供应是指提供不征收第 4A 条所述的增值税或免于第 16B 条所规定的增值税的商品和服务。

在特定纳税期内从事应纳税供应和非纳税供应业务的增值税纳税人仅可抵免与应纳税供应相关的进项税。应纳税供应必须可在增值税纳税人的账簿中得到清晰确认。

例如：

A 增值税纳税义务人从事多种供应，分别为：

a. 应纳税供应 ＝25 000 000.00 卢比，销项税 ＝2 500 000.00 卢比；

b. 无须缴纳增值税的供应 ＝5 000 000.00 卢比；

c. 免于增值税的供应 ＝5 000 000.00 卢比，销项税 ＝0。

在获得以下商品和服务时缴纳的进项税：

a. 与应纳税供应相关的应纳税商品和服务 ＝1 500 000.00 卢比；

b. 与无须缴纳增值税的供应相关的应纳税商品和服务 ＝300 000.00 卢比；

c. 应纳税商品和服务与免于增值税的供应相关的应纳税商品和服务 ＝500 000.00 卢比。

按本规定，可用于抵免 2 500 000.00 卢比销项税的进项税仅为 1 500 000.00 卢比。

第（6）款

如与应纳税供应相关的进项税无法得到正确识别，则抵免进项税的办法应以财政部部长令确定的指导原则为基准，以期为增值税纳税义务人提供确定性并使之获得便利。

例如：

A 增值税纳税人做出了如下两种供给：

a. 应纳税供应 = 35 000 000.00 卢比，销项税 = 3 500 000.00 卢比；

b. 非纳税供应 = 15 000 000.00 卢比，销项税 = 0。

当获取与总供给量相关的应纳税商品或服务的进项税为 2 500 000.00 卢比时，与应纳税供应相关的进项税无法正确辨识。按照本规定，不是所有 2 500 000.00 卢比的进项税都可以抵免 3 500 000.00 卢比的销项税。可以抵免的进项税的金额应按照财政部部长令确定的指导原则进行计算。

第（7）款

被允准使用核定利润计算净收入的企业只需做出包含总营业额和毛收入的记录。因缺乏采购记录而使可抵免的进项税无法精准确定时，财政部部长有权确定可抵免的进项税金额。

第（8）款

原则上，进项税可以抵免销项税；然而对本款所述的费用来说，进项税不可抵免。

a 项

本款在法律上给予确认，在企业申报业务进而被确认为增值税纳税人之前取得的进项税不能被抵免。

例如：

A 企业于 2001 年 1 月 3 日申报其业务活动以期注册成为增值税纳税人。确认为增值税纳税人的时间为 2001 年 1 月 5 日并从 2001 年 1 月 3 日起生效。根据本款规定，2001 年 1 月 3 日前取得的进项税不可抵免。

b 项

与生意直接相关的费用是指用于生产、分销、市场营销和管理活动的费用。

c 项

足够清楚。

d 项

本款在法律上给予确认，在企业被确认为增值税纳税人之前取得的进项税不能抵免。

例如：

A 企业于 2001 年 1 月 3 日申报其业务活动以期注册成为增值税纳税人。确认为增值税纳税人的时间为 2001 年 1 月 5 日并从 2001 年 1 月 3 日起生效。根据本款规定，2001 年 1 月 3 日前取得的因使用从关税区外获得的无形应纳税商品和应纳税服务的进项税不可抵免。

e 项

简易税务发票是指第 13 条第（7）款所述的税务发票。因为简易税务发票不包括第

13 条第（5）款所涉及的事项，所以其只能作为增值税代缴证明使用，而不能作为抵免进项税的依据。

f 项

足够清楚。

g 项

足够清楚。

h 项

在获取或使用应纳税商品和服务时，增值税纳税人或许会被要求按照发出的纳税评估书缴纳应付增值税。按本条款规定支付的增值税非为可抵免的进项税。

i 项

按照自我评估制度，增值税纳税人有责任在定期的增值税单中申报其所有的业务活动。而且，给予增值税纳税人改正定期增值税单的机会。因此，未在纳税单中申报的任何进项税不可进行抵免。

例如：

定期增值税单显示：

| 销项税 | 10 000 000.00 卢比 |
| 进项税 | 8 000 000.00 卢比 |

审计显示：

| 销项税 | 15 000 000.00 卢比 |
| 进项税 | 11 000 000.00 卢比 |

在此情况下，可抵免的进项税不是 11 000 000.00 卢比，而仅为纳税单中显示的 8 000 000.00卢比。

因此，基于审计的计算方式为：

销项税	= 15 000 000.00 卢比
进项税	= 8 000 000.00 卢比
	--------- -/-
基于审计的欠缴额	= 7 000 000.00 卢比
基于纳税单的欠缴额	= 2 000 000.00 卢比
	--------- -/-
应付欠缴额---------	= 5 000 000.00 卢比

第（9）款

本条款允许增值税纳税人因迟收税务发票等原因而将进项税与不同纳税期的销项税进行抵免。但此种抵免必须在相关纳税期结束后 3 个月内办理完毕。如逾期，仍可通过修改定期增值税单的方式将进项税进行抵免。只有在有关的进项税尚未被作为成本而进行征费，或在为获取应纳税商品和服务而支付的价格上尚未贬值，或增值税纳税人尚未被审计的情况下，上述两种抵免办法方可执行。

例如：

增值税纳税人在获取应纳税商品时缴纳的进项税，如税务发票日期为 2001 年 7 月 7

日，则此进项税可与 2001 年 7 月纳税期或其后的纳税期的销项税相抵免，但不得迟于 2001 年 10 月纳税期。

第（10）款

已删除。

第（11）款

已删除。

第（12）款

已删除。

第（13）款

足够清楚。

第（14）款

已删除。

第 10 条

（1）应付奢侈品营业税的计算方式为税基乘以第 8 条所述税率。

（2）在获取或进口归类为奢侈品的应纳税商品时缴纳的奢侈品营业税不可与增值税或按本法代扣的奢侈品营业税相抵免。

（3）出口奢侈品类应纳税商品的增值税纳税人可要求退回其在获取相关的出口应纳税商品时缴纳的奢侈品营业税。

第 10 条司法解释

第（1）款

应付奢侈品营业税的计算方式为：售价、进口值、出口值或财政部部长令确定的其他价值 × 第 8 条所述税率。

第（2）款

与在每个供应阶段都要进行扣缴的增值税相反，奢侈品营业税仅在出产奢侈品类应纳税商品的增值税纳税人进行供应时，或进口奢侈品类应纳税商品时代为扣缴。因此，奢侈品营业税不是进项税，是不可抵免的。故而，奢侈品营业税可追加到相关的应纳税商品的价格中或按照所得税法之规定作为成本记在账上。

例如：

增值税纳税义务人 A 进口了进口值为 5 000 000.00 卢比的应纳税商品。除增值税外，此纳税商品还须缴纳如税率为 20% 的奢侈品营业税。则进口该商品应付的增值税和奢侈品营业税的计算如下：

税基：　　　　5 000 000.00 卢比

增值税：

10% × 5 000 000.00 卢比 = 500 000.00 卢比；

奢侈品营业税：

20% × 5 000 000.00 卢比 = 1 000 000.00 卢比。

随后，增值税纳税人 A 使用相关的应纳税商品作为其他应纳税商品的组件。在进行供应时，须缴纳 10% 的增值税和 35% 的奢侈品营业税。因其能力不足以将已付奢侈品营业税进行抵免，故 1 000 000.00 卢比的奢侈品营业税或加到 A 生产的纳税商品的价格之中，或作为成本记在账上。

然后，增值税纳税人 A 把所生产的纳税商品以 50 000 000.00 卢比出售给增值税纳税人 B。因此，应付的增值税和奢侈品营业税的计算如下：

税基：　　　　50 000 000.00 卢比

增值税：

10% ×50 000 000.00 卢比 = 5 000 000.00 卢比；

奢侈品营业税：

35% ×50 000 000.00 卢比 = 17 500 000.00 卢比。

在上述例子中，增值税纳税人 A 可把增值税 500 000.00 卢比与增值税 5 000 000.00 卢比进行抵免。但奢侈品营业税 1 000 000.00 卢比既不能与增值税 5 000 000.00 卢比相抵免，也不能与奢侈品营业税 17 500 000.00 卢比相抵免。

第（3）款

增值税纳税人在获取奢侈品类应纳税商品时缴纳的奢侈品营业税，只要该奢侈品营业税尚未作为成本记在账上，且在相关增值税纳税人已将上述商品出口的情形下，其所缴纳的奢侈品营业税可以办理退税。

例如：

增值税纳税人 A 从某商标持有人的独家代理处以 100 000 000.00 卢比的价格购买了一辆小汽车，所付的增值税和奢侈品营业税分别为 10 000 000.00 卢比和 35 000 000.00 卢比。若此车随后出口，A 可要求退回在获取上述小汽车时所缴纳的增值税和奢侈品营业税，金额分别为 10 000 000.00 卢比和 35 000 000.00 卢比。

第五章　纳税的时间和地点及税收计算报告

第 11 条

（1）税款应在下列时间缴付：

a. 提供纳税商品时；

b. 进口纳税商品时；

c. 提供纳税服务时；

d. 使用第 4 条 d 项所述的从关税区外获得的无形应纳税商品时；

e. 使用第 4 条 e 项所述的从关税区外获得的应纳税服务时；或

f. 出口纳税商品时。

（2）若在提供应纳税商品或服务前收到付款，或在使用第 4 条 d 项所述的无形应纳税商品或第 4 条 e 项所述的应纳税服务前款项已经支付，则税款在付款时即应缴纳。

（3）已删除。

（4）如在确定纳税时间上存在困难或因规定发生变化从而可能导致不公平的现象，则税务总干事可指定某个时段作为纳税时间。

（5）已删除。

第 11 条司法解释

第（1）款

增值税代扣主要遵循应计原则，指税款应纳日期为提供应纳税商品或服务的时间，或货物的进口时间，尽管在进行提供的时候该税款可能尚未支付或尚未完全支付。通过电子商务进行的交易，其缴纳税款时间遵照本规定进行。

a 项

足够清楚。

b 项

足够清楚。

c 项

足够清楚。

d 项

如果个人或实体在关税区内使用关税区以外的无形应纳税商品或服务，则纳税时间以该个人或实体开始在关税区内使用该无形应纳税商品或服务的时间为准。

本条款基于以下事实：提供无形应纳税商品或服务的一方位于关税区外，因此其无法被确认为增值税纳税义务人。故而纳税日期和供应时间没有关系，而和商品或服务的使用时间有关系。

e 项

足够清楚。

f 项

足够清楚。

第（2）款

若收到付款的时间先于第 4 条 a 项所述的提供应纳税商品的时间或第 4 条 c 项所述的提供应纳税服务的时间，或先于第 4 条 d 项所述的来自关税区外的无形应纳税商品或第 4 条 e 项所述的来自关税区外的应纳税服务的启用时间，则税款在付款发生时即应缴纳。

第（3）款

已删除。

第（4）款

足够清楚。

第（5）项

已删除。

第 12 条

（1）对从事第 4 条 a、c、f 项所述的供应活动的增值税纳税人来说，纳税地点为其居所、驻地或业务活动所在地，或其他可由税务总干事令规定的地点。

（2）在增值税纳税人做出书面申请时，税务总干事可确定一个或多个地点作为纳税地点。

（3）在进口时，税款应在货物入境港进行缴纳，并由海关总局代扣。

（4）如果个人或实体如第 4 条 d、e 项所述的在关税区内使用关税区以外的无形应纳税商品或服务，则纳税地点应为该个人或实体之居所、驻地或业务活动所在地。

第 12 条司法解释

第（1）款

已确认为增值税纳税人的个人，应在居所或业务活动所在地进行纳税，而已确认为增值税纳税人的实体，则应在驻地或业务活动所在地进行纳税。

如增值税纳税人在居所或驻地以外有一个或多个业务活动场所，则每个场所均应申报为纳税地，且该增值税纳税人应申报其业务活动以确认为增值税纳税人。

如增值税纳税人在税务总局某办公地点管辖下拥有多个纳税点，则其可选择其中某一个地点作为所有业务活动场所的纳税所在地。

例 1：

个人 A 居住在 Bogor，其业务活动地点在 Cibinong。如在其居所处没有发生应纳税商品和/或服务的转移，则 A 应向 Cibinong 地方税务局申报其业务以确认为增值税纳税人，因为 Cibinong 是 A 的纳税所在地。与其相反，如应纳税商品或服务的提供发生在 A 的居所，则 A 应在 Bogor 地方税务局进行注册。然而，如 A 在居所和业务活动所在地均有应纳税商品或服务的供应，则 A 在 Bogor 地方税务局和 Cibinong 地方税务局均应进行注册，原因是 A 在上述两地均应纳税。

与个人情况不同的是，已确认为增值税纳税人的实体在其驻地和业务活动所在地均应进行注册，因为作为增值税纳税人的实体被视为在两地均提供应纳税商品和/或服务。

例 2：

增值税纳税人 A 有三个业务活动地点，分别是 Bengkulu、Curup 和 Manna，三个地方均处于同一地方税务局管辖之下，即 Bengkulu 地方税务局。上述三个业务活动地均提供应纳税商品和/或服务并从事销售和财务管理，因此增值税纳税人 A 在三地均应上税。在此情况下，增值税纳税人 A 应选择其中一个业务活动地，例如 Bengkulu，来申报其业务活动，并在 Bengkulu 地方税务局登记成为增值税纳税人。则位于 Bengkulu 的增值税纳税人 A 负责申报上述三个地区的所有业务活动。

第（2）款

如增值税纳税人需在多处纳税，在履行纳税义务时，其可以向税务总干事书面申请选择一个或数个活动地作为纳税地。在做出决定前，税务总干事应进行审计确保以下各项：

a. 所有地方的应纳税商品或服务的供应只在一个或数个业务地点进行；

b. 销售和财务管理集中在一个或数个地点。

第（3）款

足够清楚。

第（4）款

个人或实体，无论是否为增值税纳税人，只要在关税区内使用从关税区外获得的应纳税商品和/或服务，均应在其居所、驻地或业务活动所在地缴纳税款。

第 13 条

（1）增值税纳税人在每次提供第 4 条 a 或 f 项所述的应纳税商品时，或每次提供第 4 条 c 项所述的应纳税服务时，均应开具税务发票。

（2）尽管有第（1）款的规定，增值税纳税人仍可开具单张发票，该发票涵盖一个日历月内对同一应纳税商品买家或应纳税服务接受人的所有供应情况。

（3）如在提供应纳税商品或服务前得到付款，则在付款时即应出具发票。

（4）税务发票的开具时间、格式、尺寸、可获得性以及提交和改正的程序均由税务总干事进行确定。

（5）税务发票应包括有关应纳税商品或服务供应的信息，至少应包含下列各项：

a. 提供应纳税商品或服务的增值税纳税人的名称、住址以及纳税人识别号；

b. 应纳税商品买主或应纳税服务接受人的名称、住址和纳税人识别号；

c. 商品或服务类型、销售总额或对价、折扣额；

d. 预提的增值税；

e. 代扣的奢侈品营业税；

f. 税务发票的编码、序号和开具时间；以及

g. 税务发票授权签字人的姓名、职位及签字。

（6）税务总干事可指定某些单证用以代开税务发票；

（7）增值税纳税人可开具简易税务发票，其中的具体情况由税务总干事确定。

第 13 条司法解释

第（1）款

如发生应纳税商品和/或服务的供应活动，则提供应纳税商品或服务的增值税纳税人应代扣应纳的增值税，并开具税务发票作为扣税证明。税务发票无须做得很特别，也并非一定要区别于销售发票。税务发票可以是标准税务发票、简易税务发票或税务总干事确定的可作为税务发票使用的某些单据。

第（2）款

尽管第（1）款有规定，但为了简化行政手续，如增值税纳税人在同一日历月内所提供的商品或服务的对象为同一人，则该增值税纳税人可制作单张税务发票，称作"联合税务发票"。

第（3）款
足够清楚。

第（4）款

考虑到销售发票可能于提供应纳税商品或服务之后开具，因此税务总干事有权决定开具税务发票的时间。

同样地，税务总干事有权确定税务发票在形式、尺寸、效用、提交程序以及更改程序方面的一致性。本款中税务发票之效用的规定，意为谁负责制作税务发票表格及相关要求。例如，企业本身可开具或印刷税务发票表格，而发票的形式、尺寸和其他管理事项则

由税务总干事决定。

第（5）款

税务发票是一种纳税证明并可以用作一种抵免进项税的媒介。因此，税务发票必须正式而且实质有效。税务发票必须填写得完整、清楚且真实，并由增值税纳税人的授权人进行签署。然而，只有在应纳税商品的供应需缴纳奢侈品营业税的情况下，才填写奢侈品营业税的信息。按照本款规定，不完整的税务发票可能会导致其无法抵免第 9 条第（8）款 f 项所述的发票。包含应有信息并按本款规定填写完成的税务发票被称作"标准税务发票"。

第（6）款

尽管有第（5）款的规定，税务总干事也可在平常的业务过程中确定某种普通单据作为标准税务发票。本规定纳入法律是因为：

a. 增值税纳税人使用的销售发票已被广大公众所接受并满足行政标准要求，例如电话单或机票；

b. 要取得税收代扣证明，须有某方制作的税务发票，例如位于关税区外的应提供应纳税商品或服务的一方。出于使用来自关税区外的应纳税服务之目的，故可确定税收汇款凭单为税务发票。

第（7）款

简易税务发票亦为增值税纳税人的一种税款代扣证明，它记录着向最终消费者直接提供应纳税商品和服务。税务总干事可确定提交证明或付款证明作为简易税务发票。简易税务发票应至少包括以下各项：

a. 提供应纳税商品或服务的增值税纳税人的姓名、住址和纳税人登记号码；

b. 应纳税商品或服务的类别和数量；

c. 销售价格总额或包括税款在内的补偿金，或单独的税款总额；

d. 简易税务发票的开具日期。

第 14 条

（1）未注册为增值税纳税人的个人或实体不得开具税务发票。

（2）如税务发票已经出具，则第（1）款中提到的个人或实体应将税务发票所列出的税款额存入国库。

第 14 条司法解释

第（1）款

只有增值税纳税人方可开具税务发票。禁止非增值税纳税人开具税务发票的目的是为了防止买方遭受不恰当的税务扣缴。

第（2）款

足够清楚。

第 15 条

已删除。

第 15 条司法解释

已删除。

第五 A 章　　特别条款

第 16A 条

（1）在提供应纳税商品和/或服务时应付给增值税扣缴义务人的税款应由增值税扣缴义务人代扣、存放和申报。

（2）第（1）款所述的增值税扣缴义务人对税款进行代扣、存放及申报的程序由财政部部长令决定。

第 16 条司法解释

第（1）款

如增值税纳税人向增值税扣缴人提供应纳税商品或服务，则增值税扣缴义务人有义务对预提的税款进行代扣、存储和申报。

然而增值税纳税义务人仍有义务将增值税扣缴义务人代扣的税款进行申报。

第（2）款

足够清楚。

第 16B 条

（1）政府法规可能会决定关于以下各项的应纳税款不得全部或部分代扣，无论是暂时地还是长久地：

　　a. 指定区域的或关税区内指定地点的活动；

　　b. 对特定应纳税商品或服务的提供；

　　c. 进口特定应纳税商品；

　　d. 在关税区内使用来自关税区外的特定无形应纳税商品；

　　e. 在关税区内使用来自关税区外的特定应纳税服务。

（2）在获得未缴纳增值税的应纳税商品或服务时所缴纳的进项税仍可抵免。

（3）在获得免缴增值税的应纳税商品或服务时所缴纳的进项税不可抵免。

第 16B 条司法解释

第（1）款

税法中必须严格坚持的原则之一就是对纳税人或税收领域案件执行同等待遇，事实上，这也是坚持有效法律时的同样的做法。

为此，每项税收优惠政策，如确有必要，则必须坚持上述原则并采取措施，确保其在运用过程中不会偏离该政策被赋予的既定目标。

特许的优惠政策，其意义和目的主要是为了在重要的国民经济部门获得成功、鼓励商业界进步并提高竞争力、支持国防事业以及加快民族发展。

本条下的税收优惠限于：

a. 鼓励保税区国家重点领域出口，以及出口加工口岸区（EPTE）或关税区内其他具有类似目的的区域；

b. 涉及国家与其他国家间在贸易和投资领域的协议；

c. 通过为全民免疫计划提供疫苗推动全社会提高健康水准；

d. 保证印尼军队或警察获得所需工具，以保护印度尼西亚共和国免于外部或内部的威胁；

e. 保证印尼军队获得数据库和印度尼西亚共和国的航拍图片，以支持国防；

f. 通过以低廉价格提供关于各学科教科书、圣经及宗教教科书，以提高全民教育及智力水平；

g. 鼓励修建作业船上之居住房；

h. 保证社会下层人士可获得的住房，例如简易房、简陋房以及简易级房屋等；

i. 鼓励提高海陆空交通运输方式；

j. 在与众议院协商后，通过提供战略物资，推动民族发展。

第（2）款

以不代扣应纳增值税的形式表现的特殊待遇系指与享受该项特殊待遇的应纳税商品和/或服务的供应相关的进项税仍可抵免。换句话说，增值税仍然需要支付，但未进行代扣。

例如：

增值税纳税人 A 生产国家准予税收优惠的应纳税商品，在此情况下，商品转移时的应纳增值税从未被预提过（并非简单延缓）。

为生产这些应纳税商品，增值税纳税人 A 使用了其他应纳税商品和/或服务作为原材料、辅助材料、生产资料或其他成本组分。

在购买其他应纳税商品和/或服务时，增值税纳税人 A 向出售或提供应纳税商品或服务的增值税纳税人支付增值税。

如增值税纳税人 A 向提供商品或服务的增值税纳税人支付的增值税构成可以和销项税相抵免的进项税，则即使因国家按照第（1）款之优惠规定免扣增值税而导致销项税为 0 时，此进项税仍可进行抵免。

第（3）款

与第（2）款规定相反的是，可能会准许以免除增值税为表现形式的特殊待遇，这将导致没有销项税；在此情况下，与提供已准许免税的应纳税商品和/或服务相关的进项税不可抵免。

例如：

增值税纳税人 B 生产被国家准许税收优惠（例如在供应时免增值税）的应纳税商品。为达到生产目的，B 使用了其他应纳税商品和/或服务作为原材料、辅助材料、生产资料或其他成本组分。在购买其他应纳税商品和/或服务时，B 向出售或提供应纳税商品或服务的增值税纳税人支付了增值税。虽然 B 向其他增值税纳税人支付的增值税为可抵免的进项税，但因按第（1）款规定准许免税，从而实际上没有销项税，因此该进项税不可抵免。

第 16C 条

个人或实体在业务或工作以外进行的，自用或他用的自建活动应缴纳增值税，此规定及相关程序由财政部部长令决定。

第 16C 条司法解释

在业务或工作以外进行的自建活动应缴纳增值税，其目的是防止对增值税的避缴。

为保障低收入人群在自建项目上免征增值税，自建之定义由财政部长令进行规定。

第 16D 条

对最初所获得的非用于出售的资产的转移应征收增值税，前提是在获取资产时支付的增值税可以抵免。

第 16D 条司法解释

增值税纳税义务人最初非用于销售目的的机械、建筑、工具、家具或其他资产的供应，只要满足要求，即在获取时支付的增值税按照本法可以抵免，则应纳税。

相应地，如果在获取资产时支付的增值税按照本法规定不能抵免，则资产的供应无须纳税，除非增值税可信度由于证据不合格受到质疑，例如税务发票未能按照第 13 条第（5）款之规定完成。

第六章　其他条款

第 17 条

与税款代缴定义和程序相关的有关本法应用的事项及本法未加以特殊规定的事项，应适用于税法通则以及其他相关法律。

第 17 条司法解释

足够清楚。

第七章　过渡条款

第 18 条

（1）随着本法的生效：

a. 在本法生效前进行的所有应纳税商品或服务的提供及应纳税商品的进口，仍按照1951 年营业税法进行纳税；

b. 在本法执行规则尚未做出前，既存的且与本法无冲突的规则仍然适用。

（2）第（1）款所述的执行规则应由财政部部长做进一步规定。

第 18 条司法解释

第（1）款

a 项

足够清楚。

b 项

所有按 1951 年营业税法颁布的现存执行规则，只要尚未废除或未被本法规定所取代，且不与本法内容和目标相背的，仍然有效。

第（2）款

第（2）款规定的目的是为了克服在增值税法生效和 1951 年营业税法失效之过渡期间就同一征税对象出现的问题，例如：

——长期合同或涉及两部法律期间的合同；

——销售价格或对价剩余的未付部分；

——尚无进项税的商品库存。

在这方面，财政部部长有权决定其他不同于第（1）款的执行规则，借以减少税负上的不公平并促进本法的顺利执行。

第八章　最终条款

第 19 条

本法未尽事宜应由政府法规进一步加以规定。

第 19 条司法解释

足够清楚。

附注：

随着本法的生效：

a. 在本法生效前获准的对增值税和奢侈品营业税的延迟支付，应在准许的延迟期内结束，但不得迟于 1999 年 12 月 31 日。

b. 对油气开采业、一般矿业或以在本法生效时仍然适用的产量分成合同、作业合同或矿业作业协议为框架的矿业来说，其增值税和奢侈品营业税的征收应按相关产量分成合同、作业合同或矿业作业协议进行计算，直至上述合同或协议结束时止。